# Life With Glorious John

# Life With Glorious John

## by Evelyn Barbirolli

Robson Books

First published in Great Britain in 2002 by Robson Books,
64 Brewery Road, London N7 9NT

A member of Chrysalis Books plc

British Library Cataloguing in Publication Data
A catalogue record for this title is available from the British Library.

ISBN 1 86105 474 2

Typeset by FiSH Books, London WC1
Printed by Mackays of Chatham, Kent

# Contents

# Contents

In memory of my husband,
dear Glorious John, with love.

# Acknowledgements

*THIS MEMOIR IS* in no way a full life of my husband; I have not been blessed with the ability to write one, even if I had the desire to do so.

It is some while since my gifted and much loved friend, Michael Kennedy, suggested this memoir, and has often encouraged me to start writing. My warm thanks are due to him for giving so generously of time in his exceedingly busy life, to read and criticise. I thank also his wife, Joyce, for her sympathetic understanding.

Michael's wonderful biography of John (soon to be re-issued by the Barbirolli Society) gives a complete and deeply felt account of a great man's life; it is sensitively and understandingly written by a close friend and expert biographer.

After brief descriptions of our origins and early years, my memoir is a series of anecdotes, events and impressions from my remembrances of life with John; for the sake of continuity these are roughly in chronological order. In common with many older people, my memory is not always reliable, but these jottings are as genuine and as accurate as my ancient and limited power of recall can make them.

I have consulted John's family and friends to check my

memories; particularly I thank most warmly John's nephew Larry (Lorenzo Gibilaro). My affectionate appreciation is due to Ken Blakeley and Janyce Pringle, who read my early drafts constructively and critically, and to Jane Moore for her helpful specialist skill.

I am especially deeply grateful to my dear friend Margaret Campbell who has given me so freely of her time, knowledge and expertise. Her generously unstinting help has been invaluable, and her introductions to my encouraging publisher and his staff, and to my warmly helpful agent Andrew Best, have eased the later stages of this inexperienced biographer's work.

# *Foreword*

Evelyn has had two careers, as Evelyn Rothwell and Evelyn Barbirolli and music-lovers everywhere will be glad that she has written her memoirs of a long and eventful life. As she relates, she became an oboist almost by chance but soon the name Evelyn Rothwell was appearing in orchestral lists in London theatres, opera houses and concert-halls. In 2002 we forget how rare and difficult it was in the late 1920s for a woman to gain a regular place in a London professional orchestra and we should be grateful to three celebrated conductors, Henry J. Wood, John Barbirolli and Fritz Busch, for talentspotting the young Miss Rothwell. Barbirolli recruited her for his Covent Garden touring opera company and Busch for the Glyndebourne orchestra (mainly LSO) in the first seasons of what is now one of the world's most prestigious opera festivals.

Barbirolli soon became more than a conductor to her and their musical partnership and marriage lasted until his death in 1970. She accompanied him to New York where he faced one of the most difficult periods of his career and in this book she has much to tell about American musical politics and the prejudices and jealousies of other musicians which at times made life so unpleasant for the young English conductor.

Then came the wartime call to revive the Hallé Orchestra. The Barbirollis spent the next 27 years of their lives based in Manchester, where they both became beloved figures among a wide circle of not only music-loving friends. Evelyn's support for John and the Hallé in the exciting first year or two of their stay is recounted here. Yet she combined being a wife with her career as an oboist, appearing all too parsimoniously as soloist in concertos with her husband conducting but more often in chamber music. Many are the sonatas and other works specially composed for her artistry.

I have known Evelyn for nearly 60 years and she remains the modest, self-deprecating and loyal friend I met on her arrival in Manchester. It took a lot of persuasion to make her believe that we all wanted to know about her life, not only her life with John but her contacts with many other famous musicians. Thank goodness she eventually agreed and now we have this book, characteristically modest – but you have to expect that.

Michael Kennedy

# 1

# *John's Family and Early Life*

John was born on 2 December 1988 and was christened Giovanni Battista Barbirolli. His father, Lorenzo, and his grandfather, Antonio, were good violinists who played in the orchestra for the first performance of Verdi's *Otello* at La Scala, Milan, in 1887. John's father remembered the rehearsals; they were all attended by Verdi himself, who always sat at the back of the stalls and if he did not like anything (for instance if the tempo was not as he wanted it) would make an extremely loud click with his fingers. He knew exactly what he wanted and made sure that everyone else knew it too. He was a very practical man. Once he was asked why he had written five *piano*s (*ppppp*) in one of his works, and he answered, 'Because I hope to get two.' John often told me how much he learnt from his father about the tempi and interpretation of Verdi's music, and about other Italian composers of opera, including Puccini.

John played in the orchestra at Covent Garden in 1920 when Puccini was present at rehearsals of his *Il Trittico*. Unlike Verdi, Puccini did not take a very active part; he seemed content with the singers and orchestra and would just enjoy listening. A man of great charm and warmth, he was liked by everyone. He was a dandy and loved clothes. One day he arrived at rehearsal with a large boxful of ties. The men of the orchestra looked at them with interest and pointed out that they were all ties of famous schools and clubs, which only a member would wear in England. Mystified by this and rather worried, Puccini was soon reassured when he was told that certainly *he* could wear any of his ties. He was childishly and endearingly happy and immediately put one on.

John's mother was French. She came from Arcachon, near Bordeaux, and was always known as Mémé. She was not musical, but she attended as many concerts as she could if one of the family was involved, listening with enormous and uncritical pride. She had a very strong personality and was a materfamilias in the best Victorian sense. John adored her and their relationship was very close. She was extremely practical, and as a cook she had a touch of genius. Like many French women she was very shrewd, and often a little suspicious. Her English was enchanting; it was quite fluent, some words pronounced as they would be in French, with occasional interpolated French words. For example, '*sable*' pronounced like the fur, was sand; *fleurs* pronounced as if English, were flowers. One soon got used to this attractive, fractured English, so that communication was never a problem and always entertaining. In the family they always spoke Venetian; much more than an Italian dialect, it is a distinct language. (The plays of Goldoni are written, and should be performed, in Venetian, not in Italian.) Curiously enough, Mémé never spoke her native French in the family. She had learnt Venetian as well as developing her own idiosyncratic English.

I know that at first she did not approve of me as a wife for her beloved John. I had a career already, and when we married I was not nearly as domesticated as she would have liked. However, we soon began to get on well; her wonderful sense of humour was a great help, and possibly she realised that my love for John was deep and genuine. She was a remarkable and very dear lady, of considerable character. I grew to love and to admire her greatly.

Sadly, I never met John's father, who died before I knew John. From all accounts he was a very caring, gentle man, of considerable talent and charm. His courtship and marriage with Mémé was romantic and quite fascinating. In the late nineteenth century she had come to Paris from her native Arcachon to study millinery, and she was also considering an offer to become a *saucier* (sauce maker) in a Paris restaurant. In the evenings she often sat in the large café where Lorenzo played the violin. At first she adored him from afar, but they soon got together, fell in love and decided to marry. Lorenzo had been engaged to play in a hotel orchestra in London (I believe it was called the Hotel Cecil). He promised to contact Mémé when he had got settled. Time went on and on, and Mémé, waiting in Paris, heard nothing. Very worried, she decided to go to London to find out what was happening. Apparently, the leader of the hotel orchestra had been discovered having an affair with the hotel owner's wife and her husband was so angry that he sacked the whole orchestra. Poor Lorenzo, speaking hardly any English and without work, did not dare to send for Mémé. He had one or two Italian friends who managed to find him very modest accommodation in Bloomsbury, and he was living there when Mémé arrived in London. Apparently she and Lorenzo lived for some weeks solely on potatoes, which were cheap and nourishing. In later years Mémé used to cook a delicious dish from this early period; always known in the family as '*Patates à la Misére*'.

Mémé and Lorenzo married and in due course he found work. They had three children, Rosie, John and Peter. Rosie was an adequate pianist but not a professional in character nor in real ability. She married a very kind gentle Italian, Alfonso Gibilaro, always known as Fof or Fofo, who was greatly loved by the family. A good pianist in the light music field who was regularly engaged in large hotel orchestras, he was also a talented composer. Among other works, he wrote a beautiful song which Gigli used to sing a great deal, called *I Carretieri* (The Wagoners). This started life as an oboe solo for me, but it is really a song and not an instrumental piece.

Fof and Rosie had a family of three. Although all of them have done extremely well in various occupations, as have their children, none has inherited any musical talent. Their youngest son, Larry, is brilliant and successful in quite another way. He is Professor of Chemical Engineering at London University and also a Professor at the Italian University of L'Aquila, near Rome. He and his much loved wife, Jean, had five children, all talented in fields other than music.

John's younger brother, Peter, was a good viola player. He performed mainly in the orchestras of touring opera companies before ending his career playing for a number of years at Covent Garden. He was not at all ambitious, and was very happy to sit at the back of his section and help newcomers with his long experience of opera. He was loved and respected, and his many years in the Covent Garden Orchestra were contented and happy. His wife, Pat, although not a professional musician, was an appreciative listener. They had a talented daughter, Cecilie, who has made a great success of her life with her vital and attractive personality. She is happily married to Tim Jaggard, an ex-TV camera operator who is now retired. One of their two sons, the only musician in the family, is regularly employed in the BBC recording department and plays the French horn; the other son is a successful computer expert.

As was the habit in Italian families in John's childhood, the Barbirollis were very devoted and caring of each other and of their older relatives. Once Lorenzo was earning a reasonable salary, his Italian grandparents made their home in London with him and Mémé and the children. John's Aunt Eliza came to England to look after Rosie's children, so young John grew up among musicians. Later on, Lorenzo made quite a name for himself with the small salon orchestra he had founded at what was then the Queen's Hotel in Leicester Square. Many musicians of the day, including John, played with him in the orchestra and as soloists, and 'Barbie's Band' became a well-known attraction of the hotel. As I have mentioned, sadly I did not know John's father and never heard him play. But he was always said to be a fine musician and a player of great taste and charm, greatly liked and admired by his fellow musicians and the Queen's Hotel audiences. The famous tenor, John McCormack, gave the first performance of the well-known song, 'I Hear you Calling Me', with 'Barbie', for which he was paid one guinea. (For those who are not old enough to remember, a guinea was one pound five pence.)

All his life John was a tremendously hard worker and he became a fine cellist, but he always wanted, passionately, to be a conductor, and never doubted that this ambition would be fulfilled. From the age of five, his grandfather used to take him on Sunday afternoons to listen to the band in Lincoln's Inn Fields, where the conductor wore white gloves and used a short baton. When they went home to Marchmont Street after these band sessions, John would find a pencil to use as a baton and take a pair of white gloves from his mother's drawer (in those days women wore white gloves). Since he was rather shy about his conducting passion, he would go inside his mother's large wardrobe to perform in private. Of course, he wore the white gloves, which he thought were an essential part of a conductor's equipment. And from this early age the determination to become a conductor never left him.

## — 2 —

# Evelyn's Country Childhood

*MY FORBEARS AND* beginnings were much more conventional and less colourful than John's. My father was a tea dealer, in quite a modest way. He inherited his father's small business, which augmented a useful private income. He was older than my mother, whom he had married late in his life. He was a gentle, kindly man and a good father; intelligent, but unfortunately not musical. He used to say jokingly to me that he recognised the National Anthem and so knew when to stand up. He was an ardent fan of the Gilbert and Sullivan operas, but there it ended. He was not greatly interested in the arts, though he drew well and quite charmingly. His drawings were nearly all pencil sketches of landscapes or of trees or plants (he was a keen gardener). Unfortunately, by the time I was old enough to appreciate his talent he no longer sketched. He said he wanted to use his limited time at home seeing his children and gardening. Sadly, the sketches disappeared. My mother was a great thrower-away and tidy-upper, and I fear that she must have got rid of his drawings.

He was a deeply caring father but unfortunately, through no fault of his own, his understanding of his young family was limited. He was, by nature and upbringing, an admirable Victorian type; honest, considerate and courteous to everyone;

very conscientious, financially and otherwise, towards his wife and family. He was a reserved and private man and I don't think we ever got to know him sufficiently to realise his wonderful qualities or his deep love for us. He was a creature of habit; for example, meals had to be at exact times and he always caught the same trains each day to and from London. He was an exceptionally good shot. He liked walking, with or without his gun but always with a dog, and with a child if it were old enough. He was keenly observant of the countryside and would point out to us wild flowers, birds and animals and their habitats, so that walks with him were never dull – though sometimes they were a little long for our short legs.

My mother was utterly different – it seems remarkable to me that they got on so well and had such a happy marriage. She was much more 'modern', very attractive, lively and interested in everything and everybody. She was unimaginative and had rather a limited mind, but she was extremely practical and kind, always ready to help anyone in trouble. Before her marriage she had hoped to become a nurse, and when my brothers and I were grown up she drove the local ambulance and was expert in dealing with accidents and advanced first aid. (As there was no National Health Service in those days, I imagine that the ambulance was financed by the local hospital and doctors.)

My two brothers and I spent our earliest years in a large comfortable house on the edge of the small, pleasant market town of Wallingford-on-Thames, about fifteen miles from Oxford. We had a good cook, Nelly, and a very efficient 'house parlourmaid', Annie. Unfortunately the house had two disadvantages. There was hardly any garden – and my parents loved gardening – and my father had a tiresome and very time-consuming journey from home for his London train. The lack of a garden didn't bother us as children, for we had a gate into the garden next door, where a family of cousins lived with whom we often played. There was also an entrance into a public park so we had access to a large and excellent playground.

My paternal grandmother, who lived nearby, had a large garden where also we could play, usually after having Sunday lunch with her. Mr Marcham, assisted by a boy, kept the garden in good order and I'm sure we benefited from the vegetables and fruit grown there. I'm afraid that Marcham found us a great nuisance, but although he was gruff and slightly formidable, he was a kindly man and kept a fatherly eye on us. When we fell and grazed our knees or suffered other minor injuries, he would take us to his toolshed and treat our small wounds with a very mouldy cut potato, and any bleeding was staunched with a spider's web. Many years later John and I were fellow guests in the temporary home of the Head of the British Council in Vienna, with Alexander Fleming, who discovered penicillin. John was conducting rehearsals and concerts in the city and Fleming was giving lectures and classes, but we met for breakfast and occasionally for dinner. Fleming was a charming Scot, with a pawky sense of humour. I remember telling him about Marcham and his mouldy cut potato. He was fascinated and much amused by this very early and quite untutored use of 'penicillin'.

Mother was one of a family of thirteen; not all of them survived into adulthood and they were not all alive at the same time. The family were, as the saying goes, 'as poor as church mice'. Grandfather, our mother's father, was a solicitor whose practice was only three miles from home. Nevertheless he was often away for long periods on business, and he came home rather irregularly. As so often happens with his type (he was a womaniser and a bon viveur), he seemed to appear briefly, beget yet another child, and depart again. Sometimes he saw the children (and they did like him) but I don't think he really cared about them, nor did he worry how his very large family was able to exist on the extremely limited funds he provided.

It was not a satisfactory marriage. Grandmother was extremely untidy and was always in a muddle; he was quite the opposite. Wine meant nothing to her whereas he prided himself on being a knowledgeable connoisseur. He loved good food, but she was not a particularly talented nor interested cook (admittedly she had little time with all the children to care for!). He was essentially a bully and she could never stand up to him. These differences caused friction, and really they had little in common. They stayed together only because of the children and went their separate ways many years later.

My maternal grandmother was a splendid character, with a gentle but strong personality, much loved and trusted by everyone. She tried to do her best for her large family, but inevitably their education was rather sketchy. Some of them were far from robust, and money had to be stretched to pay for the doctor when needed. Most of the children were talented – each possessing considerable character and initiative – and naturally musical. For instance, in church or if they were together at Christmas or any other celebration, they would enjoy hymns, carols and songs, and most of the children would sing easily and instinctively in harmony. Any musical genes I might have, certainly came from my mother's side of the family.

Even in my generation we were supposed to be very proud of the one famous ancestor we possessed, great-uncle Charles Reade. He was a Victorian of many interests, who wrote books on various subjects, plays and novels, one of which, *The Cloister on the Hearth*, was well-known in its time. In my teens I had to read it and I felt guilty that I found it long and heavy going, as I still did when I re-read it in later life. I tried hard but without success to trace a book he had written and published on violin varnishes. He was a great friend of Ellen Terry and was well-known in theatrical circles. He must have been an interesting character. I wish I had known him.

I had two aunts who were particularly musical. One played the piano and the violin; she had help from friends but never any real tuition, and her playing was not good. I remember it well, it was extremely sentimental, with a good deal of sliding about (*portamento* would be too polite a way of describing it). However, she had a remarkable gift for teaching young children when they were beginners and she earned her living in this way. She had a regular job at a prestigious girls' school in the district and also took a good many little pupils at home, including myself. She really loved music and I wish that the family finances could have allowed her to be properly trained.

Another musical aunt began studying at the Royal College of Music, financed by a friend. She was learning singing and piano and getting on quite well, but because of her lung trouble and various infections, she had to resign from the College. It was a pity, because she had talent and might well have developed to a good professional standard. A difficult person, possibly because of her frustration, she was nevertheless always understanding and caring of my progress or otherwise in my student and early professional years.

Yet another aunt had just returned from teaching in India, intending to found a nursery school in England. She had trained at the Froebel Institute for Kindergarten Teaching in London, and with her intelligence and personality she was well able to achieve her ambition; in due course her school became extremely successful. Most of the children had been sent back to England by parents who were living abroad, possibly in an unsuitable climate, and who were grateful to leave their offspring with someone they could trust. 'Auntie', as she was known to everyone, used to rent a house by the sea in the summer months, and throughout the year she looked after the children in her care with great love and conscientiousness. The school, called St Anthony's, took a while to get started; at first I was the only pupil, so for a time I *was* the school! I realise now how lucky I was to have had such a wonderful teacher, one whom I loved dearly ever afterwards. She taught me the basic skills at a remarkably early age. By the time I was three and a half years old I could read and write very well, and reading became a passion which has remained with me all my life. As the school grew, at first with the advent of many cousins and friends who lived in the district, 'Auntie' continued to treat all her pupils as her family. Her discipline was greatly respected and she was much loved. Although the actual teaching from her various assistants may not have been academically orthodox, her own ideas about life and behaviour were sound and valuable, and never to be forgotten.

In 1925, when I was about fourteen, we moved from the comfortable house in Wallingford to a cottage in a neighbouring village, Cholsey. The reason was mainly financial; with two of us already at boarding school, my parents had to make sacrifices. In Cholsey, however, we had a large garden and an orchard, which delighted us all, and we were only five minutes from the main-line railway station, which meant a far quicker and easier journey for my father. We had a gardener, Mr Keep, two days a week. He had travelled extensively and loved to talk non-stop, but he was capable and hardworking and produced all our vegetables and fruit, and Mrs Keep did some useful sewing.

The cottage had small rooms and was inconvenient, with a very steep narrow staircase which our old builder called a coffin-chute. Life was not easy for my mother. In the village, there was no gas, no electricity and no mains water, and at first we had no telephone! All the cooking was on oil burners, the rooms were lit with oil lamps or candles, and water had to be hand-pumped in the kitchen from a deep artesian well. On laundry day, the water was heated by coal and wood in a vast copper. Instead of the two maids we had had in Wallingford, mother had to make do with a young 'cook-general', usually willing but quite inexperienced. Our loyal nanny came with us as my brothers were still young and needed her care. My father was very happy; he had space to grow his roses, and he got to know all the local farmers, who allowed him to walk over their land with his dog and to shoot anything he wanted. By way of payment, he gave them part of his 'bag'. He was, as I've mentioned, a particularly good shot, so our larder was enriched regularly by hares, rabbits, partridges, occasionally a pheasant, and such small delicacies as snipe and woodcock. The 'fridge' to house these excellent additions to our provender was a sunken outside larder with stone slabs on the shelves; it was remarkably efficient. Unfortunately my mother, like my grandmother, was not in the least interested in cooking and the young cook-general was usually untrained. However, mother managed to produce plain food, and the game was a great help.

One great joy was that we had pets: there were dogs (two Golden Labradors) and rabbits in hutches. There were no cats – mother had a bad allergy to them so they were avoided. The garden had a sloping lawn on which we used to play our own sporting version of croquet, a wonderful game at which my brothers became expert in later years. After a short time we acquired a car, a bull-nosed Morris, which was very exciting if slightly unreliable. Mother was the driver and a very good one. Opposite our gate there was a small farm where we were always welcome. I remember a cow producing a calf with considerable difficulty, but I had no idea at all of what had gone into its production. At fourteen or so, I was utterly ignorant of sex – how different from the young of today!

By that time I was already interested in food and drink, despite my mother's lack of interest in cooking. From a very tender age we had wine with our meals – at first with a lot of water, later with less water, and finally without any. My father was a connoisseur of wine and a buyer of port and claret for one of the City companies. In this capacity he attended wine sales and so he could often buy wines at reasonable cost. His great friend, our dear old doctor, believed strongly that wine was good for children. Our tonic after having flu or being unwell was always half port and half quinine, the basis of many French apéritifs. Father would produce an ordinary port and mother used to buy a demijohn of yellow-green quinine from the chemist with which to mix the brew, which we didn't mind drinking because it was sweet. We loved having wine with our food, certainly it did us no harm, and it left us with a love and appreciation of its qualities.

Whenever I went to tea with my godfather, who was known as Uncle Gilbert, I sampled unusual foods. He was a jolly man, a bon viveur – I think he was quite wealthy. I loved the smell of good cigars in the house, but even more I enjoyed my teas with him. In addition to the usual treats such as scones, jam and cream, and rich cakes, we had strange things to eat which I loved, even at an early age: salami and other sausages, various kinds of meat including prosciutto, pâté de foie gras, unusual cheeses, and other delicacies. I was never the worse for this sophisticated guzzling; I think it entertained godfather Gilbert to see a small child so obviously enjoying unusual adult food, so I was often invited to tea, and they were delightful gourmet occasions. (What a good preparation it was for life with John!) Uncle Gilbert lived in a large house with extensive grounds including a lake, where we went often to play, and with his wife Auntie Bets, I used to make butter. Cream or rich milk was put into a hand-churn, which had to be turned unceasingly with a handle. It was hard work, and we used to take it in turns. I can still remember the wonderful moment when the liquid ceased sloshing around inside the churn and the solid near-butter began to thump as we turned the handle. By that time the butter was almost ready, and it was delicious.

We had other occasional 'treats'. Around Christmas we were taken to London to see a play and we particularly loved *Peter Pan* and *Where the Rainbow Ends*. Unlike most children, we didn't like pantomimes – we found them ridiculous! In the summer we had a special picnic in beautiful woods a few miles away. A trap was hired, drawn by a fat, good-tempered white pony which we were allowed to drive under supervision. We learned to swim in the Thames, where the swimming lessons were fairly primitive. The boatman instructor, who stood on the bank, would fasten a cord round each of us which was attached to his 'fishing line', then throw us into the deep water while he counted 'one, two-ooo, three-eeee,' each figure being given a different tone of voice and varying in length. Perhaps surprisingly, we did learn to swim!

There was a regular dancing class for little boys and girls which we all found rather boring. I never liked dancing, even when I grew older, and funnily enough neither did John, so it was never part of our courting activities. Seeing John conduct, often people would say to me, 'What a wonderful dancer he must be.' But his choreography was confined to the conductor's rostrum; off it he was hopeless!

We were invited to various children's parties in the district. I remember one of these was given each year by the great contralto, Dame Clara Butt and her husband, Robert Kennerley Rumford, who was also a singer. They invited many children from that part of the world and we were royally entertained; there was a fantastically good tea, excellent games and competitions and a wonderfully warm welcome, with a cricket match for the older children. The Rumfords both seemed to love these occasions and certainly we all did. In later years, when Clara Butt was even more famous, I remember hearing her sing, out of doors at the opening of the local hospital. She was accompanied by the town band, which was bad and exceedingly loud. But she had an enormous voice and the band stood no chance against her!

We were given a little weekly pocket money for sweets which had to be spent with thought and care. There were large sugar balls for sale called gob-stoppers. These would change colour as you sucked them. If we ran short of sweets we had the insanitary habit of sucking till the colour changed and then passing on the gob-stopper to the next person.

Television, as yet, did not exist. Occasionally we listened to records but even this involved a certain amount of effort. On those old machines we had to turn the handle to keep the record going, and if the turning stopped or slackened, the pitch of the record dropped and the machine ground to a halt. Even listening to the wireless (as we called the radio) was not easy. It involved the sensitive placing of a wire called a 'cat's whisker' on the crystal: you were lucky to hear very much, and then only on headphones. We also had a family set with primitive speakers, but it was used mainly for the news.

In those days, we made our own amusements, and were happy and contented doing so. My young brothers were basically good friends, though they fought a good deal, as small boys tend to. I had a girl friend of my own age and we lived in a sort of fairytale world, planning fairy occupations, arranging fairy tea parties and inventing strange spells. It was a happy childhood, surrounded as we were by loving parents, a loyal nanny, caring and affectionate aunts and uncles and others in our lives.

My father's income was modest but my mother was a good and careful manager and there always seemed to be enough. If we wanted anything expensive, for instance a bicycle or an elaborate toy such as Meccano, we had to save for it ourselves – no doubt helped by presents from indulgent relatives.

It was the custom in many British families in those days to send their children to boarding school. Whether or not it was a good custom I am not sure – doubtless there are pros and cons. It was not cheap even then, and today the cost of boarding schools of any quality is so prohibitive that few parents can afford it. But eventually all three of us went away to school as boarders.

I have written about this period at some length because I have hoped to give some idea of rural life in the 1920s, so utterly different from life in the country today. The difference seems almost incredible in these days of TV, radio, the media and the internet, and early knowledge of so much.

# 3

## *The Birth of a Conductor*

*FROM EIGHT YEARS* old until twelve (the normal school leaving age at that time), John went to the council school near his home in Marchmont Street. He had bitter memories of his first day, when he was sent to school by his French mother dressed in a black pinafore, as a French child would have been. However, the teasing soon died down and he became a quiet but popular member of his class, very conscientious and serious. At that time of his life he was afflicted with difficulty in speaking. It was not a stammer or defect, but an inability to speak at all. He used to recall being sent shopping and standing in the shop quite unable to ask for what he had been sent to buy: perhaps it was a form of shyness or insecurity? At school a sensitive and understanding master soon realised that John's silence was not naughtiness or conscious disobedience. This perceptive man cured the trouble by the simple expedient of reading or speaking with John until he was confident enough to go on alone. John was always deeply grateful to this master and never forgot him. In later life he had the great pleasure of meeting him again, and being able to thank him.

Later in life, John became an accomplished speaker. He had a natural gift for words and the structure of speaking and writing. He was an avid reader, particularly of biographies, and in this way, after his short career at school, he educated himself. He started his musical studies playing the violin; the reason he became a cellist is quite well known, but is worth telling again. When he began learning the violin from his father and grandfather, at a very early age – probably only three or four years old – he got on well, but he was a restless little boy and would walk around the room as he practised. This habit infuriated his rather short-tempered Italian grandfather. One day he could stand it no longer; he went out and bought a small cello, probably quarter size, and returned with it in a taxi. He put it down in front of John and said, 'Now you'll have to sit still.' Although John loved the cello, he was always a little regretful that he had not been allowed to continue as a violinist. He used to say that his hand, very flexible with thin fingers, was born to play the violin. Perhaps it is just as well that he became a cellist and not a violinist. Despite his resolve, he might never have become a conductor!

His musical education took place entirely in England. His first cello lessons were with a Russian who lived near their home, from whom John said he learnt nothing at all. He remembered that the man spent the lesson washing his socks, while John struggled to play! Very soon, John began attending Trinity College of Music where he learnt with Mr Whitehouse, a very fine cello teacher who gave him a well-tutored basic technique. Next came the London Violoncello School in Nottingham Place, of which the founder and owner was Herbert Walenn. Mr Walenn, as John called him all his life, was not only a fine and renowned teacher of considerable personality, but also a caring and gentle man of great wisdom and character. Over many years he had a great influence on John, who always regarded him as a father figure as did many other distinguished cellists of the day. I met him, and became very fond of him many years later when I first knew John. Walenn was professor at the Royal Academy of Music, and in due course, at the age of twelve, John continued his studies there with him.

John came to know and to love the classical quartet repertory, particularly the Haydn quartets, but newer chamber music works were frowned upon by some of the older Academy teachers. Sir Alexander Mackenzie, then principal of the Academy, had forbidden the works of Ravel to be played as he said that the music would have a pernicious influence on young musicians. John and three of his friends were determined to play this music and they spent hours doing so in the men's lavatory, each sitting in a cubicle. John used to say that the acoustics were very resonant and rather unclear, and that there wasn't much room to use the bow, but they had a wonderful time! His years at the Academy developed in him a great love of chamber music and a full awareness of its value in orchestral playing.

In 1917, at the age of seventeen, he gave two cello recitals in London at the Wigmore Hall. For the first, he was accompanied by Harold Craxton, the most famous teacher and accompanist of the time. For the second, he was partnered by his then 'girlfriend', Ethel Bartlett, a very gifted young pianist who became well-known later as half of the Bartlett-Robertson two-piano duo. Both recitals were extremely successful and John was hailed as another Casals. However, he could not afford the time to build a career as a cello soloist, even if he had wanted to. From the purely practical angle, his earnings were necessary to help the family finances.

After he had left the Academy and given his two recitals, John embarked upon a freelancing life. Always a tremendous worker, he practised the cello tirelessly, becoming a player of genuine distinction. He was extremely busy with various musical activities and used to say that in those freelancing days he played

19

'everywhere except in the street'. But his ambition to become a conductor never wavered. He carried a full score to study whenever he went on journeys; with André Mangeot's Quartet, during the intervals of theatre performances, indeed at all available moments.

The first time John conducted was at the early age of seventeen, when he was in the army. Stationed on the Isle of Dogs, off the Essex coast, his year in the army was spent in that dismal spot. After a comfortable home life with his mother and the family, the army existence was hard, but John felt that it was good for him and toughened him physically. He got on well with his fellow soldiers; his Irish sergeant could not get his tongue round Barbirolli, so he called John Bob O'Reilly. The colonel in charge of the unit was a keen musician (although a bad violinist, John recalled) and, as there was very little to do on the Isle of Dogs, he formed a voluntary orchestra conducted by an untalented soldier, or sometimes by himself. Concerts were given occasionally, to friends and relatives and anyone who wished to attend. One day the usual conductor was taken ill and the colonel was away. The men of the orchestra, knowing of John's ambition to become a conductor, insisted that he should be given the chance to take charge. It was an exciting opportunity; in later years John could not recall the works on the programme (probably light, popular music) but he remembered vividly that he used the baton just as he did to the end of his life. The physical side of conducting was utterly natural and instinctive, he thought only of the music he was performing. He wrote to his father after this first experience as a conductor: 'I surprised myself at some of the effects I got without much trouble. Some of the chaps came to congratulate me and said they had never enjoyed a rehearsal so much, and what a pleasure it was to play with me.'

One engagement he recalled with pride and pleasure was

playing for the great dancer, Anna Pavlova. John was in the cello section of an orchestra engaged for a ballet company in which she took the major parts. The other cellists had no soloistic pretensions and did not want to play the cello solo, *Le Cygne* by Saint-Saëns, which was one of Pavlova's most famous dances, so John was deputed to do it. At the end of the first performance Pavlova shared her applause with John and threw down to him half a huge bouquet of tiger lilies which she had been given. She asked to see *'le petit'* who had played so beautifully and shook his hand – in a grip of iron, he said – and thanked him again. He treasured, as I still do, a plain gold earring which fell from her ear into the orchestra pit as she danced.

After his year in the army and the ending of the First World War, John continued his life of freelance cello playing. With his younger brother beginning to earn a living as a viola player; his sister happily married to a working musician; and Lorenzo becoming established with his salon orchestra at the Queen's Hotel; by 1925 John had saved enough money to set out on his own as a conductor. With the help of a few loyal friends, he formed a small chamber orchestra of approximately fifteen first-class players and ran a series of concerts in a small hall, the Chenil Gallery, in the King's Road, Chelsea. The programmes were interesting and attractive, the performances were excellent and the concerts were extremely successful, praised by the press and the audiences as well as by knowledgeable musicians. In effect John's name was made as a young and gifted conductor. Frederic Austin came to one of these concerts; a good musician and composer, he was the director of the well-known B.N.O.C. (British National Opera Company). He offered John a job immediately, with a tiny salary and minimal rehearsal time, to conduct five operas on tour, three of them in only a few day's time in Newcastle-upon-Tyne. Naturally, John and his family were very excited about this wonderful opportunity. There was only one snag: the rehearsals (just six hours for the five operas) were to be on a Friday. Italians are very superstitious, and to start a new enterprise on a Friday is to court disaster and to ensure failure.

After lengthy and serious discussions the family decided that on no account could John begin his new job on a Friday. In despair, John went to see Austin to ask if the schedule could possibly be changed, pleading an altered quartet engagement. Unfortunately, the company's rehearsal schedule had been fixed a long while in advance so a change was impossible; only three hours rehearsal could be managed on a Saturday. The first three operas were to be Gounod's *Romeo and Juliet*, Puccini's *Madame Butterfly*, and Verdi's *Aida*. John knew only a little about the Italian operas and nothing about the Gounod, but he accepted the job. It was a courageous decision, but a wonderful chance to take; all went well and his reputation grew quickly. At about this time, he changed his Christian name from the Italian Giovanni Battista (Tita to his family and close friends), to the English John.

He loved conducting opera and learnt much from it. He used to say that it is the most exacting learning experience, because anything can happen. 'If for example a door on the stage sticks, or a singer falls over, you must hold back the music as necessary, and as unobtrusively as possible.' While at work with the B.N.O.C., he fulfilled a number of other engagements. Most important among these was in the Queen's Hall, London, on 12 December 1927. Sir Thomas Beecham had been booked to conduct the London Symphony Orchestra (with Casals as soloist in the Haydn Concerto in D), but had suffered a fall and was forced to cancel his engagement at very short notice. In the time available, the L.S.O. was unable to find another conductor of similar prestige, and gave John the chance. The main work, surprisingly, because Beecham was not an Elgarian, was to be Elgar's Second Symphony. Time was short and John stayed up night and day to work at the symphony, which he knew only slightly. He was much heartened by Casals who, at the start of his rehearsal, said to the orchestra, 'Listen to him gentlemen, he knows.' This cemented a long and close friendship with the great man, whom hitherto John had hardly known. The concert was a great success. As John was leaving the stage at the end of it, a little man ran out and said: 'Don't sign any gramophone contracts. I'm Gaisberg, HMV. See you tomorrow.' This was the start of a long and fruitful friendship with the indomitable and immortal Fred Gaisberg, who almost literally *was* HMV (later EMI) for many years. John had in fact begun to record with the National Gramophonic Society, as cellist as well as conductor, but Gaisberg was to use him to accompany the many prestigious artists who came to record in England.

In 1932, after the opera engagement, John was appointed musical director and conductor of the Scottish Orchestra. Encouraged by John, it became their policy to engage the very best soloists for their regular concerts. So, at a relatively early age John was working with the most distinguished artists, such as Kreisler, Rubinstein, Heifetz, Hubermann, Horowitz, and various opera singers of distinction, including Elisabeth Schumann, Lotte Lehmann, Lauritz Melchior and Friederich Schorr. They were all delighted to be so beautifully accompanied and went away talking of the young and gifted conductor in Scotland.

In fact his reputation grew so quickly that his summons to New York in 1936 caused little surprise in musical circles. Nevertheless, it was disturbing and disappointing to his older colleague, Sir Thomas Beecham. In his freelancing days John had played under Beecham in many of his performances, some of which he had genuinely admired. Toscanini had described

Beecham as a 'talented clown'. John said that he was an 'amateur of genius', but he felt that Beecham lacked integrity and had not made the most of his great talent. Beecham evidently envied John this New York post, and in a disgraceful piece of behaviour wrote to the manager of the New York Philharmonic, Arthur Judson, and to the Chairman of the Committee, and the Ladies' Committee, telling them that he could not understand why they had engaged such an unknown upstart – and there were other derogatory words to that effect. Unfortunately, I have no copy of any of these unkind missives, but I did see and vividly remember the one to Judson and others. But in fact the effect of these protests was the opposite of what Beecham intended. The general reaction was: 'If Beecham takes all this trouble, Barbirolli *must* be good.' After John had taken over the Hallé in 1943 Beecham offered to conduct the orchestra in concerts (as he had done many times in the past). John answered that certainly Beecham could come with his own orchestra to play in Manchester (which he did) but on no account could he conduct the Hallé. After that they had no further contact.

—— *4* ——

# The Making of an Oboe Player

*WHEN I WAS* about fourteen years of age I went to Downe House, 25 miles from my Berkshire home, a prestigious and expensive boarding school which had just relocated from the home of Charles Darwin in Kent. I'm sure that my going to Downe House was due to the generosity of its founder and headmistress, Olive Willis, a remarkable and wonderful woman to whom I shall always be grateful for all I learnt during those school years. They were not particularly happy ones. I was shy and a late developer, and I excelled neither academically nor at sport, nor indeed in any way, until the oboe came into my life in my very last term.

Unusually for those days, Downe House had a good chamber orchestra, run by a redoubtable and extremely able violin teacher, Marjorie Gunn. At the beginning of my last term, it so happened that both oboists in the orchestra left unexpectedly. Since I was the only member of the school choir who was not already in the orchestra, it was suggested that I might learn the oboe. I was supplied with a poor, primitive instrument and had lessons from a keen and kind amateur oboist. I had never seen nor heard an oboe before. As I explained earlier, we had no teaching about musical instruments, we hardly ever heard a record, and of course there was no TV, nor school music programmes on the radio.

Once I had an oboe, I became fascinated by the sounds I could make on it. I worked extremely hard and progressed very quickly. Soon after I left school my violin-playing aunt discovered that a scholarship competition was about to be held for the Royal College of Music in London. I was very reluctant to enter because I could do little more than hold the oboe (I had been learning less than six months), but the family persuaded me to enter. Many students applied, with varying instruments and skills, so I did not think that I had the slightest chance. It is my firm contention that everyone has some luck in their lives and I had a large slice of it in this scholarship competition. There was a large jury of which Sir Hugh Allen, the Director of the Royal College of Music, was the chairman. To the surprise and disappointment of the other entrants, he and the jury gave me the Scholarship 'on potential' for one year. Allen said: 'If you do what I think you will, I'll renew it for three years.'

I suppose I did, and he certainly kept his word, although I did not use the full three years. The Scholarship was very generous, paying not only the College fees but three years living at a hostel, Queen Alexandra's House, literally three minutes walk from the College. Food and lodging was provided, I could practise at all reasonable hours, and very soon I made friends with other students, some of whom were musical and some in other walks of life. There were rules, of course, but one could always get permission to be late back after a concert, and I found the regulations reasonable. It was an ideal place for me at the time, since I knew only country life and was quite a stranger to London, and financially it was a great help to my parents.

The reason I did not use the full three years of my Scholarship was because I progressed extremely quickly and was soon freelancing in the profession. It seems that there was a shortage of good oboe players at the time, which was most helpful to me! In later life I regretted leaving the College as early as I did, particularly having started the oboe so late (when I was nearly eighteen years old). Perhaps I ought to have resisted the temptation to go into the profession so soon instead of staying at the College; later on there is rarely the same amount of time to practise. However, I had a passionate desire to succeed, I was prepared to work exceedingly hard and I suppose I had some natural ability, so I developed quickly as a player, and enormously enjoyed doing so. It was a great delight also to hear so many concerts. I lived for music, having heard so little earlier in life.

I'm often asked about Leon Goossens, my professor, who was the great oboe figure of the time. A wonderful performer with a dynamic personality, he was also a great innovator who transformed British oboe playing, with his beautiful sound and way of performing; and his influence is still apparent today. But he was not interested in teaching and, unfortunately, he was not conscientious about it. I remember one term at College when he gave us lessons on the first day and did not appear again until the last. That sort of 'teaching' made my first year difficult, because I had learnt quite a different method of playing from my amateur teacher. Possibly Goossens might have helped me if he could, but he was such a natural, intuitive player that he was genuinely unable to analyse other people's problems, or help them to solve them. Although he was not a good teacher in the conventional sense, I'm quite sure that we learnt a great deal from him by example. We went to hear him perform as much as possible, and on occasions we played in the oboe section with him, in theatres, for musical shows, or in amateur orchestras which needed what was called 'professional stiffening'.

While I was at College there was a remarkable incident

unrelated to oboe playing. I was one of a few students engaged by Covent Garden as extras for Mussorgsky's *Boris Godunov*. Dressed as peasants, in rags, we did not have to do much – certainly we did not sing – but we were on the Covent Garden stage with the famous bass singer, Chaliapin, so it was quite an experience. He was a dominant figure with a great, thrilling voice.

Another particularly interesting occurence concerned Benjamin Britten. Ben was at the Royal College of Music in London between 1930 and 1933, so his time there coincided with the latter part of mine. He studied piano with Arthur Benjamin and composition with John Ireland. He was not at all happy at the college; he found the atmosphere bureaucratic and unhelpful, and he resented the attitude of the officials, who would not permit him to use his Scholarship to study with Berg in Vienna. He took no part in college life and activities, so I was surprised when he asked me if I could assemble a small orchestra of students to play through a work he had written recently, his *Sinfonietta*. He gave me a list of instruments he would need, and I made sure that my friends and acquaintances would co-operate. The College staff allocated to us one of the larger rooms, and we gathered on the day and time arranged. Ben brought the parts, which he had written himself, very legibly, and he conducted most efficiently while we rehearsed and played the work. Shamefully, we little realised his remarkable early talent: some of the players complained that the parts were not well written for their instruments, nobody enjoyed the work or attempted to understand it. I remember being startled by this music, so utterly different from anything we knew, but I was impressed by Ben's conviction and the feeling of mastery and strength in what he had written.

# ——— 5 ———

# *Freelancing in the 1930s*

*JOHN AND I* both freelanced; he from 1915 to 1925, I from 1929 to 1939. Conditions did not alter much between those two periods, except that I had a greater choice of types of work, but there was a very great difference between our era and the years after the Second World War, which ended in 1945. In our times, the musical profession was not crowded. There were almost none of the competitions of which there are so many today, and reputations were made mainly by word of mouth. A young, or comparatively untried player who could handle their instrument well, was known to be reliable and to get on with their colleagues, was assured of plenty of deputising work of varying kinds. There were very few serious concerts in Great Britain at that time and orchestras only rarely played abroad. The major orchestras and concert promoters would give a limited series of prestigious performances at which internationally known conductors and soloists would appear.

There was occasional orchestral work; for example ballet companies would come to London for a limited season and would engage an *ad hoc* orchestra for that period. Amateur orchestras would often need 'professional stiffening'. I remember going to Brighton a few times and playing for Beecham (an alarming but stimulating experience) in one of his lesser part-amateur orchestras. At that time I was offered a regular job in Beecham's London Philharmonic Orchestra to 'cover' for Goossens whenever he was away. I refused; it would have been very exacting and I was not experienced enough, nor sufficiently knowledgeable about the symphonic repertory. Goossens would have been very unpredictable in dealing with his 'cover', and so might Beecham have been!

We earned a living in all sorts of ways other than playing concerts. The deputising system was generally accepted, so some of the freelance work was substituting for players who had regular jobs, for example in theatres or musicals. All theatres used live music for interludes and entr'actes even for straight plays. The size of the group could vary from a piano trio to a small salon orchestra. Most of the well-known players of the day would work in more than one theatre (the theatres were known as 'shops') and they would send their younger and less busy colleagues as deputies, only occasionally attending themselves. The pay for those theatre shows was modest but it was in cash, and regular, and usually one theatre engagement led to another when the run finished, so it was a useful source of income. My deputising often came through Goossens. He would telephone me at short notice and I would rush to the theatre concerned just in time for the start of the show. There was no chance of looking at the stack of manuscripts from which one had to play; often, the parts were written in pencil and were barely legible in the dim light of the theatre pit. It was very good practice in every way, particularly for sight reading. I remember one job where the oboist had to play unaccompanied on the stage before and during the beginning of the play. There was no music stand on the stage so I pinned the music which was entirely new to me, on to a convenient curtain. When the play started, my curtain rose high up in the flies of the theatre and my music with it. It was a horrifying moment and all I could do was to improvise as well as I could!

There were musicals of course, and I was lucky to be involved in two long runs. One was *The Dubarry* at Her Majesty's Theatre, which starred the enchanting Annie Ahlers. This ran for about a year. Nightly, as incidental music, we played Ravel's *Le Tombeau de Couperin*; exacting, but good practice for the oboist. The doyen of conductors of light music and most theatre shows was Ernest Irving, an extremely clever man and an excellent musician, alarmingly observant and critical of his players. Irving had another claim to fame for which music lovers should be grateful: he was Musical Director of Ealing Film studios and other film companies, and he made a point of engaging good composers for the scores. He was responsible for contracting Vaughan Williams, William Walton, Malcolm Arnold and many others of distinction. Irving was the conductor of my other long run, *The Land of Smiles*. Leon Goossens was first oboe and Helen Gaskell (later for many years the cor anglais player in the BBC Symphony Orchestra) was second; I was the first deputy. Irving considered that I was too young and inexperienced to play first oboe, as there were some important solos. However, one night both Goossens and Helen Gaskell were away unexpectedly; by this time I knew the solos well and was delighted to have a chance of performing them. Luckily on that night John's brother Peter happened to be playing viola in the orchestra. He went home and told his brother that he should hear me. He knew that John was looking for a second oboe for the Covent Garden Touring Company (successor to the British National Opera Company), of which he was now Musical Director. Although I was freelancing, I was still technically at the Royal College of Music and used to collect my letters there. One day I found a letter from someone whose name I read as John Barkworth, asking me to give an audition, quite soon, in the Crush Bar of Covent Garden.

I accepted of course, and John Barkworth turned out to be John Barbirolli; this was the first time I had ever seen him except in photographs. John accompanied me in the slow movement of a Handel Sonata (he was a poor pianist and I don't think he could have managed the quicker movements) and gave me some exacting sight-reading, which I did not manage too well. I was very nervous, but he was kind and encouraging and gave me the job. Sadly, the Second World War virtually ended the life of that company, but I had two tours with it, preceded by a two-week season in Covent Garden. I was twenty years old, had been learning the oboe for only two years and was still very inexperienced, so this job was an exciting and valuable one.

The repertory for the Covent Garden season included the first performance in English of Smetana's *The Bartered Bride* and the first performance, after several years, of Ethel Smyth's *The Wreckers*, which made a deep impression on me then as it did again years later, when the BBC put on a concert performance at the Proms on 31 July 1994. Ethel Smyth herself was a formidable character; she looked like someone from an earlier age. She always wore long, voluminous black skirts, and on her head the sort of floppy cap which universities present with a degree. If she had been a man, and not so eccentric, outspoken and dominant a character, I wonder whether *The Wreckers* might have had greater success. She attended all our rehearsals and bombarded John with notes about small details. He kept the last one (referring to the organ part in the finale) for many years, but sadly it has now disappeared. It said, 'I quite forgot to ask you a very important point. WHAT is the size of your organ?' John always wondered whether she had a very good sense of humour or none; he came to the conclusion that probably she had none!

She was delighted with the orchestra's keen attention and playing and said she would like to take us all out to tea after the last rehearsal. This was a real high-tea affair at the local Lyons, (opposite the Drury Lane stage door) which we attended regularly, and we all ordered extra portions of bacon, eggs, fish, baked beans and so on. Then came the wonderful moment when Ethel was to pay the bill, which was very generous of her. In those days, the cashier sat in a cage in the middle of the room and bills and change came to her on a little overhead 'railway' from some central spot. When the bill was produced, Ethel gathered up her long, voluminous black skirt to reveal long johns and a belt from which she produced her money. Very practical, no doubt, but a source of great entertainment to the orchestra.

I enjoyed playing opera for the first time and it was thrilling to be in the Covent Garden pit as an orchestra member. My first oboist was an old Italian, Pollicino. He had wonderful agility, but unfortunately a very small and unresonant sound, and so it was difficult to play quietly enough not to overpower him. But he was pleasant and helpful to me and we got on well. The cor anglais and third oboe, Bert Horton, was an elderly professional, experienced and efficient, and knew the operas well, but his unattractive tone was reedy, loud and brash.

After two weeks at Covent Garden we went on tour, spending one week, or occasionally two, in each large town. The venues included Liverpool, Manchester, Glasgow and Edinburgh. Our opera repertory was wide and varied, including *Die Walküre*, *Die Meistersinger*, *Der Rosenkavalier*, *Faust*, *Rigoletto* and *Die Fledermaus*. John conducted most of the operas and Warwick Braithwaite the others. We played an opera each night (some of the operas were extremely long) and one matinee a week, sometimes two. There was a short 'seating rehearsal' in each new venue but otherwise the days were our own. For me it was a wonderful opportunity to practise hard. My 'digs' companion, flute player John Francis, felt the same, so our 'digs' arrangements were very happy and harmonious (and quite platonic!). Most of the orchestra were in 'digs', an excellent and very economical way of living. We had a room each and a sitting room in which we had our meals, where there was always a coal fire, and we could practise as much as we liked in the house. The landlady cooked all our meals. Some landladies preferred to shop for food, others asked us to buy it ourselves and give her what we wanted to be cooked. Either way, it was very cheap and convenient. Some years later, when John and I were married, we had the most wonderful 'digs' in Edinburgh where the dear old landlady, Mrs McNab, used to cook excellent meals for us after the concerts, often extremely late at night. For a few years, we stayed with her whenever we went to Edinburgh. Sadly, she eventually retired – she was, I think, very old. We kept up with her and always went to see her when we were in Edinburgh. She appeared in John's *This is Your Life* – the long-running television show.

Rather late in my freelancing career, Sir Henry Wood re-formed his old Queen's Hall Orchestra and he engaged me as his principal oboe. The orchestra mostly made recordings and it was a great experience to play for Sir Henry. His name is known today mainly for his part in developing the Proms. There were 'Promenade Concerts' in London from 1838 but they were never a great success until Newman appointed Henry Wood as conductor of the new series in 1895. These concerts he developed and built up to become the great feature they are in British musical life today. I don't think he is remembered with enough credit for this and all his other contributions to music. He was a tireless champion of the contemporary music of his time, and gave the first performances in Britain of Debussy, Ravel, Strauss,

Schoenberg, Sibelius, Tchaikovsky, Mahler, Scriabin, Janáček and many others, long before they became well known. He was energetically against the 'deputy system' and did a great deal to improve the standard of orchestral playing. He conducted regularly and frequently, mostly in England, until his death in 1944. His hobby was painting and he was a first class artist.

He was a 'character', admired, loved, and laughed at affectionately by orchestral players. His entertaining and endearing habit of giving his instructions prematurely were delivered in his gruff cockney voice and written in his personal scores in heavy black pencil – and they had usually been repeated many times before. All the orchestral musicians who had worked with him knew in advance exactly what he would say and when. For example, John (and many others) recalled that before the first note was played of Ravel's *Daphnis and Chloe* Suite, No. 1, Henry would call out, 'Too loud, too loud!' I remember a classic saying concerning Wagner's *Tannhäuser* Overture. The first violin part is continuous and very tiring, and in order to snatch a rest the violinists would take time in turning over their parts. Henry soon put a stop to this by producing his own parts, which did not need turning. One day, he found that these were damaged (possibly on purpose) and could not be used, and he was heard to say 'My private parts, my private parts, must get 'em sewn up, get 'em sewn up.' Before my first rehearsal with him, John and all the players I knew told me exactly what he would say and when – and they were right!

But he was considerate and thoughtful to young, inexperienced instrumentalists. When he engaged me he asked if I had played Vaughan Williams' *London Symphony* (incidentally the composer's favourite). I said I had not, and he took the trouble to take me through the part privately before the first recording session. He was not a great conductor, but he had personality and an excellent clear beat, and he never wasted a second of rehearsal time. His performances were efficient and not unmusical, he always knew his scores well and made sure that his players did too. He was a great man in many ways, well liked and respected.

I played in two opera tours and enjoyed them greatly. I did not get to know John during this period, I just hero-worshipped him when he conducted! At the end of the season he gave me another audition, this time for first oboe in the Scottish Orchestra, of which he had become conductor and Musical Director. I was engaged for the 'Scottish', which had a five-month season in the winter. I had a wonderful job in the summers, first oboe in the orchestra of the Glyndebourne Festival Opera, which started in 1934. This came about in a most fortunate way. Adolf Busch, the great violinist (brother of Fritz, the conductor at Glyndebourne in its early years) was playing a concerto with John in Bournemouth. He happened to mention Glyndebourne and said that his brother was busy giving auditions to oboe players. Most of that first Glyndebourne orchestra was drawn from the L.S.O. but Busch did not like the sound made by the regular L.S.O. oboe players. They were well established and efficient but they had an 'old-fashioned' tone, reedy, acid and unattractive. John told Adolf that his brother should hear me, and so Natalie James (my good friend and a fine oboist) and I auditioned for Fritz Busch and were both engaged.

The opera engagement was invaluable. Some years later, I played for a year with the Sadler's Wells Company for Opera and Ballet, and the earlier experience served me well. The conductor of the Sadler's Wells Ballet then was the gifted composer and musician, Constant Lambert. He was a personality, and extremely musical. As a conductor he was quite adequate, or he would have been had he not been so drunk every time he appeared. We all liked and admired him and greatly regretted his unfortunate addiction. The orchestra players did their best to help him in performances and, sometimes, when these were over, we almost carried him off the rostrum and out to the exit.

One of the opera conductors was Laurance Collingwood, a pleasant man and a fine musician though not a great conductor. I remember playing in some strange sessions for him at the EMI studios in Abbey Road, recording all the old Caruso records. On the originals the accompaniment could hardly be heard because the only available microphones had been used for Caruso's wonderful voice. For the 'Caruso record' sessions, Collingwood wore headphones on which he could hear Caruso and the almost non-existent accompaniment, and we played these very simple accompaniments from manuscript parts without hearing Caruso, guided only by Collingwood's conducting.

There was one regular freelancing job which I particularly enjoyed. The BBC used to employ small salon-type orchestras regularly, usually weekly or monthly. I belonged to one of these, 'Reginald King's Orchestra', of which the leader was Alfredo Campoli – later to become an excellent soloist. The Reg King performances were always live (programmes were not recorded in those days) and the few players were excellent, so, in one respect, the job was quite exacting, but the oboe parts were usually melodic and not technically difficult, and Reg King and Alf Campoli were very helpful and pleasant. I also played with Fred Hartley's outfit. We had a year's contract with the commercial station, Radio Luxemburg, to play weekly for Rowntree's, the makers of Clear Gums. I played only one short tune somewhere in the programme, and I did the same occasionally for Lew Stone and his Dance Band, which was quite well known at that time.

One very good source of income was playing for film sessions. Being a woman, I did not do much of this! Gordon Walker (the first flute of the L.S.O.) was the 'fixer' and he and others concerned preferred to engage men. At this time, there were hardly any women in the profession at all. I did not mind that I did so little film work, because although it was extremely well paid, it was exceedingly boring and musically quite unrewarding. We had to be in the studio (these were always outside London, for instance in Elstree) by 8 a.m., and sometimes we were still there until 1 a.m. or 2 a.m. the next day. Often we just 'hung about' waiting to accompany the same few minutes of film being repeated live (they did not seem to record in those days – perhaps the quality was not good enough). I remember one occasion when we had been around all day doing very little and it was 2 a.m. My first oboe in the L.S.O., who was a dear man and generally considered rather a wit, said: 'I hope we shan't have to go on much longer because I'm suffering from ingrowing shirt tails!'

I remember one job which was delightful and musically very rewarding indeed. It was a six-week run of *Lilac Time*, playing in a small orchestra with Richard Tauber as Schubert. To look at, he was obviously utterly unsuitable, but his singing was wonderful. At each performance he used to sing a group of Schubert *Lieder*, beautifully accompanied by himself (he was a very good pianist). The songs were seldom the same and I used to sit in the pit and listen entranced to the nightly recital. He was a lovely artist.

I have mentioned earlier the few series of prestigious concerts in London at which the conductor and soloist (if there was one) were of international class. These concerts were always given in the Queen's Hall, which was tragically destroyed in the Second World War and never rebuilt. It was a large hall, but felt wonderfully intimate. The acoustics were excellent, it was comfortable and one could see and hear well from every seat. Unfortunately, there cannot now be many concert halls which are so good both for the listener and the performer. I had the great joy and privilege of playing several times in the Queen's Hall, both as an orchestral player in the L.S.O. and as a soloist in the Adolf Busch Chamber Music Players. In the orchestra one could hear the other members well, and so balance and ensemble playing presented no problems. As a soloist, in my case in a small chamber ensemble, the same applied, and one seemed able to make a good and carrying sound without effort or the temptation to force. Those of us who were fortunate enough to hear music in The Queen's Hall and to work in it will never forget the experience. We can only mourn its destruction.

I remember playing in certain orchestral concerts there which so impressed me that their memory has remained vividly in my mind for all these years. One was conducted by Bruno Walter, whose music making was warm, sensitive and inspiring. The orchestra loved working with him, and played their best. Hearing him again many years later I remember being slightly disturbed that he seemed so often to change the tempo with the mood, which rather destroyed the line. But he was older then (and so was I, and probably more critical) and I shall never forget his great warmth and utter commitment to the music. John and I came to know him many years later, in California. Once we heard him giving a wonderful recital there for charity with the great Lotte Lehmann then an elderly woman; he was a beautiful pianist. (I remembered hearing Lehmann in my earlier years in London as the incomparable Marschallin in a great performance of *Der Rosenkavalier* with Elisabeth Schumann as Sophie and Richard Mayr as Ochs.) Walter was a man of great charm and courtesy. He seemed delighted always to see us both and to talk to John, and I am sure he wished him well and that their liking was mutual. Another memorable concert with the L.S.O. was conducted by Felix Weingartner. He was a fine conductor in quite a different way from Walter. It was rather cool music-making, but with a wonderful musical line. His beat was undemonstrative but clear and logical. He used his eyes a great deal; a colleague of mine used to say his eyes came out like organ stops and fixed you! Maybe I was too young and inexperienced to appreciate his worth, but on that occasion I did not find him as inspiring as Walter.

One fascinating concert I recall was when Ravel came and conducted his own *Bolero*. He was utterly undemonstrative and seemed to be unmoved, even uninterested, by the growth of tension and sound to the vast volume of the climax. He conducted with a small, thin stick that looked like an ordinary lead pencil, and indeed may have been one. His tempo was a little slower than is usual today and his absolutely steady beat never varied at all, no matter what went on in the orchestra; his body remained quite still and his face never changed. He seemed a small, 'grey' man and it was hard to believe that he had written such lovely, sensuous music. Naturally, he had a tumultuous reception from the orchestra and the audience, but this seemed to leave him just as unmoved as had his *Bolero*. Yet in a way, his utterly undemonstrative conducting and behaviour seemed to add to the excitement.

John used to say that composers should never try to conduct their own works, because most of them could not conduct. Britten, of course, was an exception to this stricture – he was an excellent conductor of his own and other music – and Elgar too, often conducted his own works. In the 1920s John played under Elgar's baton at a Three Choirs Festival concert in Worcester, and he wrote of the occasion: 'It was wonderful to see the great man, radiantly happy amongst his friends in the Cathedral precincts, more wonderful still to play 'The Dream' [*of Gerontius*] under his direction. I remember that Elgar conducted from memory. Although he could not be called a great conductor by the highest professional technical standards, it was extraordinary how he could make you feel what he wanted if you were in sympathy with him.'

John used to recall an occasion when the famous ballet impresario, Diaghilev, had the idea that it would be interesting and instructive (as well as very good publicity) to engage composers to conduct their own ballets. The first was Manuel de Falla, who was to conduct his *Three Cornered Hat*. The poor man was literally dragged to the rostrum, protesting that truly he could not conduct. Diaghilev took no notice and signalled to the orchestra to play. De Falla managed to beat the first few bars, but when there came a bar or two of cross-rhythms he was completely undone. The orchestra went on playing but the poor man rushed off the podium protesting again that he could not do it. He was incapable of beating the music he himself had written.

The Queen's Hall concerts I remember most vividly of all were the performances in which I played the Bach Brandenburg Concertos and Suites with Adolf Busch and his Chamber Music Players. Adolf gave everything to the music and expected everyone else to do the same, which we did, eagerly and wholeheartedly. The players were very good indeed and played regularly with him. The pianist was his close friend Rudolf Serkin: at that time musicians were not so purist, and the modern piano in Bach performances was not frowned upon. The members of Adolf's renowned String Quartet led their sections in the Players. The principal cellist was Adolf's brother, Hermann, and many of the strings were pupils of either Adolf or the other section leaders, so it was quite a family affair. The oboes, horns and trumpet were engaged in London and those of us who were chosen were fortunate indeed. Aubrey Brain was first horn and his son, sixteen-year-old Dennis, was second. I was first oboe, with Natalie James and Joy Boughton second and third, and for the Second Brandenburg Concerto the trumpet player was George Eskdale and the flautist the great Marcel Moyse. The

41

recordings of these Brandenburgs and Suites have been reissued many times and are still, I believe, in the current catalogues, deservedly so I feel, because Adolf Busch's music-making was very special.

I have described in some detail the life of the freelance musician in the early 1930s. Freelancing in the year 2002 is utterly different, and it has been for many years. After the Second World War, the situation began to change. Although it is several years since I was a player myself, I still do a lot of adjudicating, which keeps me in touch with young players, so I know the difficulties they face. I must emphasise that the profession is, and has been for a long time, extremely overcrowded. For large numbers of would-be professional musicians, it is difficult to earn a decent living. True, there are competitions and these are of genuine help in 'weeding out' the less talented from those who are likely to make it to the very top. The trouble is that though a winning competitor will benefit in various ways, there are often other very good applicants who are not so fortunate. Although it is said, and truly, that there is always room at the top of the tree, the places on those branches are very few, and often unobtainable. Of course, there are more orchestras these days, many more concerts and much more recording which means that a certain number of regular jobs are available, but there are still too many players wanting to fill them. There is always a long waiting list for those who apply for a vacancy, and even when trials are given with the orchestra concerned they do not necessarily lead to an engagement. Some of the ways in which John and I earned money, no longer exist. For instance, the BBC no longer employs salon ensembles, and there is no live music in theatres. There are few amateur orchestras and those that still exist seldom need much stiffening. Obviously, I have written this chapter from my own personal experience. I had some engagements in my time which would not have existed for John, but basically the freelance conditions were the same for him as for me. It is often said that those who cannot play can always teach, but this branch of the profession is also overcrowded, and, if you have no real gift or feeling for teaching, you are unlikely to be successful, and certainly your pupils won't be happy.

Some years ago, I listened to a broadcast talk given by the great teacher Nadia Boulanger, who was discussing the difficulties of entering an overcrowded profession. She said: 'If you want to make music your life, you must want it so much that if you are told it is impossible, you feel that you would rather die.' She added, in her inimitable French accent, with great emphasis, 'And sometimes, eet ees bettaire to die.' This is a little drastic, I know, but it is a warning to would-be professional musicians that they must be aware of the difficulties they are likely to encounter.

I am most grateful that John and I entered the profession before it became so crowded and so competitive. For us, earning a living was much more enjoyable than it became later.

# — 6 —

# *The Scottish Orchestra – and 'Courting'*

*AFTER THE B.N.O.C.*, John's next permanent conductorship (following a preliminary trial season in 1932) was for the seasons 1932–36 with the Scottish Orchestra. (I have the feeling that the orchestra had a rather more elaborate official title, but it was always known as the 'Scottish'.) This orchestra had its headquarters in Glasgow, where it played mainly, apart from a weekly visit to Edinburgh. On taking over the orchestra, John made some changes in the personnel, and sacked the first oboe. As I have said, he auditioned and engaged me for this post. I started in the autumn of 1933 and stayed for four seasons. Musically, it was a very exacting job and a wonderful time of musical discovery. I knew little of the symphonic repertory and John's programmes were interesting and extremely varied. I did a great deal of practice (sometimes rather desperately; I seemed always to be catching up with solos I felt I could not play well enough!).

Personally, I was very happy, because we did our courting during those months in Glasgow. Apart from the joy of spending so much time with John, I was very comfortably settled in 'digs' only a few minutes from the hall. Mr and Mrs Quail, the proprietors, had never taken in guests before and we were wonderfully looked after. I shared with an old friend, Eileen Parry (then Grainger), an excellent viola player, and we got on extremely well. Practising was no problem; if we both wanted to work in our 'digs', there were always rooms available in the St Andrew's Halls nearby. The large hall where our concerts were held was only part of the building. One of the great halls of Europe acoustically, its destruction by fire after the Second World War was a major tragedy. We played two concerts a week in Glasgow and one in Edinburgh. The Usher Hall in Edinburgh, though a handsome hall, was not so easy acoustically, and on Mondays when we went there for rehearsal it was always icy cold, because they put the heating on only later, just in time for the concert. We used to call the day 'Black Monday'!

I had begun to know John only a little during the opera tours, but we got to know each other really well during the Scottish seasons. John's very short and unsuccessful marriage to the singer, Marjorie Parry, had foundered. She had not understood the close bond within Italian families and she was very jealous of John's deep love for his mother, who never liked her. Also I think that she lacked the warmth and sensitivity his nature needed. But the failure of a marriage can be blamed on either of those concerned.

Most of our 'courting' was done in the cold damp of the Glasgow winter. After a good dinner, usually of steak and claret, we would wander round the parks and streets of Glasgow, occasionally looking at the house where the great pioneer surgeon Joseph Lister lived. In those days, the sharing of 'digs' was frowned upon, and only if the weather was particularly bad did we go to John's rooms, where he had a dear and understanding landlady. Unfortunately, my 'digs' were on the other side of the city from John's rooms so we had to get a taxi for him to take me home. At that time in Glasgow, taxis were almost non-existent at night, and the only place where we could be sure of getting one was in a funeral parlour. We spent much of our courting time in undertakers' premises waiting for a conveyance! Only once did we actually have to travel in a hearse – a rather splendid ancient Rolls-Royce. A special treat when we had a free day was to take a twopenny tram all the way to Loch Lomond. On one memorable occasion we hired an old car and visited Iverarary.

During the Scottish season of 1935–6, John was invited to conduct the New York Philharmonic. This thrilling invitation came out of the blue. We learnt later that the many eminent soloists who had played with the Scottish had returned to New York full of praise for its gifted young conductor. In 1928, Arthur Judson, the manager of the New York Philharmonic and head of Columbia Concerts America, had met John in London; and in 1932 he wrote to him asking him to keep in touch. He was obviously interested in John even then, and his first opinion was consolidated by reports from the famous soloists.

While John was in New York, Georg Szell came to conduct the Scottish. The orchestra respected him but did not like him. He was a very good disciplinarian, with a discerning ear, but had no gift for dealing with an orchestra. He rehearsed meticulously, but the concerts really never 'lit up' and we were not inspired by him. He took a fancy to me and used to take me out to dinner frequently; I think he was probably lonely. He was an interesting man and the expensive dinners were very welcome, so I quite enjoyed those occasions. Then, to my astonishment, and not a little embarrass-ment, he asked me to marry him; I explained that I was deeply in love with John and far too involved to dream of accepting. He wrote a piece for oboe and piano for me; it was attractive, rather in the manner of Strauss, and very well written for the oboe. But I never played it and indeed it did not survive long because when John came back he tore it up and destroyed it, having

46

misunderstood my relationship with Szell (a misunderstanding which was soon resolved). In later years, Szell made a very successful career with the Cleveland Orchestra, and John and I met him and his wife again at a party in New York, when he and John were both established as distinguished conductors.

Occasionally, after John's return to the Scottish from New York, we had a weekend in York, breaking our journey from Glasgow to London. This was a great joy; we loved wandering about that beautiful city and spending time in its wonderful Minster. On one of these weekends we had an unusually interesting time. One day when we were in the Minster we noticed an old Venetian gondola anchoring-post; imaginatively, it was being used as decoration, and it looked curiously natural in its unusual place. As we were looking at it, the Dean came by and talked to us. Realising our great love for the Minster, he took us to see the reassembling of the magnificent glass windows, which had been removed and stored secretly during the Second World War. He told us that when the windows were taken down it had been noticed that many parts of them had been put together inaccurately, perhaps due to several centuries of repairs and cleaning. It had then been decided that after the war the windows should be replaced in perfect order. The Dean took us to a large room in a nearby building equipped with long narrow tables with glass tops lit from below, on which were enormous numbers of small, coloured pieces of glass. Three leather-aproned craftsmen worked there, each sorting out a tabletop. It was like an enormous jigsaw puzzle – one in which the craftsmen seemed utterly involved, carefully examining and shifting the pieces of glass with forceps. As we went into this 'puzzle room' one craftsman called out: 'Hey, Bill, have you got the virgin's head? I've got a bit of her dress and a shoe to match'.

The enterprise had obviously been organised with careful skill and efficiency, and the whole episode was enchanting. After staying for a while, fascinated, we went to the Deanery for tea. Dean Eric Milner-White was an imaginative and innovative man, whose company we felt privileged to enjoy. Quite recently, I met two old friends of his who told me that he had a distinguished collection of china and some very fine pictures. They also had been to the 'jigsaw room' and told me that the idea of it had been entirely the Dean's; it was typical of his care and love for the Minster and for everything fine and lovely.

I remember another happy occasion in York. The city had no concert hall or similar building, so when the Hallé went to play there, the concert would be held in a cinema. The orchestra always enjoyed this visit (and so did we) because Mr Prendergast, who managed the cinema, and his wife and staff, were so kind and so warmhearted. They always seemed delighted to welcome us and could not do enough to make things easy for everyone: the baggage handlers and Hallé staff, the orchestra, and John and myself. Mr Prendergast knew that John loved good ham (an almost unobtainable luxury in those days of rationing) and he arranged one evening for us to have high tea with ham and eggs after the afternoon concert. The eggs were fresh, and the first-class ham had been cured by a local farmer. The wine also was excellent though perhaps not the ideal partner for the food! Mr Prendergast had heard that John liked wine and with typical generosity he had gone to his dealer and asked him for his most expensive wine. This was a very fine Chateau Yquem, which was poured in abundant quantities into large glasses to accompany the excellent ham and eggs. It made for an unusual mixture of tastes, but one dictated by boundless kindness and generosity, and one we always remembered over the years with warm gratitude.

When the Scottish season ended in early spring, we returned to London where I continued my freelancing and John settled down to study for the New York Philharmonic's next winter season. We saw each other as often as our busy lives would permit. I came to know and love John's family; I always went to lunch on Sundays at his sister Rosie's home and most of the family would be there. We all got on very easily, and those lunches were wonderfully enjoyable. John and I used to spend happy hours wandering around London; he loved exploring old parts and seeking out fascinating places which he used to show me. Sadly, most of these have gone, either through wartime destruction or rebuilding by greedy, moneymaking builders. Fortunately there still remains a lovely group of little bow-fronted old houses in Goodwin's Court, a narrow alleyway off St. Martin's Lane.

We were both admirers of the great jazz performer and composer, Duke Ellington, and on one occasion we went together to a concert given by the Duke and his band. One piece on the programme, 'Sophisticated Lady', fascinated us particularly. My first ever present from John, a record of this song, was dedicated to 'An Unsophisticated Lady, with love'.

## ——— 7 ———

# Glyndebourne – The First Years

*GLYNDEBOURNE OPENED IN* the summer of 1934. Many people dismissed it as a mad idea of John Christie's. They said 'Who is going to travel to Sussex to see Mozart operas in the afternoon, in full evening dress?' (Evening dress was then obligatory.) Now, after more than sixty successful years, Glyndebourne is still flourishing. John Christie's son, George, is responsible for building the new, larger opera house. This is lovely to look at and acoustically excellent, and the surrounding gardens are in great taste. The larger theatre has not lost the warm, evocative atmosphere or the quality and feeling of the old Glyndebourne; it seats more people while still feeling intimate, and has all modern equipment for the scenery and stage management. We must all be grateful to John Christie for his imaginative and inspired idea, and to his son, George and to his grandson Gus who are so wonderfully carrying on the tradition and spirit of Glyndebourne.

Glyndebourne in 1934 was a magical experience for the orchestra and singers. Today, it seems almost incredible that we had two weeks of rehearsals for two Mozart operas (*Le Nozze di Figaro* and *Cosi fan Tutte*). The orchestra even played for stage rehearsals, so we could see the great producer, Carl Ebert, at work, and watch the performances taking shape. Luckily, I was able to see quite well, because the woodwind sat on the outside of the orchestra pit. The two men who made the first Glyndebourne so successful and laid the foundations for the future, were Producer Carl Ebert and Conductor Fritz Busch. They worked very closely together so that the performances achieved a true unity. The continuo parts were played with great imagination and humour by Busch himself, sitting in the orchestra pit; in this way he was able to control the speed of the recitatives and make them part of the whole movement of the opera. Busch, a lovely musician and a truly fine conductor whom the orchestra admired very much, and Ebert, a producer of well-deserved renown, worked to great effect with a small team of expert musical coaches and stage technicians. All the singers were distinguished and accomplished although not at that time world-wide stars, and both musically and dramatically the performances were excellent.

In those days everything was more intimate: the original theatre was much smaller and John Christie in his lederhosen (he was an Austro-phile) was always around in the theatre and in the garden, where we strolled in the intervals. He and his charming wife, the singer Audrey Mildmay, made everyone feel part of the whole happening. Audrey, for whom Christie had really founded Glyndebourne, wasn't perhaps a great singer – her voice was attractive and true but quite small. But she had so much vitality and charm on the stage that her performances were always musical and memorable. I remember her still as Susanna in *Le Nozze di Figaro*, and in a later season as Zerlina in *Don Giovanni*. Today, when Glyndebourne tickets are so much in demand, it is strange to recall the first performances, and the scepticism and disapproval with which they were greeted. Christie had arranged a special train from London to Lewes with a bus on to Glyndebourne. For the first performance the little theatre was nearly empty, with Christie in his box and his close friends in some of the stalls. But the press came and were duly impressed, and in a very short time the situation changed completely. Performances were extolled and soon sold out, and the transport was fully booked. Christie's apparently crazy vision became a highly successful reality.

For the orchestra, it was a most delightful job. In those early days we lived during the opera season in Lewes, the country town a few miles from Glyndebourne, at an excellent family-run hotel called the White Hart. A bus was arranged to take us to rehearsals and performances, and to bring us back to the hotel for dinner during the long interval. Today, the orchestra members usually drive back to their homes after the performances; cars are rather more reliable now than they were over sixty years ago!

In our free time (mostly during the day once the two weeks of rehearsals were over, and always Sundays) we played golf or dangerously rough cricket on the Sussex Downs. For me, it was a lovely opportunity to see John, as the family's rented house was not far away. It was an idyllic existence with only one unhappy occasion: the first rehearsal. We were in an unfinished building, sitting on a wet concrete floor overlaid with planks. There were no doors or windows, so that icy winds blew through us on this cold English summer day. We started with the Overture to *Cosi fan Tutte*, which begins with an oboe solo. The oboe and I were both dreadfully cold so the first note of my solo was extremely flat. (To explain to non-wind players, when an oboe is cold its pitch is flat.) Busch stopped and said: 'It is too deep; (i.e. too low, too flat). I began again but it was still 'too deep'. I tried to explain, but at that time Busch's limited English made it hard for him to understand me and I was nervous and unsure of myself. Most of the orchestra was drawn from the L.S.O. and as Natalie James and I had replaced their oboe players after our auditions, they were observing me critically and rather unkindly. The whole rehearsal was utterly miserable, and I was quite sure that my contract would be terminated immediately. Fortunately, my fears were unfounded! We got on well with our colleagues and soon we were invited to join the L.S.O., the first women ever to become members. At that time, women were not welcome in the profession (the L.S.O. even had a male harpist) so we were privileged indeed. My Glyndebourne contract was renewed for five seasons, but after 1938 I left to marry John in the summer of 1939. John came one evening to see Busch, and Busch said: 'Do you really *have* to get married during the Glyndebourne season? What about my oboe player?' However, we did not alter our decision: war seemed inevitable, and John was likely soon to be summoned back to New York to fulfil his contract with the Philharmonic.

I still treasure my memories of those early Glyndebourne seasons, and especially a photograph from Fritz Busch dedicated to 'The best of all oboe players'.

# —— 8 ——

# *Marriage and Honeymoon*

*JOHN'S DIVORCE CAME* through and at noon on 5 July 1939 we married. The ceremony was in the Holborn Registry Office; as John was a divorced Catholic we could not be married in church. We had our wedding lunch in an old established Italian restaurant, Pagani's in Great Portland Street, a wonderful place and truly a restaurant for musicians. There were many famous autographs and photographs on the walls and a lot of Caruso's drawings and caricatures. (He was a very talented cartoonist.) We decided to limit our guests to our families except for John's best man, and my matron of honour. Otherwise, with our many friends, the numbers would have become quite unwieldy, and we did not want that sort of celebration. I can't remember the food at our reception but I do recall that we did not join our guests in their conventional champagne; instead we drank sparkling Vouvray, because neither of us liked champagne. (I am actually allergic to it.) Sadly, Pagani's was destroyed in the Second World War, and so was the registry office where we were married.

After our wedding lunch our plan was to go to John's mother's flat in Streatham where we had left our luggage and the car, and then drive to Newhaven, where we would spend our first night, catching the ferry to France in the morning. There was a slight delay when Tom Cheetham, John's best man, left behind our passports and money and had to return to Pagani's to retrieve them. However, all was well; in those days there was never much traffic on the roads, so journeying by car was much easier and quicker.

When we reached Sussex, we visited the lovely old church in Steyning to affirm our marriage in a more religious way than had been possible earlier. And then, after the night in Newhaven, we crossed the Channel to France.

Sadly, we could not go to Italy for our honeymoon as John had planned. He had so wanted me to meet his Italian relatives and begin to get to know the country of his origin, but all this had to wait for a few years. It seems that certain aspects of the law differ (or certainly differed then) in Italy from Great Britain. Anyone born in Britain is British unless they voluntarily renounce their British citizenship at the age of eighteen. But according to Italian law, anyone born of an Italian father anywhere in the world is an Italian for life. John took advice from an acquaintance in the Foreign Office, who told him that his British passport would protect and help him anywhere in the world – except in Italy. John was warned that, should war be declared while we were in Italy, he would be conscripted into the Italian army. Obviously, this was a risk we could not take.

We took my car (a slightly better one than the smelly and noisy Singer we had used in Sussex) and explored Normandy and Brittany; it seemed wise to be near the Channel in case of an emergency that might force us to return to England in a hurry. I drove and we had a very happy two weeks. It was all very leisurely. We did not travel long distances, we stayed in small places and saw some lovely unspoilt ones. Everywhere in rural France we ate and drank excellently and cheaply. There was very little traffic, and we were fortunate to have fine weather and to find some delightful small hotels. We took with us a Michelin

Guide (we always scanned this for hotels or restaurants marked with a red R) and various maps and books, and John packed several scores. Even on his honeymoon he studied a good deal, while I explored and took photographs (in those days I was a keen photographer). It was a very happy time; the only sadness was that war seemed so near and so inevitable.

We visited the great churches in Caen and saw the Bayeux Tapestry. Here, John had a long conversation in fluent French with the old curator – mainly about the virtues of cooking on a spit, which is illustrated in the Tapestry. When we went to Caen and Bayeux we did not stay in hotels but in a very small guest house near the sea in Arromanches, later the scene of one of the D-day landings in the war. The old lady who owned the hostelry was also the cook. I remember her coming round with pan in hand to ask if we wanted a second helping; her cooking was expert, homely and delicious. I sometimes think of her and of that lovely time and wonder what happened to her in the war. We returned from our honeymoon to our room in John's mother's London flat, where we found awaiting us a cable from the New York Philharmonic insisting that John return immediately to New York, as war seemed so near and, as the cable reminded him, he was under contract. Obviously, he could not afford to break his agreement, so in August he managed to arrange a passage on a ship to America. Sadly, I could not accompany him as I had no American visa and, as the Americans had temporarily closed their visa departments due to the likelihood of war, I was unable to join him in America until October, nearly four months after our marriage – a hard time to be separated.

War was declared on 3 September 1939. While waiting to go to New York, I stayed with my family in the country, and occupied my time driving evacuees from London and helping to house them with local residents. If it was very hard for some of the poor children, it was perhaps even harder for some of their hosts and hostesses. I helped to remove all the signposts to make things more difficult for the Germans should they invade us; rolled bandages, packed dressings for the Red Cross, and dug up gardens to grow vegetables. The time went slowly as I waited eagerly for news of a visa and ship to America while writing to and receiving letters from John, who was trying hard to pull all the strings he could. Finally, I got my American visa and the date was arranged for me to sail to New York on a small American ship, on 21 October.

# 9

## *Journey to America: Life in New York*

*ON THE FIRST* day at sea, I was sitting on deck reading when a couple stopped and asked if I were John's new wife. I looked up and saw Rachmaninov and his daughter. Of course, I knew him by sight; I had seen him in concerts and played in orchestras when he was the soloist. He chatted a little and told me how much he loved making music with John who, he said, was such a wonderful accompanist. Finally, he asked me if I would like to go to the captain's tea-party that afternoon with him and his daughter. I went to the party on Rachmaninov's arm; it was a very proud moment! Thereafter, he would stop every day and talk to me briefly on deck. He was so warm and so kind, I like to think that perhaps I saw a side of this great and yet very reserved man which was not often shown. The only other contact I made on that boat trip, (apart from the North Country lady with whom I shared a cabin and who grumbled a great deal about everything), was with a very large, imposing American lady who asked me if I would find out from my husband why he never conducted the Fifth Symphony of Brahms. When I said that I knew of no such work, she was extremely annoyed and called me an ignorant fool. I discovered later that she was a well-known 'lion hunter' who gave large fashionable parties, and knew nothing about music.

On arrival in New York, I was met by John's excellent and much loved secretary Johnny Woolford, as John was conducting a concert in Boston that night. Johnny took me to our apartment in Hampshire House on Central Park South, where John arrived from Boston to join me at about 4 a.m.

Our apartment was lovely. We were quite high up, on the 28th floor next door to Yehudi Menuhin and his first wife. At twilight, when the city lights came on, the view was beautiful, like fairyland. We had a large, comfortably furnished sitting room and a very small kitchen with a tiny fridge, gas cooker and sink, equipped with pots and pans and various utensils. The bedroom had its own bathroom. There was adequate cupboard and drawer space, good heavy curtains (John liked a dark bedroom at night) and the cleaning and porter service was included in our rent. Hampshire House had been booked for us by the New York Philharmonic management, who considered that it had a suitably exclusive address. The right address was of considerable importance to most Americans; they would assume that it cost a lot of money for the dweller, and therefore that he or she was of important standing and had a large income. Some years later when John returned to the U.S.A. for guest appearances, we made a sentimenal return to Hampshire House, but, sadly, it had gone down in quality and prestige since we had lived there.

Its greatest advantage for us in New York in 1936–43 was that it was only a few minutes' walk from Carnegie Hall, where all the rehearsals and concerts were held in the days before the Lincoln Center was built. Carnegie Hall was a beautiful old hall of great character and excellent acoustics, far better, in John's opinion and mine, as well as that of many others, than the large new hall in the Lincoln Center. At one time, Carnegie Hall was threatened with destruction, but thanks to the efforts of the distinguished violinist Isaac Stern and many others who helped him, the valuable old building was saved, and it remains in use today. All musicians should be deeply grateful to Isaac and his supporters.

Johnny Woolford, our secretary, was a dear young man, deeply loyal, affectionate and caring for us both, and he was a great help to me. Hitherto, my life had been that of an orchestral player: I was ignorant about my duties as John's wife, and Johnny guided me about matters such as social contacts, which invitations to accept or refuse, who to be polite to or to trust, arranging to fill the right seats in the conductor's box for each concert: the whole situation was a minefield of social opportunities and errors. A regular visitor at that time was Elisabeth Schumann, who was living in New York at the time, not very happily we felt. She used to telephone in advance to ask for a ticket and it was always a joy to have her in the box. She used to say to John that she did not believe that he had no Viennese blood in him since he understood the music of Vienna so well.

During my first long session with Johnny Woolford he told me about the Ladies Committee and its chairman, Mrs Ruth Pratt. I should explain that the financing of orchestras in America was (and to a degree still is) organised very differently from the way it is done these days in Europe. There was little or no government financing; the necessary funds were collected from voluntary donations, and many of these were organised by the Ladies' Committee of the orchestra concerned. The members of these committees are dedicated and extremely hard-working – and a certain amount of prestige is involved. Mrs Pratt was the chairman of the New York Philharmonic Ladies' Committee; she liked John, and no doubt she was loyal to him and helpful. Although not musically knowledgeable, she was shrewd and intelligent and a powerful personality. Like many rich American women of her type, she was spoilt and adulated by hangers-on who enjoyed her lavish hospitality and relied on her influence and her wealth. She had known John well before I arrived, and he thought she had intended to marry him, or at least to have him, in modern parlance, as her 'toy boy'! Already elderly, she was not at all pleased when he appeared with a new, comparatively young wife. She resented and disliked me and made little attempt to conceal it. However, she still worked extremely hard collecting funds for the Philharmonic, and with considerable success. We often saw her at her weekly dinner parties in her New York apartment, we met her family and her close friends, and went to stay in her beautiful home on Long Island where her charming Scottish butler, McCullough, brought our breakfast and chatted to us in his delightful Scottish accent. In all, we saw a good deal of her; perhaps not as much as she would have liked, but often enough to satisfy courtesy and diplomacy. The situation was not easy, and one to deal with for which I had neither the experience nor sophistication.

There were others of her type to whom we had to be polite and in whose houses we were entertained. It made things no easier that America was very isolationist at this time, and afraid of getting involved in the war. At the various social events we had to be diplomatic and still our tongues. When even the half-American Churchill was bitterly criticised and maligned, the temptation to stand up for our country and its lonely and courageous stand was irresistible. Then the Japanese bombed Pearl Harbor and the American fleet, and things became very different. The Americans entered the war and our dinner party conversations thereafter were certainly much easier!

From the very beginning, the members of the New York Philharmonic were truly devoted to John, and their loyalty meant a great deal to him. The audiences too were happy. Many years later we discovered that attendances for John's concerts had averaged 85 per cent throughout his seven years, higher even than Toscanini had ever achieved. We got on well with the small but efficient administrative staff of the Philharmonic. The manager, Arthur Judson, a powerful and important figure in the music of America, was a reserved and taciturn man who nevertheless had, I felt, a genuine affection and admiration for John. The assistant manager, Bruno Zirato, Italian in origin, became our good friend. Maybe he was a bit of a diplomat and liked to keep in with everybody, but he had warmth and charm and I'm sure he was genuinely fond of us. Judson's secretary, Nora Shea, was Irish, attractive and charming, but possibly still hankered after Toscanini, who had been especially attached to her.

Johnny Woolford was already John's friend, and very soon he became mine. He was intensely musical and came to all the concerts and some rehearsals, and he worked in our apartment at Hampshire House taking telephone calls and messages there. As I have said, he knew all the people we had to deal with and was fully conversant with the political situations that concerned us. We were both deeply fond of him and valued fully his touching care of us. He was always there when we needed him despite John's unusual hours. After we returned to England we saw Johnny again when he came over with the U.S. Army, and once more when John guest conducted in New York. Years later, his sister wrote to tell us of his suicide. We were greatly distressed and saddened, and wished only that had we known the reason for this; we could perhaps have helped to avert his death.

The really unhappy aspect of our New York life was the virulently bad press. In John's first two years in New York the most respected critic of the time had been Lawrence Gilman. He approved of John's appointment and wrote beautifully and appreciatively about his performances. Sadly, by the time I arrived in the autumn of 1939, Gilman had died, and the most influential critic was Olin Downes, who seemed to dislike John's work and always wrote disparagingly about his concerts.

We found out later that his behaviour was aimed only indirectly against John. Judson, who had been mainly responsible for appointing John, had made the mistake of dismissing Downes from the position of commentator for the prestigious Sunday broadcasts of the New York Philharmonic. These concerts were widely heard all over the country and their commentator had a most important (and well paid) task and reputation. When Downes was dismissed, he started a campaign against John because he was Judson's protégé, the intention being to harm Judson. Nearly all the other New York critics followed the important and influential Downes. Virgil Thomson, who had succeeded Gilman at the *New York Herald Tribune*, was even more vitriolic and eventually came to ignore the New York Philharmonic altogether. The reviews were destructive and hurtful and made John's exacting task even more difficult, but the loyalty of the orchestra and the consistently good audiences were wonderfully supportive and buoyed him up to do his work.

Toscanini was not at all helpful. He had resigned from the New York Philharmonic, and we realised later that he had hoped that he would be found indispensible and be implored to return. But this did not happen because John's appointment was so successful. The N.B.C. (National Broadcasting Corporation) then formed an orchestra for Toscanini, who gave concerts in New York at the same time as John's. This was deliberately unhelpful, though the project was much less successful than those concerned had intended. At this time, Toscanini was almost deified in New York. In some ways he was a great conductor, but I feel now, as do many musicians who hear his CDs, that his reputation was exaggerated. He had enormous vitality and rhythmic strength, but there seemed to be little sensitivity, tenderness or humour in his performances. He drove these just as he drove his players, he did not seem to caress or to love the music he was making. From what one hears, he had conducted differently in his younger years in Milan. Perhaps then he was not so spoilt and adulated.

Toscanini held court every Sunday morning, attended by some of the orchestral players' wives, general gossips, and sycophants who loved to kow-tow to him. John attended one of these sessions early on during his New York time. He had known Toscanini a long while; his father had shared digs on tour with Toscanini in their early years. Unfortunately, on the morning John attended, Toscanini unleashed a long tirade against Bruno Walter and his conducting. John, who loved and admired Walter, left in disgust. Much later, at the end of John's seven-year period in New York, Toscanini telephoned him, an almost unheard-of occurrence! He said that he had not met me and would like to, and that he felt he and John should get together again. We invited Toscanini to a little Italian restaurant we knew and had just a few friends to dinner. Toscanini liked good French cognac, so I plied him with this from the bottle on the table. He became quite mellow and charming, but he was untrustworthy, and I'm sure that he did not wish John well. That night, primed with good Italian food and French brandy, he apologised for his unkind behaviour to John, though we were never sure exactly what behaviour to which he was referring.

We had some good friends in the orchestra, especially the Italian tuba player, Vincenzo Vanni, and we were fond of Nat, the backstage attendant for the Philharmonic at Carnegie Hall who looked after all backstage affairs. After concerts, he sorted out the visitors and decided who should come in, while I helped John to change. Otto Klemperer came on several occasions to see John, and always insisted on being alone with him in his private conductor's room. On his first visit, Nat was worried, as was Klemperer's 'keeper' who was always with him. Recently Klemperer had undergone a very serious brain operation, and though a full recovery was anticipated (and ultimately did take place) Klemperer was at this time really not well. When he arrived backstage he looked alarming, with his vast height and rather wild unfocused eyes. However, John invited him into his room alone and shut the door. John told me afterwards that it was a delightful time: Klemperer had held John's hand a while, helped him to change and discussed the concert with great musical intelligence and admiration; in fact he had seemed quite all right. He came again several times. John always looked forward to his visits and Nat and the 'keeper' were no longer worried.

In his free time, Nat was a keen fisherman, and he talked often about a particular fish he wanted to bring us after his next expedition. It was called, according to Nat, 'sibbus'. It took us a while to decipher Nat's very strong accent and find that it was sea bass! And when he brought it to us, the freshly caught fish was delicious.

We had some close English friends in the city. John Mundy was the orchestra manager at the Metropolitan Opera House and his wife Clytie was a well-known singing teacher who numbered Peter Pears among her pupils. (The Royal College of Music in London has a prize in her name.) Another friend was Tim McOstrich, an Irishman of great knowledge and considerable charm. A close childhood friend of mine, he was an expert and reputable dealer in antiques. As his heart was unsound he was physically unfit for the armed forces, so during the war he was sent to New York by the British government to sell rare and priceless furniture, to obtain much-needed dollars. While in New York he fell in love and married a lovely southern American girl. They had a daughter and Tim stayed on doing valuations and working for the British government.

Among our close American friends were the Steinway family, of piano-making fame. They were intensely loyal and supportive, helpful and understanding, and we became very fond of them all.

Apart from the normal repertory, John introduced the New York audiences to a lot of music which was new to them. He often included American works, which had to be played sometimes to encourage the generous donors to the Philharmonic funds! Their quality was very variable, though there were some good composers among them, for instance, John felt that Samuel Barber was really gifted. He also played a good deal of English music, which was certainly new to the Americans; for example, very little Elgar or Vaughan Williams, had as yet been performed. John included two new works by Benjamin Britten, his powerful and touching *Sinfonia da Requiem*, and the Violin Concerto with Brosa as soloist. These performances were crucially important for Ben at this stage of his career and I know that John was hurt that Ben never acknowledged them in later years.

One event was unusually memorable for me. Benjamin Britten and Peter Pears had been in New York for quite a while and Ben, a very good viola player, was longing to play some chamber music, particularly that of Mozart. He collected a quartet of good players, intending to add a viola for the wonderful Mozart Quintets. Ben invited me to come and listen if I wished, and perhaps to play in the Mozart Oboe Quartet. On the morning of our planned musical meeting, he telephoned to tell me that the leader of his quartet was ill and a replacement could not be found. Would I like to 'have a go' at the first violin parts on my oboe? As the compass and capabilities of the oboe differ greatly from those of the violin, it was with some trepidation that I agreed to take on this formidable task. When the time came we staggered through three Quintets. Ben, as I've said, was an excellent violist, the other players were musical and capable, and I managed as well as I could. It was an exciting and inspiring time of making music, even though there were some technical deficiencies. I can't recall ever enjoying chamber music more; certainly it was an occasion I shall never forget.

It was a great musical pleasure for me to listen to the rehearsals and concerts in Carnegie Hall. Many unkind words have been said about the New York Philharmonic Orchestra before and after John's seven years, but I always thought that it was a great orchestra in those years under John, and recently remastered CDs confirm my opinion. When I was listening to the orchestra 'in the flesh' their pleasure and respect when playing for John was obvious; maybe, as they were a temperamental lot, they did not always play well with anyone else! (I forget who said: 'There are no good and bad orchestras, only good and bad conductors.')

The period in New York was exciting in many ways, not least because we met – and John conducted – some of the greatest artists of the day. Kreisler we loved especially and got to know quite well. A wonderful player and a dear man, he always called John 'my musical son'. Once he came up to our flat to go through some of his well-known pieces for violin and piano which he had arranged for the Philharmonic to play at a forthcoming charity concert. He sat down at our piano, a beautiful instrument lent to us by the Steinway family. Kreisler played the piano enchantingly and it was a delight to listen to him. The rehearsal did not take long: John knew the pieces well and Kreisler loved playing with him. When they had finished, Kreisler refused any refreshment, but said: 'Do you mind if I just stay a little while? It's so happy and peaceful here.' Naturally, we were proud and delighted and after this he used to come up to our flat occasionally. We did not disturb him while he was there. He would sit quietly, or would play the piano, sometimes for quite a long time; it was a great privilege and joy for us.

His end was sad because a street accident earlier in life had left him in old age very deaf and almost blind. A few years later when John was guest-conducting in New York, we went to see him in his apartment on Riverside Drive. He looked very old and frail and when we said goodbye we felt that it was for the last time; indeed he died soon afterwards. Our memories remained warm and deeply grateful. His wife Harriet was difficult at times and certainly not obviously attractive, but he loved her devotedly and always said that had it not been for Harriet he would never have had a career. He told us that he had loved pleasure too much, had stayed through the small hours playing cards and gambling, he was lazy about practising and Harriet had made him work. In time we came to know Harriet and to appreciate her worth. She was certainly neither tactful nor apparently particularly sensitive. On that last occasion when we went to see him in New York, Harriet welcomed us warmly and when she took us in to see Fritz she said: 'Evelyn has got such a pretty dress and looks so lovely, don't you think so?' Fritz said rather sadly: 'I wish I could see her.' He took my face in his hands and felt it, and then touched the dress, as blind people do. He was not only a unique artist of the greatest quality, but one of the most lovable and dear men we knew.

Horowitz we knew and liked greatly. A brilliant pianist, he was often exceedingly nervous when he played and sometimes at the end of a performance he would run around madly, apparently unable to stop. He was very likeable, in an entirely different way from Kreisler; he was naive and childlike. But he was not the mere virtuoso pianist he was often considered to be. I remember one summer in California he told us that he had been working at the Beethoven Symphonies arranged for piano by Liszt, which even he found very difficult; he had been studying the full scores for comparison. To the great surprise of many friends he married one of Toscanini's daughters, Wanda, who had a strong and rather hard personality. It was generally accepted that Horowitz was homosexual and he was nervy and temperamental almost to the point of inbalance. The marriage was not a success; they had one child, a daughter, who we heard was difficult, but Wanda stuck by Horowitz till his death. I'm afraid that their life cannot have been easy.

Vallodio, as we called Horowitz, did not like playing with his father-in-law. Once he came to see us in our home in California because he was just about to play the Tchaikovsky Piano Concerto with John, having recently recorded it with Toscanini. John and Vallodio discussed the work briefly, they had often played it together during Horowitz's early appearances in London. Vallodio said partly in French: '*Mais pas comme Papa. He make me play so fast, and I am not free.*' He had his own technique of playing, with his fingers very flat, and wherever he went he took a special Steinway piano which had a very light action. He was a superb pianist and a gentle, lovable and intensely modest man.

Another good friend, and a great pianist with whom John loved to play, was Arthur Rubinstein. He had a wonderful command of the keyboard and tremendous, passionate vitality; he was larger than life and a great performer on and off the stage, very warm and entertaining. He and John got on splendidly. I think that probably Rubinstein was one of the artists who extolled John to Judson and the New York management, because he had worked with him often in England and Scotland, and I know he admired him greatly.

I have already talked a little about Rachmaninov. Of course he often played in New York and I saw him many times. He always looked very dour and rather miserable, but I believe he was one of the greatest pianists I have ever heard. He made a particularly beautiful singing sound on the piano and with his huge hands he could play an almost incredible legato. I heard him perform his own works mostly, and sometimes on records his rather naughty arrangements (such as the Mendelssohn Scherzo from *A Midsummer Night's Dream*). His playing was intensely musical and nobody ever made the piano sound a truly *cantabile* instrument as he did. He had a great sense of humour, though it was not always kindly. I remember on one occasion when he was in the New York artists' room with John and me. Rachmaninov had recently played his Paganini Variations with an eminent conductor he did not like, and who was not a good accompanist. One of the Paganini Variations is particularly hard for the conductor: *very* fast as Rachmaninov played it, with some tricky cross-rhythms. Rachmaninov said on this occasion in his half American accent, with a remnant of his Russian cigarette dangling from his mouth: 'I played *so fast* – he lost me.' He roared with laughter and triumph, and did not seem to mind that he had spoilt part of a performance of one of his own works.

Some years later we went to his funeral in California. The Russian Orthodox church was very small and packed with people and it was a very hot day. Each person held a lighted candle which made it even warmer. The music, sung by a fine male voice choir, was beautiful, and there were of course a good many prayers and addresses in Russian which we could not understand. The service seemed to last a very long time; there were no seats, so everyone stood, and at the end of it all, we filed out past Rachmaninov who was in an open coffin in full evening dress. His hand dangled over the edge of the coffin and most of the congregation kissed his ring, though I'm afraid we did not do so. Michael Kennedy recalls John saying to him: 'The old boy looked a bloody sight more cheerful than he ever did on the platform!'

I could tell you much more about those New York years, their difficulties and their delights. New York then was a fascinating city; then, even as now, there was a quality in the air that gave one great energy. I remember always being up very late, and having no desire to rest. On the practical side, delicatessens which sold all the essentials, were open very late, and restaurants went on serving into the small hours. One delightful side of our life in New York was 'Bronzos'. This was a small eating place; not exactly a restaurant, and was known only to intimates. 'Mama' cooked for some Italian members of the orchestra who would sit at a long table in her kitchen. She cooked for very few others mostly orchestra personnel, and all regulars. We ate privately in her sitting room with our friends, or just by ourselves. We would telephone in the morning to tell Mama whether there would be just the two of us or more people, whether we had any special dishes we'd like her to cook, and give her an approximate time of arrival. She was a wonderful cook, and she and her family were affectionate and welcoming. It was truly a home from home. We often went there with our dear old friend, the conductor Georgio Polacco. Georgio was a constant source of affection and strength to us both; now retired, he had made a great reputation as an opera conductor and director in Chicago. John had heard him and admired him many years earlier at one of his many Covent Garden appearances. Sadly, towards the end of our New York period, 'Bronzos' shut down. We heard various rumours that Mama had not paid the necessary taxes, or did not have the permits to run a restaurant, but we never discovered the truth.

After that we often cooked for ourselves in our tiny apartment kitchen. John was a naturally gifted cook (a talent probably inherited from his French mother). I loved helping him and doing menial tasks, so we enjoyed the activity. It stood us in good stead when we returned to England in 1943 to a life of strict rations, shortages and coupons.

71

## —— 10 ——

# Vancouver Holiday

*AT THE END* of the New York season in May we would go to Vancouver, in Canada. We first went because John had received an invitation from Rhynd Jamieson, the editor of the *Vancouver Province*, a flourishing local newspaper, asking him to conduct a big charity concert in aid of the Red Cross. The journey was pleasant and very restful. We went to Chicago by rail and there we changed on to a Canadian Pacific train to Vancouver. The accommodation on the train was excellent; we had what was rather charmingly called 'a drawing room', which consisted of a large cabin for two and 'facilities'. It had comfortable seats by day which were made into beds for the night. If you wished – and we did wish – you could have your meals and any other refreshments brought to your drawing room by the porter who looked after your coach. Our porter was a charming young man who ran for Canada in the Olympic Games. We asked him how he managed about training. He told us that he did two or three trips on the Canadian Pacific Railway without training at all, just to keep himself in funds, and then went home and trained hard, doing any odd jobs he could find if he needed more money. The CPR paid well, he said, and he really enjoyed the job and meeting different people. He was extremely intelligent and efficient and we liked him greatly.

The scenery was dull and flat at first; as we went through the wheat-growing districts of Canada, passing cities such as Edmonton and Calgary; but later on when we came to the Rockies, the scenery was spectacularly grand and beautiful and the weather was sunny, frosty and clear. The train moved through the Rockies at a very slow pace. We could see very well from our large cabin window, but in that old-fashioned train we could go and stand, warmly wrapped up, on a small outdoor platform, where the view was even better. In those days there was no inside observation car. At some places in the Rockies the train stopped while the guard got out and changed the points some yards away, which we liked to watch. We were always amused that he walked back to rejoin the train, which by then had begun, very slowly, to move again; his cap bore the word TRAINMAN. We did this railway trip three times, and on later trips we stopped to spend a night at Banff or Lake Louise. Now, I understand, there are grand, luxurious hotels in both places. In our time the hotels were not smart, but they were homely and very comfortable. There were no tourists – we had those lovely places to ourselves. Once when we stopped at Lake Louise it was such a gloriously cold, sunny day that we decided to go for a walk along the lakeside. On our return to the hotel we were aware that we were being followed and there was a rather ominous snuffling noise behind us. We glanced back briefly and saw a very large bear quite near. He did not seem to be at all aggressive, but we were afraid to run lest he started to run after us. Fortunately, we were not far from the hotel and the bear headed directly for the kitchen entrance. The hotel staff were amused that we had been so anxious, and told us that 'old Joe' was really quite harmless and used to come daily for food from the kitchen. We wished we had known that earlier!

We loved Vancouver and decided to try to rent somewhere to live for the next six weeks or so as we had a free period before

John was due to conduct at the Hollywood Bowl. We were both homesick for England and longing to get home. During the war this was impossible, so hearing the news read by a British reader, and being among friendly allies, seemed the next best thing, and it proved to be a successful and lovely time. During the days around the Vancouver concert we stayed at a very good local hotel, the Devonshire, where we became good friends with the owner and his wife. They managed to find an ideal house which we were able to rent from a very nice Welsh couple. The house was secluded and quiet, with a magical view over the city and the sea. We were high up, halfway up Grouse Mountain, in the then unfashionable North Vancouver. We were quite near the 'North Van' village where there were all the shops we could need. Almost all the shopkeepers were Scots and their broad Scottish accents made us feel at home. There was also an excellent Chinese fishmonger who used often to recommend us to take 'flied plawns to eat with lice'. We had hired a car, so if we wanted more elaborate shopping we used to go to the city and visit the big Hudson Bay department store. John was very fond of ham and in the delicatessen department of the Hudson Bay there was always excellent ham on the bone. In charge of it was the first horn player of the orchestra, a very keen and talented young man.

From the city we used to take short trips on the steamers which plied up and down the small creeks and inlets. They were homely little boats and the short journeys were delightful. Occasionally, our friends at the Devonshire Hotel used to drive us outside Vancouver to show us a little of the surrounding countryside. I remember one place where we often lunched by a very beautiful lake. Near our house was Capillano Canyon, a small, unfrequented park where we often walked. The wildlife was undisturbed and really wonderful. There was a salmon leap and a glacierfed pool where we could bathe, except that the water was too icy cold to be inviting. We loved to watch a colony of beavers building their dam across a stream – their skill and perseverance was fascinating. There was a very rickety-looking suspension bridge across an exceedingly deep canyon (reputedly the second longest suspension bridge in the world) which we had to cross to reach most of the park. John used to go first and then shake the bridge when I was crossing to make it even more terrifying than it was already. Such childlike occupations were a delightful part of our Vancouver life. John did an enormous amount of work and I practised a good deal. It was a restful and most satisfying time, and our six weeks went by much too quickly. We met a family of friends there whom we had known in Europe, one of whom, Jan Chenovsky, was an excellent pianist of Russian origin. His wife was an expert photographer, who had a fully equipped dark room. I was keen on taking photographs at the time but had never had the opportunity to do the processing, so I enjoyed working with her excellent equipment.

On a later visit we found two other friends who were living temporarily in Vancouver and whom we met often, the composer Arthur Benjamin, and his Canadian partner, Jack Henderson. Arthur was an expert cook and we enjoyed many a gourmet meal in his Vancouver house. He found the peace of Vancouver excellent for composing. I'm sure that he wrote other, grander works during his time in Vancouver, but he composed there for me a charming Concerto for Oboe and Strings based on the music of Cimarosa. I did not give its first performance – I wasn't playing much at this time – but oboe players everywhere welcomed it, including Goossens. It has remained very popular and I always enjoyed playing and recording it.

When the time came to move we were very sad to leave Vancouver but other pleasures awaited us in Hollywood.

## —— *11* ——

# *California –*
# *Making Music: Hollywood Bowl*

*WE HAD ARRANGED* to buy a car from our good friend Bernard Herrmann, who lived in Beverly Hills, Los Angeles, so we took back our hired car in Vancouver and went to California by train. Our rented house in Beverly Hills was not quite ready for occupancy, so for the first week we stayed with Bernard and his first wife, Lucy. They were a wonderful host and hostess and we became very fond of them both. Benny earned a good living writing music for Hitchcock's films, but he hoped to become known generally as a fine composer, not just a good movie musician. This never quite happened, though John performed his epic choral work *Moby Dick* during the New York season and it was well received. Benny was a remarkable man, a rough-seeming character of exquisite taste and great knowledge. He loved all things English: music, literature, pictures and eighteenth-century furniture, of which he had some fine examples. We had a very happy week with him and Lucy.

When we moved into our rented house we were given the opportunity to employ the maid who had looked after it. This seemed a good idea, so we engaged her. Unfortunately, she proved arrogant, lazy and difficult. I was much too lenient with her and one day John overheard her being very rude to me. To my delight and surprise he dismissed her furiously on the spot. Her successor was a dear large black lady who worked well and was always charming. She had an enchanting little son who sat and watched TV while she did her cleaning.

The word cleaning reminds me of a generous present given to us by a man we had met somewhere in Beverly Hills. He loved hunting red deer and asked if we would like some venison. We said we would, and thought no more about it. Very late one night, after we had gone to bed, our doorbell rang and John went down to investigate. He found nobody there, but on the doorstep was the large carcass of a deer! Fortunately, this generous present had been skinned and eviscerated, but obviously it would not go whole into our freezer or fridge. I went to sleep intending to leave it till the morning, but John couldn't resist dealing with it immediately. In his teens he had always wanted to be a surgeon; all his life he was deeply interested in medical matters, and many of our closest friends in England were doctors. He had, he said, a wonderful time cutting up the carcass into neat manageable pieces. The only place he could 'operate' was the kitchen floor. In the morning I came down to find a huge pile of tidy joints and chunks ready to go into the freezer or fridge. But the kitchen floor was a sea of blood, mostly dried. We thought that our cleaner would be truly horrified and wonder what we'd been up to, so we cleaned the floor together. The venison, marinated in red wine, made a fine addition to our larder.

We had moved from Vancouver to Los Angeles mainly for professional reasons, because John had been engaged to conduct concerts in the Hollywood Bowl. This vast natural canyon had been made into a remarkable 'concert hall' holding, I believe, many thousands of people. It has wonderful natural acoustics, a shell had been built over the orchestra, but that was all. I was told that it was a quarter of a mile from the stage to the most distant seats. On one occasion I sat in one of those seats, and I could hear everything perfectly. The only disconcerting effect was visual; because sound and light waves travel at different rates, the conductor's baton moved at a different speed from the music, so that one did not see what one heard. The Bowl concerts, as they were called, were very prestigious affairs, and only artists of great repute used to appear in them. In the summers when we were there, 1940–42, the concerts were particularly distinguished. Several famous musicians had been forced to leave Germany and other Nazi-run European countries, because they were Jewish or had Jewish sympathies. Many of them had come to make a new life in America and some were in Hollywood for the summer.

In Beverly Hills we got to know really well a lovely family of Italian-American origin, the Marafiotis. Every Sunday we went to lunch there and had a swim in their pool. They were known as our *famiglia* (family), and in a way they were, for we loved them all dearly and felt completely at home with them. Mario, the man of the house, had been secretary to Caruso, and had many tales to tell about him. Caruso was, evidently, an extremely kind and generous man, very helpful to his colleagues and to all who worked for him. Mario Marafioti told us the story of 'The Coat Song'. In a performance of Puccini's *La Bohème*, the bass singer taking the part of Colline had a bad cold and was losing his voice. By the time his big aria (known as 'The Coat Song') was due, in the last act, he was unable to make a sound. Caruso, whose tenor voice had a remarkably wide range, told his colleague to turn his back to the audience and he, Caruso, would sing his aria for him. He did it so successfully that nobody noticed the substitution. Caruso had a private recording of the bass aria made for Mario Marafioti, who kept it for years. When the incident became widely known, Caruso was asked to make a commercial recording of the aria, but he refused because he thought it would be harmful to bass singers. This was typical of his generosity, and it was only later, after his death, that his 'Coat Song' record was released.

The *famiglia* comprised Mario, his wife Clara – a charming and warmhearted American of Italian origin – and their two daughters, Fiora and Ileana, of whom we became particularly fond. The whole family was a delightful part of our lives. Ileana has twice come to England recently with her husband and it has really been a joy to see her and to find her the same dear affectionate person, long and happily married to Klaus a warm-hearted man who I like greatly.

Those summers in and around Los Angeles were wonderful, unique times. We used to make music among friends, most of the well-known European musicians knew each other and we used to go to their rented houses and play just for ourselves. I recall a long session at the house of José Iturbi, a first-class virtuoso Spanish pianist with a great reputation until in mid-career he deserted the serious concert world to make films and play popular light music. At this time, he was living in Beverly Hills with his talented and charming sister, Amparo. That afternoon and evening Iturbi and Horowitz played all the Mozart works for one piano and for two, which was truly a wonderful musical experience. The 'audience' consisted only of Wanda Horowitz, Amparo Iturbi, John and myself. Finally, Amparo cooked a delicious meal for us all.

When John and I held musical evenings, our quartet was a distinguished one, led by Zino Francescati with Bill Primrose playing viola, John cello, and Rudi Polk second violin. John was the cook and he had the most distinguished page turner (incidentally, in Norwegian a 'leaf louse') Edward G. Robinson, well known as a tough, ugly actor in gangster films. He utterly belied his film roles; he was a gentle, sensitive man who loved pictures and had a distinguished collection of Impressionist paintings, for which he had built a fine gallery. He collected these paintings long before they became fashionable and sought-after; he bought them because he loved them. Eddie became our good friend and enjoyed coming to our musical evenings. He did not read music, but used to sit by John and turn over the cello part when John nodded, and so he became part of the ensemble.

One evening we visited Emmanuel Feuermann, with Lauri Kennedy and his wife Dot. Lauri the grandfather of violinist Nigel Kennedy, was a wonderful cellist, who had led the BBC Symphony Orchestra cellos for some years and had now retired (or so he said, though he still played beautifully). Feuermann was himself a great virtuoso cellist who died when tragically young. John used to say that there was literally nothing that Feuermann could not play. We never heard him in a concert so I don't know if his musicality matched his virtuosity, but by general reputation it did. We went to his house that evening because he wanted John and Lauri to try a cello he was thinking of buying, and while we were there they asked him if he would play his famous party piece. This was a performance of the first movement of the Mendelssohn Violin Concerto on the cello, but at the violin's proper pitch. It was incredible – we were all flabbergasted. He was modest and charming on that occasion, but unfortunately, we never saw him again.

A party of a rather different type was given by Wanda and Vallodio Horowitz in their large, grand house. The party also was large and grand; we were all formally dressed and a huge number of people were there, of whom we knew only a few. We were told that Charlie Chaplin would be coming, so we all waited eagerly for him. He arrived, rather late, in a huge chauffeur-driven Rolls-Royce wearing full evening dress. On arrival, before he met or talked to anyone, he stood and addressed us all, and this first impression disappointed most of us. The formal speech seemed pointless and insincere and was littered with platitudes, it was really rather embarrassing. However, afterwards he went around and met the guests. When he came to John he asked in a real cockney voice: ''Ow's Lambeff?' (Lambeth was the part of London whence he came.) Then he changed utterly; John and he chatted about London and its sad destruction from bombing, then Chaplin did an impersonation of a seedy down-and-out drunkard leaning against a pub wall. A filthy cigarette end appeared to be dangling from his mouth, his colour seemed to change and he became pathetic, touching in a way. It was incredible. In full evening dress as Chaplin was, in that smart party atmosphere and without any make-up or other props, he seemed literally to become that hopeless down-and-out drunkard. We never forgot it.

Heifetz held a musical party in his large house by the sea, near a place called (euphemistically) Venice. Bill Primrose was viola, the leader of the Los Angeles Philharmonic second violin, either John or Lauri Kennedy played cello, both of them when the Schubert Quintet was performed. The party was a very cold and regimented affair, a marathon of quartets and quintets. Of course, the playing was marvellous, but there was no enjoyment. Heifetz allowed no pauses between works to savour the beautiful playing, he seemed to have no love of the music. His children came in to say hello and were coldly dismissed without any apparent affection. I know that the few listeners did not enjoy that occasion and nor did the players. I only hope that Heifetz got some pleasure from it, but he showed no sign of it.

Arguably one of the greatest violinists ever known, Heifitz, the man was cold, ruthless, difficult and exacting. John had accompanied him many times and never had any trouble with him until the summer of 1941, when an important concert was to be given for the Red Cross in a vast hall called The Shrine on the outskirts of Los Angeles. It was a Tchaikovsky concert, with Heifetz and Horowitz playing the concertos, and John conducting the Los Angeles Philharmonic. Heifetz was very difficult all through the arrangements: he wanted his name in bigger print than Horowitz, he wanted to play last on the programme, although musically the Piano Concerto was obviously the more effective finale. When at the rehearsal the point in the last movement was reached where the oboe player takes the lead, Heifetz did not say anything to John but spoke directly and in an unpleasantly critical way to the oboist, who happened to be the elderly and very distinguished Henri de Busscher. (Leon Goossens used to say that he learned to play from listening to de Busscher when he was in London.) John was annoyed, but said courteously to Heifetz perhaps he could tell him what he wanted? Heifetz answered rudely that he preferred to speak to that very bad player himself, and walked off the platform. The orchestra clapped and shuffled and John apologised to dear old de Busscher who, of course, had played beautifully as always. John told Heifetz after the rehearsal that he would conduct for him for this concert, but never again. And he kept to this: he never did conduct for Heifetz again, although Heifetz asked him to do so many times.

During our first visit to the Hollywood Bowl the schedule was not arduous and we had time to see the several eighteenth-century Missions, not far from Los Angeles. They were built and founded by Spanish monks who wanted to convert the natives. No Mission was further than a day's walk or ride from the next, so, in a car, it was possible to see them all at our leisure. They are very beautiful: some were well kept and a few were still used as monasteries or as religious schools; others were derelict and almost falling down. I hear that nowadays they have all been restored and are a tourist attraction. We were alone in our exploration of the Missions, and saw nobody in most of them. We spent a few nights away on this trip, stopping outside small towns in motels which were well equipped and comfortable. The privacy and quiet was just what we wanted. It was an interesting and extraordinarily pleasant few days.

There was a certain amount of publicity regarding the Bowl concerts. One particularly tiresome affair was the public breakfast at which artists made speeches and photographs were taken. John had not felt able to refuse the breakfast invitation as this would seriously have offended the manager, a formidable and very energetic lady called Mrs Irish. However, he got out of making a speech by saying, when the moment came, 'At breakfast I speak only to my wife.' The audience laughed and appeared to bear him no resentment for not having said his piece. We had an interesting visit to the film studios of MGM (Metro Goldwyn Mayer). The head of their Sound and Acoustics Department was the knowledgeable and interesting Douglas Shearer (the brother of one of their well-known film stars, Norma Shearer). He showed us how a series of raised dots and dashes on paper could sound notes and he predicted that in the future performances could be artificially made, so that a particular sound, for instance that produced by Kreisler, could be reproduced to order. In 1939 we found this rather alarming, but he said it would be a very long time yet in the future. We had lunch in the MGM canteen with Louis B. Mayer's characterful secretary. She insisted that we try the special chicken soup which was so full of chicken that it was like a rich stew. We were told that when Mayer became prosperous many years before, he determined that no penniless actor or actress or stagehand should ever be hungry for lack of money, as he often used to be. If they were desperate they could eat the soup and pay when they were able. It was a nice idea and the 'soup' was excellent – a meal in itself.

We used to go to lunch occasionally at the Montemezzis. Italo Montemezzi, a charming Venetian composer, loved to talk Venetian with John. Among other works Montemezzi wrote an opera, *L'Amore di Tre Re* (The Love of Three Kings). This was quite well-known, more often performed in America than in Europe, though it was given in Milan and at Covent Garden. John and I never heard it, but Michael Kennedy told me that it is 'not bad at all'. Montemezzi's wife, Catherine, was a vigorous New Yorker who felt strongly that Italo had never had the success which was his due, and she tried hard to remedy this. Italo didn't mind at all: he lived comfortably and adored playing golf. I had the impression that he no longer bothered to compose (I think Catherine was wealthy). He was likeable and attractive. Catherine's lunches were well-known, and she often invited famous people in the hope that they would do something for Italo's music. The lunches always took place out of doors (it hardly ever rained in that part of California, so planning could be done well in advance without risk). The table was long and very narrow so that you could talk comfortably to your opposite neighbour as well as to the one next to you. I remember one luncheon when Stravinsky was sitting opposite John; he looked even more dour and dismal than usual and was taking no part in the conversation. John told him that in the *Firebird Suite*, which he had conducted recently at the Bowl, he had found a misprint in the score and in one of the parts being used. The misprint was an obvious mistake, which is probably why nobody had bothered to correct it, and John only told Stravinsky about it to amuse him. However, the great man took it seriously. Coming alive, he walked briskly around the long table to our side of it. He took a thick black pencil out of his pocket, gave it to John and asked him to write out the offending part. John wrote out the relevant part of score, after which Stravinsky took back the pencil, crossed out the wrong note with vicious intensity, smiled benignly and went back contentedly to his seat. The only place where they had been able to write was the white tablecloth on which we were lunching. We begged for permission to take it away, but Catherine would not relinquish the such notable autographs. I hope she did not send the cloth to the laundry by mistake!

Then it was back to New York, to Hampshire House and concerts in Carnegie Hall. These were part of the New York Philharmonic's centenary season, and would mark the end of John's seven-year tenure.

## —— 12 ——

# A Year of Change: 1942–43

*THE NEW YORK* Philharmonic Orchestra was 100 years old in 1942. It seems surprising that so young a country should have the second oldest orchestra in the world (though, as I understand, the Vienna Philharmonic and the Hallé are not far behind). John had had talks with Arthur Judson, who knew that his great desire was to go back to England, and that John had already set in motion his idea of doing so in the summer of 1942. There was another reason why Judson hesitated to renew John's contract, and the two of them had discussed this at length. The new director of the American Musicians' Union had changed its rules, which now decreed that all soloists and conductors must join. John had been a member of the Musicians' Union in England when he was a cellist, and he would have had no objection to becoming a member of the Union in America, but the new laws made it obligatory for everyone joining to be an American citizen, or to promise to become one. John had taken out First Papers on accepting the New York Philharmonic post, but this was only a formality to facilitate obtaining the visa necessary for any non-American who worked in the U.S.A. The new ruling was much more binding and permanent. At that time, John would have had to change his nationality and become an American citizen in order to take a permanent position in America, or any post lasting an appreciable period. Neither of us could change our nationality when our country was at war. Judson was fully appreciative of this, and understood our feelings. He offered John eighteen guest concerts and discussed with him the list of distinguished conductors for the centenary season.

John had become more and more homesick for England and was longing to see his mother and the other members of his family. At that time, travel across the Atlantic by any means was impossible for anyone not on important official business. John had written to various colleagues and others in England with an offer to pay all his own expenses and to conduct without fee any orchestra, anywhere, for the benefit of the musicians concerned. The one who helped him most was the Welsh tenor, Parry Jones. Parry knew A.V. Alexander, who was First Lord of the Admiralty in Winston Churchill's War Cabinet. Alexander explained John's offer to Churchill, and Churchill's reply was short and to the point. 'If he's fool enough to want to come, let him come,' so in due course, the journey was arranged and John sailed from New York on a small Norwegian boat with a cargo of bacon. The journey was hazardous, the boat was one of a large number of small ships travelling very slowly in convoy, escorted by warships. Sadly, the U-boats were all too efficient and many ships were attacked and lost. John particularly remembered two things about this trip (which, he said, he really enjoyed!). First, the Norwegians had been issued with thick, heavy rubber suits which would offer some protection were the boat to be sunk in that cold water. John said that although the suits were not uncomfortable, they were exceedingly difficult to put on, so he and most of the crew wore them all the time. He got on excellently with the Norwegians, finding them splendid people with a great sense of humour. The second memory was a sad one; he recalled how deeply upsetting it had been to look at the convoy in the morning and see the gaps where ships had been destroyed overnight. John himself was quite fearless, he did not worry at all about the dangers of the journey, nor had he any doubt that he would arrive unharmed in England to see his family.

When he left New York, officials told me that the trip would last ten days or less. In fact it took 23 days, so for two weeks I lived in constant dread of hearing of John's death – if not at sea, then perhaps from bombs in England. It was a terribly anxious time. There had, of course, been no chance of a passage for me – I was essentially non-essential!

While John was away I stayed as a paying guest with Johnny Woolford's adopted mother in Rochester, New York State. When this arrangement was made, Johnny had thought that he would be there to keep me company, but unfortunately he was drafted into the American army. His delightful sister was not there either. Johnny's mother, Mrs Woolford, was an unsympathetic woman, who seemed to delight in making things difficult and unhappy. She was utterly unhelpful in what was an exacting and trying situation for me. In order to kill time usefully, I took a typing course at a local secretarial college. This was very successful and I learnt to 'touch-type' at good, accurate speeds. I practised a lot and became quite efficient. I also managed to kill some time on John's behalf. He wanted to create a concerto for clarinet, and another for viola using material from Handel, along the lines of the 'oboe concerti' he had put together for me so successfully from the music of Corelli and Pergolesi. Rochester has an excellent music library, so I spent many hours there going through the collected edition of Handel's works. I found some suitable music for the 'concerti' and had many pages photographed for John, who did make those 'concerti' later on.

There is an excellent school of music in Rochester, the

Eastman, one of the best in the U.S.A. At the time I was in Rochester, the school had a particularly well-regarded oboe faculty. Unfortunately, Mrs Woolford did not like my practising the oboe, nor did she let me invite any friends or colleagues to her house, so the pleasure of playing my oboe and spending time with fellow musicians was denied me. Many years later, when I had retired from playing, Bob Sprenkle, a famous American oboist, came to London for a holiday in his retirement. He had been a member of the oboe faculty at Eastman when I was in Rochester, and he told me that he had very much wanted to invite me to Eastman, but the telephone answers Mrs Woolford gave him had been so off-putting that he presumed I did not want to be disturbed. When we did finally meet in London, and when I gave master classes at Eastman, it was a delight. He was a charming man with some interesting and original ideas about playing and teaching the oboe.

To go back to 1942, time passed slowly, and having occupations was a great help. Little did I know how useful my typing ability was going to be in the near future. John was away for about two months, I think – but it seemed longer. When he returned, it was after a particularly hazardous journey. He travelled in a small Fyffes banana boat which was going empty to America to stock up with food. The convoy was attacked by U-boats and three ships were sunk extremely near the one in which John was travelling, but fortunately his ship escaped unscathed. This journey lasted longer than I had anticipated, but this time I was not so worried: Parry Jones had managed to find out the approximate date of John's arrival in the U.S.A. and John actually appeared in Rochester just before the expected date. After one night in Rochester we set off to Los Angeles for his next concerts, which were to be at the Hollywood Bowl.

It was wonderful to hear about John's English visit. Both

families were flourishing and Mémé had accompanied him everywhere. He had conducted the L.S.O. and L.P.O. in London, Bristol, Newcastle, Wolverhampton, Bradford, and the BBC Orchestra in Bedford, where the organisation was stationed during the war. (A concert in Manchester was cancelled due to his ship's late arrival.) The concerts were all ecstatically received and John was acclaimed everywhere. The whole venture had been utterly worthwhile, and certainly John was much the better and happier for it. A.V. Alexander spoke at his final concert in the Albert Hall, London, and John gave a party for him at the Savage Club before leaving for America. We did not know then that we should both be back in England by the Spring.

Back in California we did not rent a house because our time there seemed likely to be shorter than usual, and the outlook was uncertain. We stayed at the Beverly Hills Hotel, very comfortable, with a large swimming pool. Sadly, our rooms were burgled while we were out. The thieves took all John's personal jewellery, nothing else of his, and nothing of mine. Their haul included a watch given to him by the New York Philharmonic Orchestra, the watch his family had given him on his 21st birthday, and some lovely cuff links from old Polacco in New York, among other items. They were all irreplaceable possessions, and were never recovered.

It was a great pleasure to see our Californian friends, especially our very dear Marafioti *famiglia*. After the Bowl concerts there were guest engagements in the Los Angeles season and in Chicago and Seattle, all of which were happy and successful. John particularly enjoyed conducting the Chicago Orchestra – an ensemble of great tradition and repute – with an enthusiastic audience, and he also liked the Los Angeles Philharmonic, some of whose members he had worked with many times, and were old friends. So the time passed quickly and pleasantly until his final concerts in New York early in 1943. These were very exciting and emotional events – the last one ended with a long, heartwarming ovation of farewell both from orchestra and audience.

After New York we returned to Los Angeles knowing that it would be only a temporary visit, as negotiations with the Hallé Orchestra in England were already under way. In New York on 23 February a cable had come asking 'Would you be interested in permanent conductorship Hallé? Important developments pending.' This was indeed a timely request, for we were both longing to get home. John cabled back, 'Am always interested to consider a permanent conductorship of an orchestra with as great a tradition as the Hallé.' We were aware that the management of the Los Angeles Orchestra were likely to offer John their permanent conductorship, but the Union's new rule would have precluded John accepting the post; he could only have been guest conductor. In wartime it was understandable that the Union rule was strict. I understand that nowadays the situation is quite different.

During this brief and unsettled period of transition in Los Angeles we stayed with our very good friends Anthony Collins and his partner Cissy. Tony had been principal viola of the L.S.O. but had left to concentrate on conducting, and he and Cissy had decided to come to California with the idea of staying there permanently. They were generous and delightful hosts with whom we felt truly at home, and I think they were as glad of our company as we were of theirs.

## —— *13* ——

# *Journey Home – Forming The Hallé...*

*WE HAD A* very good friend Ken Helder, a man of Dutch origin, whom we saw regularly in London and New York. We knew that he worked part-time for Rodex coats in London, but he was very secretive about his main job. We presumed that perhaps he was in some organisation such as British Intelligence, because he seemed to have considerable influence in government quarters. So when we knew that we would be going back to England, probably at short notice, we contacted Ken, who managed to book our passage to Lisbon, on a small neutral ship, with a British flight on to England. Except for one suitcase each, we shipped all that we could to Manchester in advance. Luckily, two lovely pieces of furniture which had been wedding presents, eventually arrived safely, but our pictures, books and all our papers and clothes were lost at sea.

We had a pleasant journey on the small Portuguese ship, the *Serpa Pinto*, accompanied by Ken Helder (who would be staying in Lisbon for some days) and various fellow passengers. The weather was lovely; it was late May, and I remember that we landed for a few hours only in Madeira, where the beautiful jacaranda trees were in full flower. As we walked from the ship into the town, small boys ran alongside advertising their sisters for the obvious services, calling out in English the extra inducement 'All pink inside like Queen Victoria', which made us all laugh! When we arrived in Lisbon we reported to the British government office where flights to England were arranged. We were told that our earliest possible flight would be on Tuesday; as it was only Friday, we decided to leave Lisbon for a quiet weekend in Cintra. We had only just arrived at our hotel when a staff member of the government office in Lisbon telephoned to ask if we would be prepared to leave very early next morning (Saturday), rather than on the following Tuesday as arranged. Naturally we were delighted to accept, as we were eager to get to Manchester and we both wanted to see our families before going there. Our flight was uneventful. We landed at Avonmouth, where we went through a long and exhaustive inspection of our luggage and our papers. Ken Helder always had a stock of not-too-polite stories, and he had written out one or two of them which I'd unthinkingly put in my handbag. John was very worried about them and said I ought to destroy them; he thought the customs inspector might be suspicious – or shocked! While we were waiting to be interviewed I went to the Ladies', tore the paper into small bits and pulled the chain on them – most effectively! When the search of our belongings was over, we telephoned our families and took the first available train to London. John stayed there briefly with his family and I caught a train on to the country to see mine, after which we met to travel to Manchester, again by train. We spent our first night in Alderley Edge, at the home of the chairman of the Hallé, Philip Godlee, and his wife. We all got on well and it was a happy start. The manager of the Hallé had booked us into a hotel in Bowdon, outside Manchester, where we stayed for quite a while until we found somewhere more permanent to live.

We were greatly distressed to find out that the Tuesday plane from Lisbon (on which we had originally been booked) had been shot down, and everyone on it killed, including the actor Leslie Howard who had asked to change places with us in order to see the premiere of his film *Mädchen in Uniform* in Lisbon. We had an illogical feeling of guilt, because many of the passengers killed had travelled with us on the *Serpa Pinto*. We never knew the cause of the tragedy, if indeed anyone did. One theory was that Howard's manager, Chenils, bore a slight resemblance to Churchill, which had given rise to the rumour that the great man was on board, and thus made the plane into an enemy target.

We had wanted so much to come to England that we did not enquire fully enough about the Hallé post. Philip Godlee and R.J. Forbes, an influential member of the committee and at that time principal of the Royal Manchester College of Music, had told John that enough money and guarantees existed to make the venture financially sound, and it did not occur to us that an orchestra would not be ready and waiting. The reality was horrifyingly different. Harold Holt, the concert agent, negotiated a contract for John, but I doubt if this was ever honoured because there was in fact neither money, nor any guarantees of funds. Worse still, there was virtually no orchestra, and a week's concerts had been booked in Bradford to start on 5 July (the anniversary of our wedding day), only a month after we had arrived in Manchester.

The most urgent undertaking was to appoint an orchestra, with time to rehearse it. Godlee and Forbes had expected (too optimistically, I think) that the 35 players who had left the Hallé to join the BBC would come back to the Hallé. Sadly, only fourteen players did so – which was understandable since the BBC had offered them an increased salary and improved conditions. Godlee had advertised for players but with negligible results. The invaluable nucleus of the 'new' Hallé Orchestra consisted of a small, but enterprising and courageous group of players who had abandoned the tempting financial prospects of the BBC to throw in their lot with the Hallé. Fortunately, among them was our leader Laurance Turner, who had led one of the BBC sectional orchestras and was an excellent and experienced violinist. He was also a loyal man, who became our dear friend and was a great support to John and the Hallé. In addition to Laurance as leader, the nucleus consisted of our assistant leader, Arthur Percival, the leader of the second violins Philip Hecht, principal double bass Arthur Shaw, violinists Norah Winstanley and Jane Marcus, cellists Haydn Rogerson, Stuart Knussen and Gladys Yates, harpist Charles Collier, bassoonist Bert Mitton, Patricia Stancliffe cor anglais, Arthur Lockwood trumpet, and tuba player and orchestral manager, Wally Jones, who was a tower of strength. In the early days, one of the Hallé Committee asked Wally what he thought of the new conductor. He was heard to reply, 'Well – he's a sod on the box [i.e. the conductor's rostrum] but a toff outside.' John treasured this opinion, and he and Wally became great friends.

Finding players was not easy at that time. Many of those who would normally have been available were in the Forces, or perhaps doing war work in factories. John gave auditions for many hours daily to everyone who applied. The result was an extraordinarily mixed bunch of men and women, some of whom played quite well (though their previous experience had perhaps been as amateurs rather than professionals) and many others who could play hardly at all. John heard everyone himself. I attended almost all the auditions and some of them were tragi-comic. There were dismal days when nobody who came to play was a remote possibility, but there were golden days when we found some players of real quality. One of these was the day we heard the wonderful flute player, Oliver Bannister. He was only sixteen years old, the son of a postman, but was truly first class. Of course he was engaged immediately and he stayed with the Hallé for some years before going to London to play first flute in the Covent Garden Orchestra. There is a charming sequel to that Manchester audition. One day, very recently, there arrived for me an enormous bouquet of red roses, and a little later there came a telephone call from Oliver Bannister. He had sent the roses on the fiftieth anniversary of his first playing for John. I was greatly touched by this lovely gesture, which would have meant a great deal to John, as it did to me.

Others engaged after auditioning included Patricia Stancliffe, an excellent cor anglais player who had given up her job at Sadler's Wells . She was a great asset and her later departure to get married was much regretted. Two horn players were engaged. Livia Gollancz (daughter of the publisher) became first horn; she was not a marvellous player, but was very musical and extremely intelligent. She coped remarkably well, and she was a popular and entertaining member of the orchestra. Enid Roper, who had been a school teacher, came in as third horn. She was an invaluable member of the Hallé's horn section for many years and a very good player.

If ever anything was made of 'bricks without straw' it was this first 'new' Hallé. The double bass section was a major problem, since most of the applicants came from theatre orchestras where only very limited skills were required. The stories of the double bass auditions are well known, but I can't resist repeating them! One elderly man played the Scherzo of Beethoven's Fifth Symphony with enormous rhythmic vitality, but he never moved his left hand, so it was all on one note. Another was asked to play the famous double bass solo from Verdi's *Otello*, a notoriously difficult piece. The elderly man applying for the job had several unsuccessful attempts. Finally,

John played the solo on the double bass. The player looked and listened, astonished, and said 'What, oop theer? Ah've never bin oop theer before.'

Finally John had an orchestra. It was like the curate's egg – good in parts – but, trained by John, it had to be ready to give concerts in early July, less than three weeks ahead.

## —— 14 ——

# Early Hallé Years: 1943 Onward

*CONDITIONS WERE FAR* from easy for the orchestra and John. The first Hallé concerts were held all over the place and in some unlikely venues: cinemas on the outskirts of Manchester were used and, in Bradford as well as Manchester, Methodist and other religious buildings. The acoustics were often poor and so was the accommodation for the orchestra personnel. Travelling was difficult with no petrol available, there were no orchestra buses, and public transport was limited and frequently unreliable.

Once a week there was a concert in Sheffield. These concerts were held in a fine hall, and attended by a good subscription audience, but unfortunately the acoustics of the hall were unresonant and unhelpful, and the orchestra on the platform was divided by two enormous lion statues standing centre-stage (these were later removed), which made ensemble playing difficult. In those early days the journey home from Sheffield was by train. You had to change at Chinley where the incoming train was often late; the station was extremely cold and no waiting rooms were open. On arrival at Didsbury station in Manchester, John had a long walk home with his suitcase, and no doubt the members of the orchestra had equally inconvenient journeys. It was only a good deal later that petrol was available to provide buses for the orchestra and a car for John, and concert venues began to be heated more reliably.

Our own lives became a little more settled, because Laurance Turner knew the manager of a block of flats in Rusholme, and he arranged for us to rent a small flat. The soundproofing was inadequate, but the building was not far from the city centre and it had one great advantage – central heating. Spoilt as we were, coming from America, this was wonderfully welcome. We had no furniture and everything we could buy was rationed requiring coupons, of which we had only a very limited amount. However, our friend Tim McOstrich in New York had told us that his London flat had been badly bombed and that we could take away anything that was usable. I went to the government depository in Lupus Street, behind Victoria Station, to assess the position. All Tim's furniture was covered in soot and most of it was damp and badly damaged, but I was able to pick out two beds, a table and chairs and one or two other oddments, and had them sent up to Manchester. By the time everything was cleaned it did not look quite so depressing, and we had enough essentials to manage for the time being. Food rationing was strict, so when shopping I used to look for the few off-ration foods. I remember that on one occasion when John was guest-conducting in Liverpool, he was walking from the station to the Philharmonic Hall when he happened to see a butcher's shop with a lot of pigs' trotters in the window. These were off-ration and John bought eight of them to take home. In those days wrapping paper was non-existent, so the butcher packaged the feet as well as he could in newspaper. John arrived at the large, smart artists' room to find the whole Liverpool Committee waiting to greet him formally. He put down the untidy newspaper bundle full of pigs' trotters on the table, but unfortunately the package came undone, leaving the pigs' trotters naked and unashamed. The Committee members, John said, were shocked and looked away, but when I arrived later for the concert, I was as delighted as John that he had bought such a useful addition to our larder! I think English pigs must be bred differently from French ones because those trotters were not nearly so meaty as the French ones Mémé used to buy in London before the war. But still, they made stock and were extremely valuable. One of John's fans, a little elderly lady who lived in the country in Wales, used to send us eggs occasionally, which were more than welcome for stretching our rations.

On the administrative side of the Hallé, we had an excellent chairman in Philip Godlee. Philip, with the strong support of Robert Forbes, had been mainly responsible for engaging John. Some said it was an 'act of God' but Philip used to say that it was an 'act of Godlee'. He was a fine musician and a good viola player who had bred three string players to make up a very good family quartet. Robert Forbes was deeply involved, even though his letters had been optimistic to the point of being grossly inaccurate (John described them later, without malice, as 'almost fraudulent').

When we arrived, the manager was R.B. Hesselgrave, an elderly, apparently lazy man, and obviously quite incapable of running a large number of concerts to be held in various venues. He soon departed. There was a safe in the office to which Hesselgrave had held the key and combination. Philip Godlee came to the office to open it with me; we expected to find money or valuables, or both, so the anticipation was exciting. Sadly, the safe was entirely filled with bird seed. It was disappointing, but at least we could laugh! We were fortunate indeed that Hesselgrave's place was taken a little later by Ernest Bean, who had been in the circulation department of what was then the *Manchester Guardian*. He was musical, very intelligent and extremely efficient, with a quick and likeable sense of humour.

He stayed for a while but left in 1951, to our regret, to become manager of the Royal Festival Hall. Before Bean started, John had a disagreement with the administration, which then consisted of just Godlee and Forbes. A piano soloist had been booked for every one of the six opening concerts in Bradford. John was very angry because he had not been consulted. He wanted the Hallé, not piano soloists, to be the 'draw' for concerts. He threatened to resign if the pianists were not cancelled and he retained only one, his old friend, the great Clifford Curzon.

With the practical inconveniences I have described, I may have given the impression that this was a time of unremitting and unrewarding hard work. Certainly the work was hard and unremitting because so many concerts were planned and a great deal of rehearsing was necessary, but life was far from unrewarding. The concerts were remarkably successful – nearly all of them sold out in advance – and the audiences were very enthusiastic. John had a remarkable gift for creating a rapport not only between himself and his orchestra, but also between the orchestra and the audience, a feeling that was particularly strong in the early Hallé days. At that time, during and just after the war, we felt we were on a crusade. There was a sense that music, and the arts in general, had become very important and would be even more so when normal life returned. The arts had indeed begun to matter and music especially flourished. For those early Hallé concerts, the audiences were excited and elated – the thrill and the electric atmosphere will never be forgotten by anyone who attended them. Rehearsals were necessarily hard, because the hotch-potch of players had to be welded and perfected into a real ensemble before the Hallé could take its place as the great orchestra it was to become. John's rehearsals were always lively. The players respected his personal touch, his ability to lead them and make them play better than they ever thought they could.

They appreciated his sense of humour and admired his capacity for hard work and his total commitment to the job. They knew he would never ask them to do anything that he was not prepared to do himself, and they appreciated his sharing the discomforts and inconveniences of travel and unheated halls.

The lack of a rehearsal room had been a problem. Fortunately, a large upstairs room was found in a run-down building in Hewitt Street. It was no more than adequate, but it had to do. It was hardest for the baggage handlers who had to haul up the large instruments and music with a primitive rope pulley. Nothing better could be found for some years, and gradually the orchestra got used to trailing up all those stairs and being either too hot or too cold when they arrived at the rehearsal room at the very top of the building. John, with everyone else, eventually acquired a grudging affection for the Hewitt Street rehearsal room, and at least it solved one problem. Another important problem was to find somewhere in central Manchester in which to hold the Hallé's regular subscription series of concerts until the Free Trade Hall could be rebuilt after the bombing. It was decided to use the Albert Hall (which is not quite so large and grand as its name implies) in Peter Street, almost opposite the ruined Free Trade Hall. It was a religious building and was rented to the Hallé by the Methodist church. It was smaller than was really needed, but it was central and the acoustics were acceptable. That old hall did valiant service for some years, until the Free Trade Hall was ready for use in November 1951.

Now the Hallé schedule was taking shape. In addition to the weekly subscription concerts in Manchester, there were weekly visits to Sheffield, slightly less frequent but regular concerts in Bradford, and occasional concerts in Hanley (where there was a fine old hall) and Leicester (which had a good hall and a loyal audience). In the late summer, the Hallé toured the south of

England, playing mainly in cathedrals. There was a week in Harrogate and one in Edinburgh, and later on, the Hallé visited Wolverhampton, Newcastle and occasionally London. Gradually the schedule filled up and the number of concerts increased, so that the workload for John and the orchestra became very heavy. Later, John used to complain that he kept training young, inexperienced but talented players, only for them to be enticed to London by better pay and lighter work.

Cinemas were still used for occasional concerts around Manchester and in other cities without concert halls. The cinemas were not ideal: they could be used for concerts only at limited times because they had their own schedule of films to show. Probably the most inspiring and exciting Manchester concerts were those held in Belle Vue. This was a very large circular hall which held approximately 5,000. It had been built for the circus and was still used for the same purpose. It was situated in the middle of a zoo, whose denizens could often be heard by audiences. Built mostly of wood, its acoustics were a little resonant but good. The wooden seats were uncomfortable, hard and close together, but Belle Vue had a friendly, warm intimacy which was quite remarkable in a hall of that vast capacity. John's artist's room was labelled 'The Ringmaster's Room', which gave him considerable amusement, and the performances in Belle Vue always thrilled and delighted him, as they did the large and loyal audiences. Choral works were often performed there (Handel's *Messiah* was put on regularly), along with concerts that featured the most famous soloists of the day (at least those who could be relied upon to fill that extremely large hall). I remember the occasion when Casals was the soloist. It was his first appearance in England for several years and there was excited anticipation of the concert. When Casals arrived at Belle Vue, John apologised to him for it being rather a curious building and an unusual venue.

Casals said immediately, 'But Barbirolli, I *love* circuses.'

It was a truly unforgettable concert and, like most Belle Vue concerts, was held in the afternoon. Afterwards Casals came to our tiny flat for a meal. We had gathered together our rations and kind friends had supplied some precious bottles of wine. Casals was an enchanting companion and I think he enjoyed this homely occasion as much as we did. We gave him an old playbill of a concert in the nineteenth century which mentioned Beethoven and a performance by 'Master Liszt'. He was delighted, and we were greatly touched when he said he would put it in his 'room of sentiment' where, he told us, he kept objects he treasured. When we took him to catch his sleeper train, we found the station packed with young soldiers who had obviously been on leave celebrating. They saw Casals with his cello and one of them shouted, 'Give us a tune Mister.' Casals answered with a smile, 'No, the train is due, so there is no time,' then he turned to John and said, 'I think they will not be so 'appy in the morning'.

Many years later, John went to Puerto Rico to conduct Mahler in the Casals Festival. At the first rehearsal Casals was deeply touched by John's music-making and embraced him so fervently that he broke John's glasses, which were hanging round his neck. John treasured those broken glasses and I took them to our Viennese optician, who ground his own lenses. He quite understood John's wish to have the bits put together but said, sadly, that it was beyond his skill.

Among other artists who came to play with John and the Hallé was Jacques Thibaud, the great French violinist. John knew him well but had not seen him for some years, so when Thibaud came onto the platform to rehearse they embraced fervently, in French fashion. The perceptive Thibaud sensed the shocked disapproval of the tough Lancashire players and said: 'It's all right – 'e could be my son in 'ot country.' Thibaud loved women, sometimes too fervently, to the detriment of his performances; on occasions he had even been known to forget to appear at a concert. But at his best he was a wonderful player, unique and incomparable; I don't remember anyone playing the Debussy Sonata as he did. He formed a magical trio with Cortot and Casals; fortunately, we can still obtain CDs of their playing. When the trio was on tour, Casals was very serious all the time – too serious for Thibaud, who was lighthearted and at times a practical joker. As he later recounted to John, he thought one night he would lighten the proceedings, so he removed the 'Messieurs' ('Gents') notice from its rightful place, stuck it on the door of Casals' bedroom and removed his key. In the morning, Thibaud asked Casals how he had slept. Casals said, 'Very little. It was most extraordinary, because all night men came into my bedroom, apologised and then went away immediately. It was most disturbing and I could not lock my door.' Thibaud replaced the notice and Casals remained unaware of the practical joke.

Thibaud and Kreisler were very good friends and there is a charming anecdote which illustrates the difference in their characters. When war was imminent, they both happened to be in Paris. It was a beautiful day and they were walking together in the park. Kreisler, in a philosophical mood, full of foreboding, said, 'How lovely it would be if we were like those two little dogs in front of us, with nothing to do but skip around and be happy, no troubles, no responsibilities.' Thibaud replied 'What! Spend my life sniffing your arse? No thank you.'

While I'm telling stories about violinists, I'd like to say something about Ysaÿe, a great player from a slightly earlier age. John met him at one of a series of concerts given in Paris to honour Ysaÿe, in which works written for him were performed. In this programme the work was Chausson's Concerto for solo violin, piano and string quartet and John was the cellist. Ysaÿe had ceased playing by this time; he was old and ill and had lost a leg through diabetes. He personally thanked the artists who had taken part in the concert, including young John. John said he looked like a lion, of enormous size and with a personality to match, full of warmth and charm. It was a great occasion. Ysaÿe had a delightfully childish and endearing sense of humour. When his doctor insisted that he must reduce his wine-drinking to one bottle a day, Ysaÿe found that he had a very large bottle made to hold eight. Then he invited his doctor to dinner, pointed to the table and said, 'You see Doctor, only one!'

A much less appealing incident concerns two other violinists of considerable repute, Mischa Elman and Heifetz. They had both studied with the great teacher Leopold Auer. When he died, they found themselves sharing a carriage in the funeral cortege. Elman was very hurt and angry that Heifetz had, quite rightly, been chosen to play at the funeral service. Elman stayed sullenly silent for some while and then delivered himself of an acidly ungenerous – if philosophical – comment: 'One good thing. Today there can be no applause.'

But I have digressed with all these anecdotes. I must emphasise that the 'new' Hallé concerts quickly became prestigious events in which it was important for the most famous artists of the day to perform, just as it had been in the past. True, the 'new' Hallé concerts were often held in unconventional and sometimes far from ideal venues. True, many members of the 'new' Hallé were not yet of the highest class. But John had a wonderful gift of teaching his players and welding them into an ensemble to sound better than they did individually. As I have said, he quickly developed a bond between his orchestra, himself and his audiences. In due course he became a respected 'character' in Manchester and not only among those Mancunians who were interested in music. He succeded in gaining not only admiration but affection from those tough Northerners, who always took a great deal of convincing. Here is an example. John always signed autographs in aid of the Musicians' Benevolent Fund after concerts, but not during the intervals. At a concert in Hanley, one young soldier had to catch his last bus to barracks and couldn't stay till the end of the concert, so John made an exception for him. The boy came in during the interval, seized John's hand in a grip of iron and said with heartfelt enthusiasm, 'Woonderful concert – *so far.*' With typical Northern caution, he was not going to commit himself any further!

Once John was ill in hospital and the fact was announced in the local press. As one of the Hallé violinists was getting on to a bus, the conductor noticed her violin case and said, 'How's the boss today? Better I hope.' The days had gone when one newspaper published an unkind description of 'The fat little man from America with the funny name'. John was well known now, particularly in Manchester and the North, and was respected and admired by music lovers all over the country.

During the summers in the late 1940s John rented a house in Seaford, Sussex, for the family. Seaford was then still a small, quiet seaside town with almost empty beaches, set in beautiful unspoilt countryside. Occasionally, we went into Brighton or Lewes, or explored little villages in the neighbourhood. The local shops provided all our needs and Mémé cooked for us, assisted by other members of the family. There were vegetables and fruit in the small garden and the house was very comfortable.

John and I walked a good deal in those days, nearly always on the Sussex Downs. Sometimes, when we had extra time and energy, we would walk over the clifftops from Seaford to Eastbourne. We also took little trips in my old 'banger', which was noisy and smelly but surprisingly reliable. It was an ancient Singer for which I had paid £5. Its only defect seemed to be a faulty clutch which caused it to emit clouds of malodorous smoke when I changed gear, but it took us to some lovely places and on many family picnics. We came to know and love that beautiful country. They were halcyon days.

Our much loved Kathleen Ferrier (whom we always knew as Katie) stayed with us once in Seaford. She was the perfect guest, enjoying everything and fitting in completely with our family life. She walked, came on picnics in my little car, sat on the beach, kept us in fits of laughter with her stories and played with the children; and, of course, she was adored by them and by everyone else. She seemed so well at the time. If only it had lasted. As an artist and as a person she was unique, and very dear. We were lucky indeed to have known her, and to have shared with her a few of those wonderfully happy days in Sussex.

## —— *15* ——

# *Other Possibilities*

*AS SOON AS* he returned to England, John was inundated with offers of permanent appointments and guest-conducting engagements. In the early years he refused these, feeling it was too soon to leave the newly formed Hallé even for short spells. However, there were two major and permanent offers which had to be considered. The more tempting one was the musical directorship of Covent Garden Opera, which was soon to be reopened. The general administrator of Covent Garden, David Webster, used to come to Manchester frequently to see John and ask him if he had changed his mind about coming permanently to Covent Garden. We enjoyed lunching with David at the lovely old eating house, 'Sinclairs', which had escaped bombing, and where the wartime food was edible. But as John's answer to David was always 'No – he would stay with the Hallé' – the offer was never officially made. John loved opera and was a born opera conductor, but his Hallé 'baby' was little more than newborn, and was only just beginning to develop its character and quality, its audiences and its reputation. John felt that it would be disloyal – and probably fatal – for him to leave it so soon. The same applied to an offer from the London Symphony Orchestra in May 1944. In fact he was to remain loyal to the

Hallé for more than a quarter of a century. At first it was, in a sense, a crusade: later, it was a fulfilment for John, and finally, it was his musical memorial.

The other major offer was a very firm and official one, to become musical director of the BBC and chief conductor of the BBC Symphony Orchestra when Sir Adrian Boult retired in 1950. John's manager, Kenneth Crickmore, encouraged him strongly to take it, but it never appealed to John and he refused it unequivocally. He abhorred the idea of making programmes with a committee; and to perform mostly in studios without a visible human audience did not appeal to him at all. Also, though perhaps unjustly, he suspected the power of red tape and officialdom in such a large and important organisation. He wanted no part of such a world.

## —— *16* ——

# The Hallé's 'Finest Hour'

*IN THE HALLÉ'S* critical early years, Ernest Bean did a splendid job of management. He did not spare himself, working ridiculously long hours, and at that difficult and crucial time he was invaluable. In due course the unremitting, stressful work began to take its toll on his health, and it became obvious that help was essential. In 1951 Anthony Hughes joined the Hallé's administrative staff, and his duties largely included working with John on the planning of concert and rehearsal schedules and programmes. Tony was an excellent musician, a beautiful pianist with a remarkable gift for improvisation which used to fascinate John, who often asked him to play. Apart from his musical talent he was most efficient and a great help to John, who valued his opinions highly. We greatly regretted his leaving for a successful career in Australia.

During the early days I worked long, unpaid hours for the Hallé, partly in the office and partly at home. This job kept me from other war work and was indeed a blessing, as I was able to stay in Manchester with John. Until we were able to find a suitable professional I was John's personal secretary as well, so the work was hard, albeit interesting. How fortunate it was that I had taken that typing course in Rochester the previous summer!

As the years went on the Hallé grew more accomplished and established, and better managed. So it became possible for John to do some guest-conducting and for the Hallé to play outside England. John knew that it was stimulating for the orchestra to go on tour occasionally. Over the years he took them to many countries, including Austria, Germany, Italy, Portugal, South America and Rhodesia (for the Cecil Rhodes Centenary). Towards the end of the war, over Christmas 1943 and early January 1944, John took the Hallé on a memorable and momentous trip, to play to the troops of the British Army in France, Belgium and Holland. During the previous autumn he had spent a short time in Bari, Italy, conducting the local orchestra in concerts for the British Eighth Army. He had realised then how greatly orchestral classical music was appreciated and enjoyed and on his return to England he suggested to Walter Legge (the head of ENSA, which organised entertainment for those serving in the armed forces), that he might go overseas with the Hallé. Up to this point, ENSA had done good work in sending small ensembles and soloists to entertain the troops, but had never sent an orchestra. Now that the war appeared to be nearly over, this major enterprise did not seem quite so difficult or dangerous. Legge, an imaginative man, agreed with the idea, and elaborate arrangements were set in motion by ENSA. John asked the members of the Hallé if they would go, and warned them of the discomforts and difficulties they would face; their consent was unanimous and enthusiastic.

The discomforts began early when the SS *Canterbury*, on which they were to cross the Channel, was delayed by dense fog. The ship was far too crowded with members of the Hallé and troops to permit the normal use of the cabins or other rooms, so John and the orchestra spent two nights on deck in bitter cold. During the day they played an impromptu 'concert', in dreadfully cramped conditions, but morale was high and complaints non-existent. On the other side of the Channel the difficulties continued. Unexpectedly for all concerned, Hitler had just launched his Ardennes Offensive (commonly known as the Battle of the Bulge). As a direct result, transport put aside for the orchestra had to be used for rushing troops to places where they were urgently needed for the Allied response. There was one vehicle for the ladies, everyone else rode in primitive trucks – including John, who insisted on travelling with the men of the orchestra. There were no seats in the trucks, only hooks from which one had to hang. The roads were very rough, the cold was bitter, and the flapping canvas of the trucks was of little protection against the icy winds. But the stirring emotions and inspiration of the concerts, and the obvious joy of the troops, made everything worthwhile, and in a strange way John and most of the others greatly enjoyed it all.

Unfortunately, at the very beginning of the enterprise I fell off the unlit stage of the concert hall in Brussels and broke my arm; John also fell but fortunately he landed on top of me and was quite unhurt. For this reason I missed one or two concerts, so I am particularly indebted to Major Dare Wilson, who was present at one of them, for his vivid and moving account of it, which is to be included in his forthcoming book, *Whither the Fates*. The Major recalls some of the items which were played: Beethoven's *Leonora* Overture No. 3, Schubert's 'Unfinished Symphony', Sibelius' *Valse Triste*, and Strauss' Overture to *Die Fledermaus*, among other popular works. He also recalls John's brief speech to his enraptured audience before the last of many encores. At the end of an extremely lengthy concert. John himself was in tears, but he managed to say: 'We have had a memorable evening together: you have been a wonderful audience and the orchestra have loved playing for you. I am sure that many of us will remember it for many years. We would love to continue playing for you, as you would wish us to, but in a little while I would become aware that the orchestra was no longer sounding its best. Then they themselves would know it, and you might detect it. None of us would want this to happen, so we shall finish after the final encore.' This was the *Londonderry Air* – often known today as 'Danny Boy' – and it moved everyone deeply.

The Hallé had given thirteen concerts in fifteen days, and after two weeks or so of physical discomfort and rewarding and moving performances, John and the orchestra returned home. John described the trip, in the words of Churchill, as 'Their finest hour'. ENSA must be thanked and praised for making the event possible. Its oft-quoted nickname 'Every Night Something Awful', would on this occasion have been dreadfully unjust and quite untrue.

## —— 17 ——

# *Australian Jubilee*

*JOHN'S FIRST SUBSTANTIAL* guest engagement away from the Hallé was for a most important occasion – the Jubilee of Australia in 1950. He was booked for six weeks of their Jubilee summer and made a repeat visit in 1955.

Flying from London to Sydney in the 1950s, was utterly different from today. The journey was much more time-consuming – it took four days and four nights! For the first three nights we slept in comfortable hotels or hostels. I recall that we landed, in order to sleep, in Karachi and again in Singapore and there was another stop which I can't remember. On the fourth night we slept in the plane, in extremely good beds converted from the seats. There was never any lack of room – it was very restful and luxurious. The Australian airline, Qantas, was excellent: the whole flight was well managed and arranged, even the food was good! Certainly travel is much faster today, but it is also much less relaxed and not nearly so enjoyable or comfortable.

In Australia in 1950 the orchestras were effectively in the charge of the ABC (Australian Broadcasting Commission), which did a capable job of financing and advising them. Sydney and Melbourne had well-established, capable orchestras: those in Adelaide, Brisbane and Perth were comparatively new and less experienced.

The ABC asked its guest conductors to spend at least two weeks with each orchestra for training and to gain experience. On our first visit John worked with the orchestras in four of the five major cities – Sydney, Melbourne, Adelaide and Brisbane – Perth was added for the 1955 visit. It was hard work for John, but interesting and rewarding, and we both enjoyed the two visits. During the summer of 1950 our visit coincided with the British cricket team's tour of Australia for the Jubilee test matches. The team was a distinguished one, including such players as Hutton, Washbrook, David Sheppard, Bedser, Evans, Wright and Simpson, but despite this galaxy of talent we lost, sadly and surprisingly, to the Australians 4–1. The British team was very popular, especially their captain, F.R. Brown. I remember seeing a placard on an outdoor fruit and vegetable stall in Sydney on which was written 'Buy my lettuces – hearts as big as Freddie Brown's'. I do hope that such tributes compensated him for his cricketing team's lack of success. John and I were both passionately interested in cricket. I watched some of the 1950–51 Tests in Australia but John, unfortunately, had too little free time to go very often.

The quality of the Australian orchestras was variable. At that time Sydney's was the best – a good ensemble with a regular audience. Something very strange happened before the first concert there, which was also John's first in Australia. The final rehearsal had taken place in the afternoon. While John was changing into evening dress, the manager of the orchestra telephoned, in a state of considerable panic, to tell John that all the orchestral parts, and his personal scores, had been stolen from the hall. Fortunately, the Sydney Conservatory had some useful material, including Brahms' Second Symphony, and it was possible to choose a programme which would be known to the orchestra and could be played reasonably well without rehearsal. The situation was explained to the supportive and understanding

Above: L-R, John, John's Italian Grandfather, John's sister Rosie, aged 7.
© Author's private collection

Below left: John aged 9.
© Author's private collection

Below right: John aged 16.
© Author's private collection

Left: John in 1917, just after enlisting in the Army.
© Author's private collection

Below: John and Evelyn in New York, November 1939.
© Author's private collection

Above: In California, playing for pleasure, summer 1941.
© Author's private collection

Above: With Kathleen Ferrier on holiday in Sussex, summer 1950.
© Author's private collection

Below: In Australia, 1955; rehearsing with two members of the Sydney Symphony Orchestra and Conductor Walter Susskind playing piano for a charity performance.
© Author's private collection

Left: Studying at home in Manchester, 1960s.
© Author's private collection

Right: Cooking in Manchester in 1946. The apron was made by Ileana Marafioti of our California 'Family'.
© Author's private collection

Below: In New York with Danny Kaye, January 24 1940 on Evelyn's birthday.
© Author's private collection

Above: Inspecting some new recording equipment at an American factory while on tour with the New York Philharmonic in 1940.
© Author's private collection

Below left: John always called this picture 'Tell the Doctor Everything'.
© Author's private collection

Below: With Evelyn, John's mother, pianist Arthur Rubinstein and his wife Nela in Manchester, at the opening of the rebuilt Free Trade Hall, November 1951.
© Author's private collection

above: Greeting the Queen Mother, with the Lord Mayor of Manchester looking on. At the opening of the rebuilt Free Trade Hall in Manchester, November 1951. © Author's private collection

below left: John with his mother, 1950s. © Author's private collection

Conducting at rehearsal

© Author's private collection

Above: With Vaughan Williams and his wife Ursula when the 8th symphony was first performed in 1956. © Author's private collection

Below: Speaking in acknowledgement of being made Freeman of the city of Manchester, 1958. © Author's private collection

Above: L-R, Laurence Turner (Ex-leader of the Hallé Orchestra), Martin Milner (Leader), John, Clive Smart (Manager), Manchester 1963, when John received the Gold medal of the Hallé society (for 20 years service).

Below left: Conducting in New York at a rehearsal with NY Philharmonic

Below right: With the great viola player Lionel Tertis and our dear friend Lady Ruth Fermoy after a concert at the Kings Lynn Festival, examining Lionel's Royal Philharmonic Society's Gold Medal which John also received.

Above: Rehearsing in the 1960s
© Author's private collection

Above: John conducting.
© Author's private collection

Below: At a party after a concert, with Augustus John, 1950s.
© Author's private collection

Above: A sketch by the Bristol artist Barnard Lintott, in New York

Left: A great friend
Wolfgang Stresemann,
Intendant manager of the
Berlin Philharmonic.
© Author's private collection

Below: Evelyn with Peter
Ustinov, Chancellor of
Durham University, being
shown how he once
played the flute. She had
just been given an
Honorary Doctor of Music
by the University.
© Author's private collection

Left: John communicating with engineers on the recording studio telephone. Young Daniel Barenboim was the concert soloist.
© Author's private collection

Below: Sculptor Byron Howard at work on his bust of John. This was unveiled on 2 December 2000.
© Author's private collection

Conducting in New York, January 1958.

audience, awaiting patiently the long overdue start of the concert. The performances went splendidly. As soon as we had returned to our hotel the much-relieved manager of the orchestra telephoned again to tell John that all the parts and scores had been returned. A man had telephoned anonymously and said that the music was well wrapped up on the steps of one of the hall exits, and this had proved to be true! The caller was asked his reason for such an apparently stupid action and he gave a rather disarming reply. He said that he was an ardent Australian and a great supporter both of his own country and of John's conducting, and he wanted the world to know about this important Jubilee concert. Reuters published the incident and so readers of newspapers all over the world were aware of it, but it was rather an inconvenient way for him to show his admiration!

The remaining concerts in Sydney and those in other cities took place without incident. The orchestras performed excellently and we got on well with people everywhere. One wholly delightful sightseeing occasion was the visit to the Koala Reservation. Having already bought toy Koala bears for all our young relatives and friends, it was a great joy to see the live Koalas, and they were just as enchanting as we had imagined. They eat only one kind of eucalyptus leaf (out of the hundreds of species in Australia) which is grown in the reservation where the Koalas are encouraged to live and breed contentedly. On arrival at the reservation the keepers handed a Koala to each visitor; they smelt very clean, with a hint of eucalyptus, and were apparently quite content to remain hugging us. They have the endearing habit of clinging closely and apparently affectionately to a tree, or just as happily to a human being. They are marsupials and carry their young in a pouch. We stayed and watched for some time and saw one mother carrying her baby in this way. It was a memorable and quite enchanting episode.

I made great friends with the oboist Jiri Tancibudek. Many years ago he had left his native Czechoslovakia to make his life in Australia, where he has had a most successful career. Jiri is a very fine oboe player; Martinu's Oboe Concerto was written for him and he has recorded it on CD, having studied it with the composer. (Of the two published editions of this work, the version which matches his CD is the authentic one). Jiri came to Europe to introduce the work himself, but could not stay long enough to play the first performance in England, so I had the privilege of introducing this fine concerto at the Proms in London and other European cities.

On our second visit to Australia in 1955, Perth was added to the other four cities we had visited on our first tour. We loved this small but spacious city, its parks and rural life. Good wine is made there and excellent lobsters are caught. On his arrival John happened to mention to the press that we both liked lobster. Thereafter, every day, two lobsters, freshly cooked and prepared, were left outside our door by a kindly anonymous donor. I don't remember ever enjoying so much lobster – and probably I never shall again!

One great difference between our two spells in Australia was the accommodation. In 1950 we had found the hotels comfortable, but their dining hours were very difficult for John, who liked his main meal (the only meal he ate all day!) quite late in the evening. At that time, all the hotel dining rooms and restaurants were long closed, so for some weeks we had lived rather boringly, and possibly not very healthily, on bread, cold meat and cheese, with fruit and wine bought from the rather limited delicatessens. Before accepting the 1955 engagement, John made the condition that a furnished, fully equipped apartment should be booked for him in each city, and transport provided. The ABC were very anxious for John to return, so they were willing to comply with this somewhat unusual request.

Travelling with us was Bernadette (Bernie) Hammond, a New Zealander who had been the nurse-companion to our beloved Kathleen Ferrier during the last years of her life. It was a sad time for Bernie, who had recently lost not only Kathleen but also her husband, to whom she had been married for only a short while before he died. We were very fond of her, so her presence made the tour particularly happy for us, and I hope Bernie felt the same way. When the tour was over she returned to her native New Zealand, where her son was born. We saw her only once again when she came to England for a brief stay and after that we relied on letters and an occasional telephone call. However, in 1999 I had the genuine joy of meeting her son and his wife when on holiday in England and we are both keeping up a correspondence now that Bernie has died.

# —— *18* ——

# *Guest Conducting and Travelling*

*THROUGH THE YEARS*, we spent a great time travelling for John's guest-conducting engagements. John enjoyed conducting the great orchestras but sometimes he accepted engagements where the orchestra was not of the very highest standing, but the place itself was delightful, for instance Venice. Or sometimes he would choose to conduct in a city where he had special friends, such as Genoa. John was a wonderful guest conductor because he had the great gift of achieving a rapport with an orchestra in an incredibly short space of time, and getting from the players his own sound and general style of playing – even of behaviour. I used to call him *il mago* (the magician), for somehow the transformation always seemed like magic. One cannot explain this phenomenon any more than one can list the indefinable qualities of any other great conductor. I always listened to the first rehearsal of any orchestra John went to conduct, particularly if it was one he had not worked with before. By the time the interval came, about an hour and a half after they had started, there would already be an obvious change, and the orchestra would be well on the way to becoming John's orchestra; all the while greatly enjoying it. This happened with orchestras of fine quality, as well as with lesser ensembles. Sound was a passion with him and he always managed to get out of any orchestra the warm, beautiful, singing sound he wanted.

On tour we tried always to make our hotel room a temporary home, where we would often eat late at night, picnic fashion. John ate no breakfast, and very little or nothing for lunch (except occasionally a small sandwich). As I have said, he liked his only real meal of the day in the evening. As this could be taken only after all his work was done – often after a concert – he sometimes ate very late. John disliked even the better restaurants at that time; waiters tended to be indifferent and the kitchens could never produce the kind of simply-cooked food he preferred, so we formed the habit of having cold food in our hotel room. We always travelled with knives and forks, a corkscrew and possibly a tin opener, salt, pepper and mustard, plastic plates, napkins and tea cloths (one of which would serve as a tablecloth). While John was working I would explore the town and buy bread, wine, cold meat, cheese and fruit. John liked ham if it was good and flavoursome, and salami and prosciutto if I could find an Italian delicatessen. Cheese would be mature cheddar or good parmesan; he disliked what he called 'strong, smelly cheeses'. When we got to our room after the concert, John would change into pyjamas and a dressing-gown and have a leisurely aperitif while I 'laid the table'. There was almost always some sort of table in our hotel room, and if not, piled-up suitcases would serve. I would open the wine, spread the table with a tea cloth and lay out the food on plates so that it looked particularly appetising. John really enjoyed those suppers. The food was not very varied, but at least it was nourishing and John was able to feel relaxed and at ease. In any case we were seldom away from home-cooking for more than one or two weeks.

Usually I had no difficulty in buying whatever we needed, but on one occasion in Budapest when John was shopping with me (he loved to do this if he were free), we were faced with an important looking array of wines and could not make anyone understand what we wanted, which was a dry red table wine. We bought an expensive bottle which had a very long, detailed label, unfortunately all in Hungarian; and the glass was dark so we did not know whether the wine was red or white. It turned out to be white, very heavy and very sweet – just what we did *not* want. I took a Hungarian dictionary with me the next day! Of course, we did not always picnic. There were times when we had to accept invitations, and in Italy, and more rarely in France, it was often possible to find a friendly trattoria or simple restaurant open late, where the food was good and the service caring.

I have read many biographies of musicians and entertainers in which the description of their travels consists simply of a list of places and engagements, which are usually of little interest to the average reader. In my resolve to avoid such a dull catalogue I have written only generally about our guest-conducting travels. But I must make one exception, an unforgettable week of great pleasure in San Francisco during a long tour of the U.S.A., when we spent many hours with the gifted and enchanting Danny Kaye. We had previously met Danny only once, at a party in New York. It was my birthday and I always remember Danny singing 'Happy Birthday' to me in a voice which mimicked that of a small child. During our week in San Francisco, John was conducting rehearsals and concerts with the San Francisco orchestra and Danny was giving nightly performances of his one-man show. He came to John's rehearsal every morning and we went to his show each night. Although Danny was not a trained musician, he was so naturally talented, with such innate rhythmic sense, that he 'conducted' very well. During one of John's rehearsals he asked John to give him a lesson on how to manage the opening of Beethoven's Fifth Symphony. At his show, he would sit alternately at the front of the stage, chatting to the audience, or turn round to conduct the little band on the stage. Remembering his conducting lesson, he would direct his little band in the opening of Beethoven's Fifth Symphony. After each performance he turned round to the audience and said: 'Was it all right Johnny?' He did this several times, and the audience was fascinated, imagining that he must have a stooge in the theatre.

After his show we would have supper together at Trader Vic's. Danny was fond of Oriental food and this 'Trader Vic's' was the original of the chain. They were delicious and hilarious evenings. I recall one occasion when a large and rather ignorant lady came to our table for autographs. Danny introduced John as Mitropoulos, the famous conductor (who was 6ft 7in tall, whereas John was only 5ft 4in). I was supposedly Kirsten Flagstad, the great Wagnerian singer. To our great amusement the gullible lady swallowed it all whole. Apart from the fun of being with Danny, we came to realise what a dear man he was. I saw him only once again, in London after John's death. We enjoyed a Chinese meal and a host of reminiscences. I remember him with the greatest admiration and affection.

John loved pictures, but found visiting galleries too tiring in the midst of work. Instead he loved to wander about the old part of the town we were visiting. In Europe this was easy, though in America much less so! In Vienna it was wonderful to visit the homes and birthplaces of great composers. We had a favourite place at the back of the Dom (the cathedral), where a narrow stone staircase with very worn steps leads to two small rooms where Mozart used to play quartets with Haydn. When we went, it did not seem to be a museum – the rooms were empty and nobody took any notice of us – but it was touchingly evocative, as may be imagined. There must be other such places in Vienna – it is a city for musicians and of musicians.

Just after the war we went to Italy to see John's Italian family. In Rovigo there lived Uncle Toni and his wife. They were a very dear, simple couple, both charming. Toni took us around the town, (in which there are some interesting buildings), and introduced us to his friends. I remember one of them vividly. We met him in a large church where he was kneeling on the floor saying his prayers, with his shopping bags scattered around him. Uncle Toni nudged him and he leapt up to greet us, but after a short conversation he went back to his prayers. It was all utterly natural, and the church was obviously part of his everyday life. We went to lunch next day with Uncle Toni and his wife, who were worried because their flat was so plain, with an open fire on which they cooked. When we arrived, there was veal turning on the spit and the most delicious smell foretold how good it was going to taste. A cousin of John's lived with his wife and family in a rather grand house just outside the town. We stayed the night there and John's nephew drove us next day to a bus en route to Padua, to visit several more cousins. So soon after the war, travelling was awkward and we were touched to be met from our rather ramshackle bus by a large family. With considerable difficulty they had prepared a delicious meal for us. As they had fuel for cooking only at certain times of the day, they had cooked the meal earlier and kept it warm in hayboxes. Most of the cousins were quite elderly and all were absolutely delightful, very cultivated and intelligent. I went twice to stay with them after John died. Sadly, they are all dead now, but I remember their warm and affectionate courtesy so well.

John's other relatives were in Rome. Uncle Bibo lived with his adopted daughter Irene and her husband and their fourteen-year-old son, on whom she doted. We stayed with them on our first visit to Rome. Uncle Bibo had been, I understood, an important executive on the railways. When I met him he was already very old, but still extremely handsome and charming. Irene, the adopted daughter, was very sweet and selfless, and did not spare herself in looking after everyone. We did not take to her husband, and on our second visit we became aware that he was charging us more than if we were staying in a first-class hotel suite! John had been very generous, but he did not like being 'done'. By now old Uncle Bibo had died, so we stayed after that at the British Embassy, where we were beautifully looked after. We were very fond of the Ambassador, Ashley Clarke (who was later to marry the wonderful Frances) and also of a successor, Pat Hancock and his very dear wife Beatrice, so it was always a great pleasure to stay there. The staff were charming and there was a beautiful swimming pool in the garden (it had been presented by Hitler to the occupant during the war). I saw Rome in great luxury because I used to go around in an Embassy car with Lady Hancock, an old and dear friend, once a fine violinist. The car would take us and wait for us everywhere, so I saw, in great comfort, much more of Rome than I could have seen by myself. Pat, Beatrice and Ashley have died unfortunately but I still keep in contact with Frances, Ashley's widow, who is extremely active in the Venice in Peril organisation and spends most of her time working in Venice.

Before leaving family matters, I must tell of one of our many visits to Dublin, where John used to love conducting a fine choir which had a particularly lovely sound. We got to know Father Andrew Griffiths, the manager of this choir, very well, and one day he said jokingly: 'I think it's time you two got married.' When we were married in 1939 it had been in a registry office. This time Father Andrew arranged a private service in the private chapel of the Archbishop and with his approval. Father Andrew took the service, with just two friends from the choir as witnesses. This was in 1970, only a few months before John died and when he was already far from well, so we were deeply happy that we were then 'properly married'.

# —— *19* ——

# *Berlin*

*THE ORCHESTRA WHICH* John most loved to conduct was the Berlin Philharmonic. For the last ten years of his life he went to Berlin at least twice each season. It was a very special relationship: even the press talked of the 'love affair' between John and the orchestra and each time he went they called it the 'Barbirolli Festival'. Ecstatic receptions from packed audiences and intelligent reviews from knowledgeable critics added to the joy of making music with that great orchestra, which gave so generously in responding to him.

The Intendant of the Berlin Philharmonic Orchestra, Wolfgang Stresemann, was greatly respected and admired. He was the son of a most distinguished statesman, Gustav Stresemann (who might conceivably have saved his country from Nazism had he lived longer and been in better health). Wolfgang was not only a remarkable manager but a very fine musician who had himself been a conductor. A diplomatic and powerful man, he was well able to deal with the members of the orchestra, with Karajan (who was Musical Director for life), and with the officials of the Senate of Berlin, the council that largely financed the Philharmonic; and he held his post with distinction for many years. He was sensitive, understanding, critical and extremely knowledgeable. He admired

John's music-making and shared with him an especial love of Haydn, and they became very good friends. In the latter part of his long life, after his retirement, Stresemann became a distinguished writer, whose books include a definitive biography of his father. I would like to quote from an earlier and smaller book, *The Berlin Philharmonic from Bülow to Karajan*, which, fortunately for me, has been translated into English. In the section entitled 'Prominent Guest Conductors', Stresemann wrote:

Sir John Barbirolli deserves special mention here. For almost a decade he conducted four programmes each season and very soon became a great favourite with both the orchestra and the public. His deeply moving performances of Mahler (particularly the Ninth) are unforgettable; he conducted all the Symphonies with the Philharmonic except the Seventh and the Eighth. (Shortly before his death he had programmed the Seventh for the next season.) Of Italian-French descent, Sir John was a full-blooded musician who combined temperament with a deeply-felt lyricism. He possessed a remarkable instinct for inner musical relationships, for the mysteries which lie behind the notes, and thanks to his inspiring personality always succeeded in conveying the emotional message of the music to both players and listeners. Within a short time he had created a large following in Berlin and it received his concerts with the greatest enthusiasm. Berlin concert-goers and orchestra members alike will long remember Sir John and the many memorable evenings he gave them.'

I know that this phenomenal success in Berlin, time after time, did much to build John's self-esteem and helped to heal the scars left so many years ago by the cruelly unjust criticisms in New York. So deep was his innate modesty and lack of self-confidence that he was never convinced that he would be successful the next time he went to Berlin and before each visit he suffered dreadful attacks of depression. Of course he was always successful, and if anything he was received more and more ecstatically each time, and once he was conducting the Berlin Philharmonic he was no longer doubtful but happy and fulfilled. His contact with the orchestra was immediate. Stresemann told me about John's very first rehearsal, of Mahler's Ninth Symphony. The Philharmonic did not like Mahler at the time and were not looking forward to this performance with a conductor they did not know. Stresemann was attending this rehearsal and at the interval, a deputation from the orchestra came to see him. They said, in effect, 'do not delay to engage him, we must not lose him', which touched John greatly.

After John's death I stayed a short while each year with the Stresemanns, which was a great joy for me. Sadly, Wolfgang has died; he was a great man whose friendship we both valued deeply. Jean, his widow, is still a close friend. During visits to Berlin I always went to a Philharmonic concert. Of course none of the current members of the orchestra had been there in John's time, over 30 years ago, but there are always a few older players present at the concerts who welcome me, and even the newcomers talk to me of John and his music-making and quote the little jokes he used to make. He did not speak the language, but in his 'pidgin German' he used to manage little sayings and jokes with which he amused the orchestra. They also remember the flip-up dark glasses he wore at rehearsals (he was always sensitive to light), known as the 'James Bond' spectacles.

After John died the Berlin Philharmonic gave a wonderful memorial concert for him, to a packed hall, conducted by Daniel Barenboim with Clifford Curzon as soloist. The programme contained the following beautiful tribute by Wolfgang Stresemann, which I have quoted without alterations.

Stresemann spoke excellent English and his meaning is always clear, even if at moments his English wording is unusual. (The tribute in the memorial concert programme was in German; this English translation is Stresemann's own.)

'Sir John Barbirolli was one of the most loved guest conductors of the Berlin Philharmonic Orchestra during the periods 1960/61–1969/70 till he died, 29/7/1970. A memorial concert was given on the 11/12 February 1971 conducted by Daniel Barenboim with Sir Clifford Curzon as soloist. From this occasion the following printed obituary is taken from the programme: 'I don't want to be an old man'. That was the answer Sir John Barbirolli gave me to my question whether he would begin to take care of his health. He never had a vacation and days without work he found depressing and lost. In spite of several slight heart attacks he worked until the last moment. Happily returned from two rehearsals he died in the middle of his work, faithful to his own law. John Barbirolli lived only for the music to which he hung with all the threads of his heart. Each performance meant to him a highly personal adventure which again and again he had to formulate and for which he fought to be successful. If he reached whatever he wanted – and he nearly always did – then the success was emphatic. Only few have the gift to give the music experience to the orchestra and the public with equal great intensity. This experience included the music in its full multitude.'

As with all genuine musicians John Barbirolli was not a specialist. He was a heroic interpreter of heroic music. His lyric understanding made him the ideal interpreter of German romantic music. He found his way to the mystery in the music, but he also proved that he was a full-blooded musician when he par exemple, conducted Dvor˘ák. Full of temperament and yet so incredibly sensitive, filled with deep religiosity – with what a humble glory did he conduct Verdi's Requiem. He was always determined to find the inner realm of the music. But at the same time he knew with awake understanding and high intelligence the structure of each work, which he always displayed clearly in his interpretation. The most important aspect in his musical performance was the wide humanity which was expressed deeply in his reproductions and which was felt often in a nearly overwhelming way by those who were around him.

No wonder he succeeded very quickly in Berlin. Already after the first rehearsal he found a very close contact. When Barbirolli, after several cancellations because of illness, returned to Berlin in the season 1960/61 the friendship was quickly resumed and it lasted to the end. When Sir John arrived to the platform very soon a wave of love streamed out to him as well as for himself as his musicianship. He was met with the same warmth from the orchestra for whom he stood like an authority combined with the feeling of true solidarity. Since his young years he was a passionate cello player. He loved the quartet playing with members of the Hallé-Orchestra. As he once said: 'The best recreation after a concert!'

He always had his own bowings marked in the works, and now and then he showed the cellists (not without pride) the fingering of difficult places. Often he himself took one of the cellos in the orchestra and played the passages in question for the musicians.

The same interest he showed for the wind, especially for the woodwind. No wonder! His amiable wife, a great musician too, played as 1st oboist in her early days in The Scottish National Orchestra and the London Symphony Orchestra. Sir John has conducted the Berlin Philharmonic

Orchestra at more than 70 concerts. His repertoire ranged from old English music (which often was arranged by him) over Bach, Haydn, whom he loved enormously, until Bartók, Hindemith and Schönberg whose *Verklärte Nacht* and *Pelléas and Mélisande* he specially loved to conduct. Berlioz *Fantastique* was one of his favourites. At all times he was fascinated by French music, especially Debussy and Ravel. That he was very strongly familiar to the German music from Mozart until Strauss (he was regarded as a second to none in his Brahms interpretations) is an obvious thing.

But he also found his way to Bruckner whose 9th Symphony he conducted on the memorial concert of Bruno Walter's 90th birthday. On a concert where Barbirolli conducted Bruckner's 7th Symphony he returned to the conductor's room trembling and nearly with tears in his eyes in spite of the great applause. He wasn't sure if he had given honour to Bruckner and the orchestra. 'It is my first Bruckner performance in Germany' he said. It nearly sounded like a confession. He was very serious about his responsibility being the transformer who receives the light from another. You always felt John's affection to the composers. That too was characteristic for his art of interpretation.

On one occasion where a changing of the programme was necessary I proposed Beethoven's *Pastorale*. John Barbirolli wrote that he had to restudy that wonderful but difficult work which he had not conducted for a long time and for which he for the moment was short of time. Without such a restudy he did not want to stand before his Berlin-friends. An answer which honoured Barbirolli.

Especially mentioned must be his efforts for the works of Gustav Mahler. Not until his late years a friend made him aware of the Mahler symphonies. Through the years, so he told, he was occupied with the gigantic scores until this maybe the most human subjective music with its nearly inaudible *Ecce homo* cry was revealed to him. The tie to Mahler was never broken. Significant to Sir John's deep humanity was that just he, son of an Italian father and a French mother, an Englishman himself deeply united to the English music from Byrd till Britten, became the big apostle of the Austrian composers. Unforgettable was his interpretation of the 9th Symphony with its transfigured farewell tones performed by Barbirolli so slowly that the music, nearly coming to a standstill, seemed to touch eternity. Just as touching was the Adagio finale of the 3rd Symphony, this too kept restrained until the last moment, yet filled with a unique deep experience. And great was the interpretations of the 4th, 5th and 6th symphonies where Barbirolli possessed the same strong understanding of the tragic breakdown. During his last period with the Berlin Philharmonic Orchestra he conducted the 1st Symphony of Mahler and was by no means guilty to the singing melodious tone, its parodic elements as to the stormy temperamental Finale and showed again that he was the greatest Mahler-conductor of his time. When we talked about the programmes for 1970/71 he said that he after several years of studying the 7th Symphony now was prepared to conduct it.

His last Mahler performance took place in Stuttgart where he conducted the *Resurrection Symphony* which he earlier had performed in Berlin. The following is an impression a shaken listener had: 'As when the great old man was jerking the gates of heaven.'

We say farewell to John Barbirolli with great gratitude. Those who have known him will never forget him. His time now belongs to the music history to which the word of the poet also applies:

> Don't cry why it is over,
> Smile why it has been.

# —— 20 ——

# *Houston*

*ANOTHER MAJOR GUEST* engagement during the last ten years of John's life was with the Houston Symphony Orchestra. This was, perhaps a little unexpectedly, an extremely happy experience. John was engaged as musical director as well as principal conductor of the orchestra, so we spent, of necessity, rather longer there than for the usual guest engagements. The orchestra was a good one, trained and appointed mainly by Stokowski, who had been followed by other fine conductors, though none had stayed long. At the time John took over, it was a sound, well-knit ensemble, and very few changes in personnel were needed. The atmosphere among the players was excellent, and they were all delighted to be led once more by a great conductor. Our periods in Houston varied in length: the first few times we went for four to six weeks, later perhaps for only ten days or so. John's contract was flexible, and he was able to work with them for whatever period he wanted.

The manager, Tom Johnson, had been largely responsible for appointing John, a decision warmly backed by the musically intelligent and supportive president, Miss Ima Hogg, and the equally supportive chairman, General Maurice Hirsch. During John's long tour of guest concerts in the U.S.A. a year or so earlier, Houston had been one of the orchestras he had conducted. They had recently been looking for a new permanent conductor, and Tom Johnson immediately flew to London to book John. The first time he went to Houston the concerts were well-attended, and though the hall John used at the start was not ideal, a fine new hall, the Jones Hall, was soon built. John had complete control over all musical matters, with the unstinting support of the management and committee. Financially it was lucrative for us and a wholly delightful time. The rehearsal and concert schedule was always sensible, much easier than that of the Hallé or most guest orchestras in Europe; this was good for John as he had time to study and to plan his next schedule with the Hallé. We both used to enjoy shopping together, cooking, and occasionally going to a movie or to one of the city's repertory theatres; occupations for which normally we had no time. Before John arrived, Tom Johnson had made it clear to all concerned that we did not want to be entertained or attend social functions. The Texans observed this dictum loyally and respected our privacy. It was lovely for both of us to live at a slower pace, relying on a sympathetic manager and staff to do the 'donkey work'. It was very easy and relaxing. In addition to the Johnsons, we made some other good friends. I was very fond of Ray Weaver, the fine principal oboe, with whom I had some enjoyable oboe sessions, and Wayne Crouse, the distinguished principal viola, was our special friend.

Tom Johnson and his wife Kathleen did everything possible to make our life easy and untroubled. On each visit to Houston they met us at the airport and took us to the apartment they had rented for us, which was always convenient and fully equipped. Freezer, fridge and bar were filled with everything we could possibly need, and the hired car was waiting outside the door ready for me to drive John to work. It was like walking into a first-class hotel suite, without any of the troubles staying in a hotel might involve.

Houston in the 1960s was a thriving, fast-growing city. Texans are different from Americans elsewhere in that vast country. They are independent and proud of it, cherishing their distinguished past, sensitive and friendly. We grew to like them greatly and always loved our times among them. I remember going to the annual cattle show and rodeo, which was quite an experience. After a brief and untutored look at the enormous bulls on show (one was called Barbirolli) we watched terrifyingly expert 'cowboys' trying to stay on unsaddled, untrained horses that bucked wildly. It was quite alarming, but very exciting, to watch such an exhibition live rather than on television!

The Houston Symphony Orchestra tour with John was rather hard going for me. I played the Strauss Concerto twelve times in fourteen days – finishing with a performance in Carnegie Hall in New York – and we had the honour of being entertained at the White House by President Johnson and his wife, 'Lady Bird'. He was a Texan and had kindly arranged for the whole orchestra to be entertained in another room of the White House. Our lunch was an intimate one, Miss Hogg and General Hirsch being the only other guests. The President left soon after it for a meeting, but we stayed on for a little while. 'Lady Bird' asked Miss Hogg if she would advise her about some special chairs in the White House as Miss Hogg was an authority on early American furniture. (When she died she left her collection to the city to found an imaginative and comprehensive museum of American furniture. All the pieces are beautiful examples. Each floor of the museum is devoted to a different period). On this occasion at the White House she took a chair, turned it upside down to examine it thoroughly and pronounced that the set had been made by a well-known maker near Boston, in the early nineteenth century. She advised about its maintenance with great expertise. 'Lady

Bird', (who, I presumed, was not knowledgeable about antiques, as Jackie Kennedy had been) was most grateful.

Our last visit to Houston was a short one because John's heart trouble had started and he was having blackouts, but we both remembered our times in Houston with genuine pleasure and gratitude, especially to Tom and Kathleen Johnson.

$$—\ 21\ —$$

# Working and Recording

*THE MODERN TERM* 'workaholic' is often used to describe John, and perhaps he merited the description. He was a tremendous and relentless worker, because he was truly a perfectionist. He wanted to do his best for the composers whose work he was performing, and to this end he worked himself long and hard, with concentrated thought and effort. He would not give up until he felt that no more could be done to improve a performance. This perfectionism was applied to anything he was doing, even activities such as cooking, and he kept it up even if he were ill or exhausted. Musically, not only did he study works which were new to him, but he would study again works he had conducted many, many times, such as Beethoven's Fifth Symphony. If anyone in the orchestra was heard to say 'Surely there's no need to rehearse *that* again,' John would remind the speaker that there was sure to be at least one person in the audience who would be hearing Beethoven's Fifth for the first time, saying, 'It's got to be as good as possible for that person, and for Beethoven.' He tried never to leave anything to chance; a perfunctory performance was outside his ken, even at rehearsal. Knowing the notes thoroughly was not enough, he needed to get inside the heart of the music. In the chapter about Berlin I quoted

Wolfgang Stresemann, who expressed it eloquently when he said that John had 'a remarkable instinct for the mysteries which lie behind the notes'. Certainly he had an instinct, because of his innate musicality, but I feel that his endless study and thought also had much to do with his understanding of the 'mysteries'.

He always worked lying on his bed, using a special table to hold his scores at the requisite angle. He had a theory that if his body were at rest, his brain would work better. He never studied at the piano, and never listened to anyone's recording of a performance until he had decided on his own interpretation of the work concerned and he would not perform a work until he felt he knew the heart of it and its true character.

This made him an ideal interpreter of the Mahler symphonies. They demand great control of length and shape with their varying moods of tragedy, humour, full-blooded warmth and at times bucolic vitality, all within a mighty structure. John used to say that to conduct Mahler symphonies you need a great heart, and to wear it on your sleeve. True, but the structure is just as vital, and demands all the many hours of thought and study he gave to it.

There were some great works that John would not conduct for many years, because he did not feel ready for them. Beethoven's Pastoral Symphony was one of these. Although he conducted all the other Beethoven symphonies, he found it difficult to understand the Sixth, and to reach its heart. And it was a long while before he finally performed Bach's wonderful St Matthew Passion in his own edition and with his own instrumentation.

He was very careful in planning his programmes and rehearsals, a factor of vital importance in the early days of the new Hallé. For example, if a work had been programmed which he knew would need a lot of rehearsal, he would plan the programmes near it to contain pieces that would need less time. Often planning was done a long way ahead, and when a complicated work was programmed he would encourage the players to take their parts home to practise. He held regular sectional rehearsals (known in the orchestra as 'JB's sexuals!'). When a three-hour rehearsal was scheduled for the orchestra, John would work with the strings alone for three hours, giving the rest of the players (woodwind, brass, percussion and harps) only slightly less time. The string players used to refer to themselves with some envy as the P.B.S. (poor bloody strings), but there was less wind playing in the score and solo wind players had to find more time for individual practice. These sectional rehearsals entailed only the scheduled six hours's work for the orchestra members, but demanded nine hours for John. He was indefatigable, but the results were excellent and really reduced the overall rehearsal time needed.

Another rehearsal time-saver was his marking for the strings. He bowed, and even occasionally fingered, the string parts, so that all the players were playing in the same part of their instrument at the same time. Being a good cellist, John could bow the parts expertly to obtain precisely the sound he wanted. Sound was a passion with him. He preferred to do his marking in the middle of the night; he slept very little and seemed not to need more, and he loved to work when everyone else was asleep. He would point out that it was the most peaceful and productive time. There were no letters, no visitors, no telephone calls, and I was not constantly appearing with sandwiches or telling him to come to rest, since I was asleep myself! He would mark one 'master part' for each string section and the marks in this would be copied by the librarian and helpers, (or occasionally, in times of urgency, by me.)

John loved making music with others and this was a wonderfully sympathetic aspect of his conducting make-up. He did not care for the word 'accompanying'. He felt that it implied that the conductor and orchestra were subservient to the soloist, whereas in truth he and the orchestra were making music together with a fellow artist. He preferred to choose the soloist himself when putting together a programme, but this was not always possible, for example in guest-conducting engagements when the soloist had already been booked by the concert promoters. I remember only one occasion when he gave in to having a soloist he had never heard. His Swiss agent, Schulhess, a man whom he was happy to trust, assured him that the pianist was exceptional, but that her poor health had prevented her travelling to perform outside her own country. The concert was to be given as part of the Lucerne Festival and the name of the pianist was Clara Haskill. John gave in and accepted her, as everyone was so insistent, and as soon as she started to play he realised that she was indeed a very special artist. Thereafter, he engaged her as often as her health would permit, and it was always the happiest possible collaboration. She was enchanting, truly a wonderful musician and it was tragic that her health so limited her appearances. (I believe she had a tubercular spine.) Whether for Clara or for any other soloist, he always allowed plenty of rehearsal time for their concerto. The result was a co-ordinated musical whole, satisfying for all concerned.

John did not mark his personal scores at all elaborately, only at vital points. This is purely a matter of personal preference; John knew his scores so well that he did not need a lot of reminders, but I can think of one great pianist whose solo parts were so covered with markings that one could hardly see the notes. John wore glasses for rehearsals so that he could more easily deal with queries from orchestra members regarding the score, or direct them to restart at a certain point (usually one marked with a letter). But he never wore them when conducting a concert, for he felt that they created a barrier between the players and himself.

I am asked sometimes if John ever conducted from memory, that is without a score. The answer is no, never. When he first started conducting, he set himself the task of writing out from memory every note in the score concerned, but he soon realised that this would be impossible if he were to have the varied and interesting repertory he wanted. In fact, he knew his scores so well that he could have done without them more often than not, but he would never take the risk. Toscanini, who had appallingly bad sight, once said to him, 'If I were not forced to conduct from memory, I certainly would not do so.' He could not see the score at all when conducting, and if, for example, he were to be asked about a note at rehearsal, he had to hold the score right up to his eyes, touching his nose. Fortunately for him, he had a naturally phenomenal memory, which had of course developed further through his obligatory use of it over many years.

Once John became well-known, many would-be conductors would beg him to teach them, but he always refused. He had never had a conducting lesson himself and he felt strongly that conductors are born, not made, and that they need special qualities within themselves. They must have strength of personality and a gift for dealing with players; they need enough physical stamina for the endless hard work that the job involves, and a natural manual facility for conveying their own musical ideas through their physical actions and leadership. John was fortunate in possessing all these qualities, plus the will and commitment to work hard and unremittingly. He would encourage would-be conducting pupils to come round with him on tour, or wherever he was working, so that they might learn in the real situations of rehearsals and concerts. Of course he did not charge these would-be pupils, but they had to pay their own expenses for living and travelling. He spent a lot of time with his students, always making himself available so that they could feel free to talk to him. He would give them tips on reading and studying scores, and would expect them to listen frequently to rehearsals as well as to concerts and recording sessions. But he would *never* consent to give them lessons, because he was so sure that it was useless. His greatest scorn was reserved for the method of teaching conducting which involves the use of records and perhaps a mirror. He pointed out that as one of the hardest parts of the conductor's art is to set and hold a tempo, waving one's arms to a ready-made tempo on a record is a useless occupation.

John was not fussy about batons, though he always conducted with one. He felt that it was much clearer for the players than if he used only his hands, eloquent though they were. He preferred a medium-length baton, well-balanced and very light in weight with a slender handle; lightness was the quality he really cared about. Sometimes, he was lucky in finding a craftsman who would make batons for him. I remember a wonderful man in Scotland whose profession was making wooden-shafted golf clubs, in the days when wooden shafts were the norm. (I think that he used a wood called 'Dangawood'.) After this craftsman died, John found a maker in Texas who produced beautiful lightweight and well-balanced batons, but they would always break too easily to be really useful. If, during a concert, a baton broke or flew out of his hand, John was not at all disturbed, he just went on without it. As I have described earlier, the physical aspect of conducting was for him entirely natural and instinctive. His movements and types of beat were dictated by the music he was performing, and he thought only of the music. He never had to work at the physical side of his craft, or even consider it.

John always gave interested in his players; he knew about their trials and their joys; they were all people making music with him. He conducted every orchestra in the same way as he conducted his own Hallé: he encouraged and inspired, but never drove, never bullied or forced. Musicians always enjoyed playing with him and gave him their full attention and musical co-operation. His performances had warmth, spontaneity, vitality, colour and passion in the creation of which the orchestra took a full part, and the listener could feel a genuine ensemble of the highest order.

Recording was always part of John's life. As a cellist at the age of eleven he made discs for Edison Bell with his sister Rosie. They played popular short pieces such as Thomé's *Simple Aveu* and Van Biene's *Broken Melody*. The playing is old fashioned in style but very musical. Rather later, in 1925, when he was starting to conduct, he took part in recordings with André Mangeot's Quartet, of which he was again the cellist. Around that time he also made records for the National Gramophonic Society, having been engaged by its director, Christopher Stone, the original disc jockey, a famous and influential man. Some of these were recordings with Ethel Bartlett, of Bach Sonatas and other works for cello and piano. Others, his first recordings as a conductor, were made with his own chamber orchestra. When Gaisberg of HMV started to use him, John accompanied great singers and instrumentalists such as Chaliapin, Elisabeth Schumann, Lotte Lehmann, Lauritz Melchior, Frida Leider, Kreisler, Rubinstein, Heifetz and Suggia. Over the years he made innumerable recordings with orchestras including the Berlin Philharmonic, the Vienna Philharmonic, New York Philharmonic, the London Symphony Orchestra and other London orchestras, as well as his own Hallé. Only days before his death he was recording Delius. I do not intend to give a catalogue of his recordings – they are far too numerous and too varied – but it may be of interest to go a little more deeply into this particular aspect of his hardworking life. *NOTE*: Malcolm Walker's wonderfully comprehensive discography of all CD's currently available is to be found on page 228.

He made a recording exactly as he conducted a concert: I don't think he felt that recording was any more special or more nerve-racking, except perhaps for the players. In his early days, recordings had to be made in four minute 'takes' and if anything needed altering or adjusting, the whole four minutes would have to be recorded again. Technical advances have now made it easy to redo small bits of the whole and insert them – to 'patch' any faulty moments. Of course, this is extremely useful: it saves a good deal of time, and the players worry less about an exacting passage, knowing that they can redo it if necessary. But this universally used method has its dangers too. So often, the quest for a flawless performance can overcome the musical flow and impetus of the whole. There are, I know, reputable artists who record in short sections and who then repeat them again and again until they consider the performance to be perfect, but often the heart of the music gets lost on the way. John deprecated wholly this way of employing a technical advantage and used it only when really necessary. He would record in long sweeps, and never stop for any imperfection. At the end of a long 'take', he knew exactly where it would be essential to 'patch', usually to correct a small imperfection of intonation or ensemble. John had complete faith in his producer; usually this was Ronald Kinloch Anderson, himself an excellent pianist with a sensitive ear. At recording sessions, Ronald sat with the score and made a note of any slightly faulty moment. He would then discuss this with John and they would listen to that part again, and if necessary redo it or 'patch' it. For many years – maybe even to this day – John held the record for the longest 'take' ever made at EMI (I believe that it was the complete slow movement of Mahler's Fifth Symphony). This way of conducting a recording, just as if he were conducting a concert, is, I think, why John's recordings are so warm and so 'live', and have such a wonderful flow and line.

But he had one unfortunate habit, of which he was utterly oblivious. In moments of great emotion or excitement, he would 'sing', or rather grunt and make noises, while recording. The noise was barely audible at a concert, but over a sensitive microphone in the recording studio it was disturbing, and it used to worry the producer and the engineers. On certain sessions, for instance some of these with Jacqueline du Pré, Suvi Raj Grubb was the producer instead of Ronald Kinloch Anderson. In his book, *Music Makers on Record*, Suvi writes an enchanting description of an unsuccessful attempt to stop John 'singing'. As John was utterly unaware of what he was doing, he was of no help and on a few of his recordings I'm afraid one can just hear the vocal noises!

Only a few years ago we used to accept that while painters, sculptors and writers could leave us a legacy of their talents, the work of performing artists died with their performances, except for a short while in the memories of those who heard them. Today this is not so: skilled remasterers can process old records and put their music on to CDs, keeping the sound quality and the musical character, without the coughs, scratches, and other unwanted noises. Some of these experts are musically very sensitive as well as technically accomplished, and they can avoid the pitfalls of achieving perfection at the cost of losing the sound and character of the original. I am personally deeply grateful to one of the greatest of these remasterers, Michael Dutton, who has done so much invaluable work. With his sensitive expertise and the valuable support of Pauline Pickering, and Paul Brooks, Chairman and Vice Chairman of the Barbirolli Society, many of my husband's recordings have been reissued on CDs. I am so thankful personally that many old recordings of John's are still 'alive', and I am everlastingly grateful to the Barbirolli Society who have made it possible to hear them.

## —— 22 ——

# Composers, Influences, Friends, Staff

*I HAVE DESCRIBED* in previous chapters many of the friends and colleagues John and I were so lucky to know over the years. In this chapter I would like to mention some others who for various reasons have so far been omitted, but with whom we were fortunate to share happy and creative times.

John was not a composer. He told me that he had tried when he was young, but as anything he wrote came out as weak Delius he gave up this exercise. He loved 'making' works from the music of others, which he did with great taste and skill, with considerable success. There are two charming works for Oboe and Strings made from the music of Corelli and Pergelesi which are often performed and have been recorded. He made also others for Viola and for Clarinet. Now the Barbirolli Society is going to record a work by Arnold Bax which John arranged freely with Bax's complete approval and pleasure. John always had a particular affection for Bax's music. He criticised it because, he said, Bax never knew when to stop and all too often a work could be spoiled because it outstayed its welcome.

In his cello playing days John often took part in the Bax Quintet for Oboe and String Quartet and he was always worried by Bax's attempt to get too much out of the single strings by double stopping and divisi, which sometimes made the texture thick and unbeautiful. When Bax was still alive (he died in 1953) John suggested adding a double bass part and recording the string quartet to make a work for Oboe and String Orchestra. Bax was genuinely delighted and begged John to do this. The project did not come to fruition for many years – John was always so busy – but later in his life he did reorganise the Bax Quintet and we played the new version at a Promenade concert. Sadly this was the only performance, because I never felt I wanted to play it again without John, but I am happy that this one live performance is to be recorded on CD, and will be appearing soon. It is a very lovely work and, as Bax was slightly controlled by the stamina and sound of the wind instrument, it is not too long.

I wrote in Chapter 3 about John's early days learning the cello with Mr Whitehouse and Herbert Walenn, and his partnership with Ethel Bartlett at the Royal Academy of Music, and I have described his busy times as a freelance cellist after he left the Academy. One of the jobs I have mentioned in passing is John's time as cellist with André Mangeot's Quartet, which was a real musical pleasure for him.

André was a fine musician, a Frenchman of considerable charm and knowledge. John loved him and said that he learned a great deal from him, though at times he wished that André had spent more time practising the violin and less time in research and in writing letters seeking engagements! He could have been an excellent violinist, technically as well as musically. An interesting musician, he was passionately fond of the Purcell Chaconnes, which he edited and played in his quartet concerts.

During the days of the B.N.O.C. opera, on tour and in the short London season, John made some close friends among the singers, such as Percy Heming, an excellent baritone and a lovable man who died much too young, Gladys Parr, a gifted Mezzo-soprano (and a first-class actress), and the Welsh tenor Parry Jones, limited vocally but an extremely musical singer and a very good performer.

One of John's good friends in Glasgow when he was conducting the Scottish was Charles Parker with whom he went to Bayreuth. He was a journalist who shared John's great love of Elgar's music. Parker suggested to John one day that they might go to see Elgar, and in August 1933 they went to Marl Bank, his home in Worcester. Elgar was delighted to see them, and played his own recording of *Falstaff*. At the side drum solo, Elgar said, 'Well that's a good bit anyway.' When they left, he hugged John with great warmth, thanking him for enjoying and understanding his music. Soon after this, Elgar was diagnosed with cancer. Sadly, John never saw him again.

Of course Elgar already knew of John's work. His friend, Frank Schuster, had heard John's performance of Elgar's Second Symphony in 1927 when he deputised for Beecham at an L.S.O. concert. Schuster wrote to Elgar: 'I must just tell you that to my thinking Barbirolli gave a remarkably good account of your No. 2, playing it as it is written and what's more as it is *felt* – no exaggeration but very cohesive and round and rich. But it appears that in spite of a most enthusiastic reception, the highbrows don't agree with me. Am I wrong?' Elgar then wrote John a letter which gave him intense pleasure: 'I hear splendid accounts of your conducting of the symphony concert on Monday last; for your kind care of my work I send you very sincere thanks. I should have sent a word before the concert had I known of it, but I was unaware that anything of mine was being given.' And in 1929, at a dinner when John was present, Elgar spoke of him as 'a rising hope of music in England for whom I have great admiration and in whose work I have every confidence. As long as we have conductors and musicians like Barbirolli, this country has nothing to worry about.' John played one of the early performances of the Cello Concerto (in Bournemouth in 1921) and he was one of the cellists in the orchestra in 1919 at the first performance. This was a disaster, due to the conductor, Albert Coates, being so greedy over his rehearsal allowance, and leaving too little time for Elgar to rehearse the Concerto with the soloist, Felix Salmond.

In October 1927 John made his first Elgar recording, of the *Introduction and Allegro*, under the auspices of the National Gramophonic Society. Compton Mackenzie, the author and playwright, sent the record to Elgar who replied to him, 'I hasten to say that I think the record excellent in every way. I know that Mr Barbirolli is an extremely able youth and, very properly, has ideas of his own, added to which he is a remarkably able conductor.' In 1929 John made a second recording of the piece and his fine interpretation inspired Elgar to say, 'I'd never realised that it was such a big work.' John loved Elgar's music, and it moved him deeply. But some of the critics and musicians of the day were disapproving of his heartfelt way of conducting Elgar. Daniel Barenboim (of whom more later) said perceptively: 'During his lifetime, people in England often criticised his musical personality in general and his Elgar in particular. They considered him too emotional and thought he took too many liberties. But I felt that he brought a dimension to Elgar's music which is so often lacking, a kind of nervous quality which he had in common with Mahler. There is almost a certain over-sensitivity in some of Elgar's greater works, which is sometimes sacrificed for the conventional idea of Elgar as the perfect English gentleman.'

As is well known, John was inspired by the symphonies of Mahler, which he came to know and to love quite late in his conducting life. (The well-known writer and critic, Neville

Cardus, had suggested to John that the symphonies were made for him.) He once had a brief meeting with Mahler's widow, Alma, after he had guest-conducted a Mahler symphony with the New York Philharmonic at Carnegie Hall, New York. Alma embraced him and said she had been so greatly moved by his performance that it might have been Mahler himself conducting, so complete was John's understanding.

John had a great love for Grieg's music, especially for some of the songs. When he was conducting in the charming town of Bergen in Norway, we used to go to the composer's home. The house in which Grieg lived with his wife, and where he worked, was within easy reach of the town, and it was a joy to visit. The Griegs lived in lovely, lonely country beside a lake, and he used to compose in a small hut in the grounds. This contained a modest piano, a chair and a writing table, and from the window could be seen the most beautiful view of the lake and countryside. On the door hung Grieg's tiny coat (he was very small) and his hat. It is easy to imagine Grieg writing those inspired songs for his wife (a well-known singer) in the peace of that little hut, with so much tranquil beauty around it. The second time we went to the hut, the guide left us alone for a few minutes and John took the opportunity to play a little on the piano and to touch the coat. It was an evocative and memorable visit.

Another attraction of Bergen was more mundane. Excellent prawns were sold every morning on the old quayside, near our hotel. The prawns had only just been unloaded from the boats and cooked, so that they were deliciously fresh. I never had to shop around in Bergen for our picnic meals, I only had to buy bread and butter and wine to go with the prawns, which we enjoyed every day! The only slight difficulty was getting rid of the debris from our warm hotel room. John was able to deal with this problem once he found a statue of his much-loved Grieg in a small park only a few minutes away. He would take off his hat and bow in homage to Grieg each day, while he dropped the package of prawn debris from its hiding place under his hat into a conveniently placed rubbish bin.

John knew several British composers of his time; Arnold Bax, John Ireland, Edmund Rubbra, E. J. Moeran and William Walton were good friends and all of them used to promise John the new work for which he had asked them. But disappointingly those works never came. Walton always said he was lazy, Ireland said he was too slow. John played quite a lot of Bax, and of Rubbra whose music he admired and liked. One great composer he knew well and for whom he had the greatest possible musical admiration was Ralph Vaughan Williams. John had always played his music, but he got to know him personally only during the latter years of Vaughan Williams' life, when John was nearing the end of his own. It was a very happy association for John, as I am sure it was for Vaughan Williams. They first came together with the Seventh Symphony (the *Sinfonia Antartica*). VW, as we called him, had made into a symphony some of the music he had used for *Scott of the Antarctic*, the film of the ill-fated Scott expedition. John liked it greatly and with the Hallé he gave it a splendid performance, with which VW was delighted. He had come up to Manchester for the concert and we were able to arrange a small celebration for him. (He did not care for large functions but he loved small intimate parties, usually over a meal.) On this occasion VW wrote in John's programme, 'For Glorious John, the Glorious Conductor of a Glorious Orchestra, with love and admiration from Ralph.' This was the first time that the epithet 'Glorious John' was used, and John was vastly proud and happy that it was so generally adopted thereafter. VW came to Manchester on several occasions for rehearsals and performances of his works. On one occasion he conducted his own *Sea Symphony* and John played in the cello section, an event which gave VW much pleasure. Each time he came to Manchester with his dear and gifted wife, Ursula, we arranged a little party for him in a good hotel – our own flat was much too small. The last party we held for him took place during the Cheltenham Festival, in a hotel at the top of Cleeve Hill. It was a lovely summer evening and I can see VW now, before supper, standing quite still, gazing over that beautiful countryside he loved and knew so well.

VW was the most considerate, courteous and kindly of men. For example, he would sit through the new works of younger composers and give them as much encouragement as he possibly could. He was very modest and worked hard until his death. Every morning he would compose at his desk, whether or not he felt inclined to do so. He would not throw away the result till the next day, even if he felt that it was of no value. He was a true professional, very self-critical, and unsparing of himself. Many celebratory dinners and functions were given for him on his 85th birthday but his deafness made these affairs very tiring. I recall one such event which he had said he would only attend if John and I were placed on either side of him. He explained that he did not want to talk and knew we would not mind. But as it turned out he talked all the time, and most entertainingly! He had just seen in a musical dictionary an entry for Harriet Cohen, Bax's mistress, which said 'see under Bax', and this amused him greatly. Not long before that, I was engaged to play his oboe concerto at the Leith Hill Festival and he was due to conduct it for me. When I arrived, he apologised that he could not conduct the work after all because, he said, he could not remember it. Explaining that he had a very bad memory, he told me that when he was younger he used to bicycle a good deal in the Malvern Hills. He found that bicycling was most conducive for beautiful tunes to come into his head, but the trouble was that by the time he had alighted from his machine and found a pencil, he had always forgotten the tune. I remember saying to him that perhaps God would send him the tunes again when it was more convenient but he said, very modestly and touchingly, 'No, I think that was God's way of weeding out my bad ones.'

After the *Sinfonia Antartica*, the next symphony, the Eighth, was written for and dedicated to John, who loved it and performed it with heartfelt pride. At first VW had doubts about the symphony but John arranged a private run-through in Manchester in 1956. After it, VW wrote to John, 'Dear Glorious John, I expect it was your magic, but if you approve, I propose NOT to scrap the symphony.'

VW trusted John, and when he considered revising certain parts in some of his works, he would ask John's advice about scoring, balance and tempo. He even asked me about a difficult passage in his oboe concerto which he intended to alter. There are, I'm sure, many interesting letters from VW among the collection of John's letters in the archives of the Royal Academy of Music, but I am going to quote one he wrote to me, because it shows his consideration for his friends and colleagues and his wise attitude about first listening to new works. The letter was dated 22 July 1956.

My dear Evelyn,

It was wonderful of John to send us that splendid telegram. I am so glad that you were with him and you know, what we all know, how essential it is that he should have a good rest and get quite well to go on with his great work: and if anyone can make him, you can. Also, you have got to keep well yourself, dear Evelyn, and go on playing beautifully. We listened to your record the other night, and it is lovely. I cannot imagine anything better in the way of a performance. Thank you again.

I hear on all sides how splendidly they all played under their inspirer not only in my tune but in everything. I listened in to most of it. A wonderful performance of Beethoven 7 and the other works had fine send-offs, though I can never judge of the quality of a new work at first hearing.

Love from us both to you both,

From Ralph.

Although VW was in his eighties when we knew him, he never seemed an old man. He was so interested in everything, took so lively and active a part in all that life had to offer. He and Ursula married when he was eighty, and were looking for a house in London; Ursula went to an estate agent to find out more about one they had thought a likely possibility. When Ursula returned and found VW eager to know the result of her enquiries, she said: 'There's one snag; we can only have it on a lease of twenty years.' VW's instant reply was: 'Oh well, my dear, we can always renew it.' He was a man of enduring and endearing charm and warmth, and as listeners in the world of music have wisely decided, a truly great composer. We were privileged indeed to have known him.

John enjoyed the company of women and had some close friends, particularly during the latter part of his life. When I was re-reading Ursula Vaughan Williams' fascinating life of her husband, *R.V.W.* I came upon a quotation from one of his letters to a friend in which he said: 'You know I like being appreciated, and make no pretence about it!' I think that this is true of all of us, and particularly of most artists. John was no exception, and I think that women are better at flattery, if one can call it that. No doubt his particular pleasure in it came from his basic insecurity, his innate modesty, and self-doubt. Norah Winstanley, an attractive violinist in the Hallé, became very close to John over a few years and I confess that I found this association worrying. But the bond between John and myself was too deep and too strong to be seriously disturbed. Another woman friend, late in his life, was Audrey Napier-Smith. Audrey and I had been at the Royal College of Music together and were good friends, and I know that John's friendship gave him, and Audrey, much pleasure. She was not a flatterer, and I liked her greatly. She had a long pen-friendship with the poet John Masefield and they exchanged a fascinating series of some thousand letters. Later she exchanged many letters with John; she was very intelligent and intensely musical. Her violin and viola playing was limited, but she was a valuable member of the Hallé and a good friend to both of us. Recently I was deeply sad to find out that she had died of a severe stroke, but it perhaps was better so: she was so alive and interested in everything and everybody that it would have been terrible for her to exist having lost her faculties.

Our dear friend Ruth Fermoy was not only the beautiful and much loved grandmother of Princess Diana, she was an excellent pianist. She had studied in her younger years with the great French pianist, Alfred Cortot, and was a gifted and extremely accomplished chamber music player. She founded the King's Lynn Festival and was active in running it for many years. Every year a chamber music concert was held at which she played one of the major works for piano and string quartet, and they were great performances: she played like a top-class professional. John enjoyed these concerts and always played the cello in the quartet, which was led by Martin Milner, the leader of the Hallé, and included two other Hallé players. Sometimes we played a work for oboe and strings. These concerts were a highlight of the festival and were greatly appreciated by the audience. Ruth was a lady in waiting to Queen Elizabeth the Queen Mother, who always attended the King's Lynn concert in St Nicholas Church when she was staying at Sandringham. In those days there was no withdrawing room and no marquee outside and the conductor's room in the church, (in other words the vestry), was very small indeed. So the Queen Mother and all her attendants and friends, used to congregate during the interval in the churchyard among the tombstones. Curiously enough, I don't remember that it ever rained for those concerts, but I do recall one very cold summer night. John came out after the first half of the concert, and naturally he was quite hot after conducting. The Queen Mother, worried lest he should catch cold, immediately took off the flimsy feather boa she was wearing and wrapped it round him. It was delightful, such a thoughtful, caring gesture, and typical of her. The very thought warmed John! Needless to say, all those present took off their own wraps and offered them to the Queen Mother.

We especially loved Kathleen Ferrier, as a musician and a friend. I have described her visit to the family in Sussex in Chapter 14, and she also often stayed with us in Manchester. We saw a great deal of her during her tragically short career. Surely very few artists, if any, have merited their place in public admiration and affection as she did. Even people today who never saw or heard her, know her name and love her records. Certainly, she was blessed with a lovely voice, she was intensely musical and a great artist. But more than that, she had a personality of such warmth, such generosity and humour, that she seemed to draw the listeners into herself. Even on records these qualities come through and so keep her memory alive. We used to go to her home in London to play chamber music (she was a good pianist), to eat and drink and laugh. The tragic circumstances of her early and untimely death are well known, but even in her last years, when she was fighting the cancer that would kill her, she was always full of life, and apparently so happy, that it was hard to realise that we would not have the joy of her friendship for much longer. John adored her as a person and an artist and they worked a lot together. He conducted the last performances of her life in Gluck's opera *Orpheus and Eurydice* at Covent Garden, produced by the great dancer and choreographer, Frederick Ashton. She managed the first two performances wonderfully, unforgettably, but at the very end of the second, the cancer overtook her and she could stand only supported by her fellow singers. She was unable to do the last performance, but had to stay in hospital where she died. The end seemed so tragically early for such a great artist, so gifted and with so much courage. She had such a sense of humour, such a capacity for bringing joy to others, and such enjoyment of life herself.

Janet Baker now retired, is another great singer whom John admired profoundly and of whom he became very fond. Janet knew, as did many friends and musicians, that John had wanted fervently to record Elgar's *Dream of Gerontius* with Kathleen Ferrier as the Angel. This was not possible because their recording companies (John's was EMI and Kathleen's Decca) could not agree. So when Janet recorded it with him in 1964, she knew that she was second choice, even though Kathleen had been dead for eleven years. However, this feeling was soon dispelled; John loved Janet's singing of the work and soon felt deep affection for her personally. Both Janet and her husband Keith Shelley are dear friends and very special people.

Two other dear friends were Sam and Annie Oddy. When we bought a little mews house in London, we came to know Sam, who had a garage in the mews where he sorted his fruit and vegetables. Sam was a real Cockney who had been brought up using rhyming slang and still spoke it. He was the modern equivalent of a 'barrow boy', as he had a lorry filled with vegetables and fruit which he took round for sale and delivery. As the saying goes, he was truly the salt of the earth. We were very fond of him; as we were of his wife, Annie, who sounds like a Cockney herself but who is actually German, and a sterling character. (Their happy marriage was the result of a wartime meeting.) Sam occasionally mispronounced words or used the wrong ones, and I remember a most endearing example. Once he was going to Brighton for the weekend despite having a bad cough. On his return, John asked how he was. Sam replied that he was much better, and added: 'It must have been all that there embracing air.' The extra 'em' made it so much more convincing!

Daniel Barenboim is a great musician and a loyal, much-loved, friend. I remember well when we first heard him play the piano. John was conducting the Israeli Philharmonic in Tel Aviv and Jerusalem. He always enjoyed working with that orchestra, which was full of intelligent, accomplished musicians. In general, when John was guest conducting on tour he made the rule that he would not accede to the many requests made from players asking him to hear them, but so many of the Israeli orchestra had told him of a tremendously gifted young pianist called Barenboim that he decided to waive his rule. We went to the Barenboim home outside Tel Aviv and Daniel, then I think a boy in his mid-teens, sat at his own piano and played. His repertory on that occasion was enormously varied, including piano works of extreme technical difficulty and musical profundity, in which this boy showed a deep, instinctive understanding remarkable at his age. He played on and on, despite suggestions from his parents that he might be wearing John out, but John was enchanted by such a tremendous talent and happy to go on listening. Daniel's father was a reputable piano teacher and his mother, Aida, a very dear and musical lady. We finally left their home full of music and fascinated by Daniel's great gifts. When Daniel began performing in public all over the world he often played with John conducting and this was always a musical joy for both of them.

Today Daniel is not only a great pianist but also himself a fine conductor. I am always touched by his loyalty to John, from whom he often says he learnt so much, particularly about orchestral playing and the preparation of works for performance. Daniel used to listen to John rehearsing whenever he came to play a concerto. They would always talk together and Daniel would study John's scores and orchestral parts. John knew of Daniel's ambition to conduct as well as to play and I'm sure he would be proud and happy indeed to know of Daniel's success in both fields. I have the greatest admiration and affection for him and I am so deeply appreciative of all that he does for John's memory. For example, he organised and played in a concert in aid of John's Memorial Trust, in the Royal Festival Hall, and he came to Manchester for the centenary of John's birth to take part in a symposium (see Appendix 3) as well as giving a magical and unforgettable performance of the First Piano Concerto of Brahms. My only worry about Daniel is that he does too much. He is director of the Opera in what was East Berlin and of the Chicago Symphony (where he took over from Solti when he retired), and in addition undertakes piano performances and guest-conducting engagements in abundance. I hope he will not burn himself out.

I knew his first wife Jacqueline du Pré well, and during her years of illness I used to see her about once a week. It seemed a wicked shame that she should be incapacitated so early and die so young. The word 'genius' should be used rarely and sparingly, but I do think, as did John, that Jackie had a touch of it. She was great fun to be with and had a very naughty sense of humour, which she used often to shock and tease her wonderful nurse-companion, Ruth Anne. Whenever friends spent the evening with

161

her she would insist on listening to records of her own performances. At first I found this distressing, but I very soon understood that it was a kind of compensation for all that she had known and could no longer enjoy. She was a born performer and it was tragic that so much of her life and genius had to be taken from her. She played often with John (who had given her a Suggia award at a very early age) and accepted any suggestion he made. She once told me that she adored and trusted him, which I found very touching. His only tiny criticism about her playing was that sometimes she gave *too* much. She was, after all, very young when she became so famous. John used to calm her down just a little, and she was always grateful. John, in turn, loved conducting for her and was very fond of her. Her performance of the Elgar Cello Concerto with John conducting is, in my opinion, a truly great recording and confirms the epithet of genius.

We were fortunate to have some fine secretaries over the years. Our first, in Manchester, was Sidney Rothwell (no relation of mine – it is a fairly common name in the north of England). We really liked him, but he was about to get married and wanted a nine-to-five job, which John's certainly was not! Judy Smith, then quite a young woman, was an excellent secretary in every way and we liked her particularly, but she left us to move to London, to our genuine regret. I still see her often and it is always a great pleasure. She is an intrepid and adventurous traveller, and she often has an unusual hobby. These hobbies have ranged through buying and selling secondhand books, repairing old clocks and automata and, most recently, making furniture. Rosalind Booth, another excellent secretary at first, became devoted to Ken Crickmore, manager of the Hallé 1951–60. His part in our lives is examined in the next chapter. Brenda Coupe, née Bracewell, was our last secretary and a first-class one. I shall never forget her loyalty to us both. She was most efficient and I was glad that she married a kind man when her work with me in Manchester was over. I am still in touch with her regularly as a friend.

As I have mentioned, all his life John was interested in medical and surgical matters. In his early adult years his great ambition was to be a surgeon. Fortunately, this ambition was never considered seriously, because the family had no money to finance it, but John's deep interest continued throughout his life. One of our closest friends in Manchester was W.R. (Bill) Douglas, a well-known surgeon and head of the Manchester Christie Cancer Hospital. We were extremely fond of him and of his wife, Meg, and he was a great support both to John and to me. During our Manchester years he operated on each of us! Bill was an enchanting man with a great sense of humour, a healthy liking for good food and wine, and, most important, a caring, gentle consideration for his patients. John loved watching surgical operations and he had seen Bill operate several times, but after some years he had never seen him do the operation for which he was famous at that time – since so few surgeons were performing it, a block dissection of the neck. Bill finally arranged for John to attend this operation and John read it up carefully and made copious notes about the procedure before he went, fascinated, to watch Bill doing it. John was full of admiration for Bill's expertise and artistry, and gave him his careful notes. Bill said that they would have done credit to a fully qualified surgeon. John felt very proud. This preparation was typical of his thoroughness in everything he did.

In my Acknowledgements I have thanked our dear and gifted friend, Michael Kennedy. He and his enchanting and courageous first wife, Eslyn, were our close friends in Manchester over many years. This friendship meant a great deal to us both. Now that John is no longer living, Michael's close friendship means even more to me, and I am deeply grateful for his loyal and loving memories of John. We first knew Michael when he was young (in his late teens, I think, when he was just about to go into the Navy and soon to marry Eslyn). After the Second World War ended Michael rose quickly in the hierarchy of the *Daily Telegraph* and today he is music critic of the *Sunday Telegraph*. He is an author of distinction and has written great biographies of Elgar and Strauss among many other books, including a beautiful biography of John. Michael is remarkably erudite and his research is exhaustive but he writes so well and so vividly that his beautiful prose is easy to read as well as being reliably informative. I see him and his dear and greatly supportive second wife, Joyce, on the rare occasions when they are not rushing round the world reviewing festivals, operas or new works. Despite his well-deserved reputation as an author and music critic, he remains unspoilt by success; he is the same warmhearted friend I have always known, one who gave much affection and loyalty to John and still does to his memory.

Martin Milner, leader of the Hallé (and of the King's Lynn Quartet), was a dear and supportive friend. In John's last years when he was often away guest conducting, he relied upon Martin to look after the Hallé string sections as well as leading the orchestra. John trusted him implicitly and his trust was amply justified. At the Manchester symposium celebrating the centenary of John's birth, Daniel Barenboim spoke about Martin with great warmth. 'One has to say that Martin Milner was not just a normal leader of the section. He was really one of the most consummate leaders of the string sections that I have come across anywhere and his knowledge and his help in the music-making went far beyond his playing the violin.' We were all delighted to know that Martin was in the audience (in the wheelchair that had become necessary after he suffered a severe stroke) and he received a well-deserved standing ovation from the audience, which must have meant a great deal to him. He died, alas, a few months later.

In Manchester we had a wonderful cleaning lady for many years, Nellie Richardson, who was excellent in every way, caring, warmhearted, loyal and efficient. She became our friend, as did her husband Reg. After Reg died, her health deteriorated and she had to leave us. Her health is still very poor but she lives in a home now, always thinking of others, never complaining, and grateful for anything done for her. She is a sterling person of whom we were very fond, as I still am.

When Nellie had to retire we decided that it would be sensible to engage a married couple, as we were away a good deal and in our present home there would be a nice flat for them. Kenneth Crickmore arranged for Phyl and Joe, his mother and stepfather, to take the post. They were very good and we liked them. Unfortunately, they left without notice at a most inconvenient time, when we were in America and I had just broken my arm. Naturally, I suppose, their loyalty was to Crickmore rather than to us, and our association with him seemed to be nearing its end at the time. But it left our large Manchester house empty until our secretary Brenda came and stayed alone in it for some weeks – a kind act I shall never forget.

Phyl and Joe were succeeded by Mary and Roy. They were loyal and efficient and we all got on excellently. Mary gave invaluable help to Brenda in sorting out John's affairs after his death. Roy was a taxi driver but he drove us only occasionally; the Hallé driver (also called Roy) looked after John at work with the Hallé. Both Roys were good drivers and considerate companions and I was sad to let them go when I moved to London a year or so after John's death.

# Crickmore: An Unhappy Association

*KENNETH CRICKMORE WAS* manager of the Hallé for nine years and our personal manager for a much longer time. He had come into our lives during the early days of the Hallé. In the season 1943–44 he was the extremely competent manager of concerts in Sheffield, where the Hallé played weekly. John soon got to know Crickmore and came to appreciate his efficiency. He told us that he was an ex-RAF fighter pilot who had later flown bombers before being invalided out of the service. Among other episodes he claimed to have taken part in the Battle of Britain, and said he had been short-listed as a bomber pilot to go on the 'Dambusting' raids. He had a talent for persuading people to believe his claims and, stupidly I fear, we never checked on anything.

He was so capable that John arranged for him to become involved in the Hallé management. Crickmore succeeded Ernest Bean as manager in 1951 when Bean left to become manager of the Royal Festival Hall, and he was extremely successful until he resigned through ill health in 1960, when Clive Smart took over. Undeniably, Ken was talented and efficient. As time went on, his association with John developed and he became John's personal manager. He took charge of all our affairs, financial and otherwise, and looked after guest appearances, recordings and fees. In fact, he took over the business side of our life so completely that John needed only to think of his music and I had only to look after John. It seemed a satisfactory state of affairs. Our secretary, Rosalind Booth, lived and worked with Ken. We both trusted them utterly and never questioned anything they did. Often I feel ashamed to realise how completely we were taken in, how stupid and how ridiculously trusting we were. When Ken developed cancer which necessitated the loss of his leg, it only consolidated our trust, because it became mingled with compassion. The only thing we ever asked of him was to submit monthly accounts of his management. These always seemed satisfactory but we did not scrutinise them closely.

Finally, when no accounts were sent for several months, we became worried. In 1963 or thereabouts, we went to America for one of John's guest-conducting engagements. Ken and Rosalind were also over there, trying to arrange Ken's divorce from his first wife. (Such matters were easier to manage in certain states of America or in Mexico than in Britain, and in the end Ken and Rosalind married.) As time went on and we still received no accounts we became suspicious and consulted our friend, the lawyer Tony Jackson, in whose Beverly Hills house we were staying at the time. Tony went to see Ken and Rosalind, who were living in rented accommodation near Los Angeles. By the time Ken died in 1965, Tony had filed a court case on John's behalf which was defended unsuccessfully by Rosalind, then Ken's widow. We were paid some money, but it was not so much the financial loss that upset John so deeply, it was the fact that a man whom he had thought a loyal friend he had trusted implicitly, had turned out to be untrustworthy. It was a dreadful let-down, and naturally John felt guilty that he had allowed it to happen. I felt even more guilty because I should have checked on Ken and Rosalind. It is so easy to be wise after the event. If only he had used his considerable abilities for honest purposes, how valuable he could have been. But perhaps it is a tribute to John's loyalty, even if misguided in this case, that he wouldn't listen to the many people who warned him about Kenneth Crickmore.

# —— 24 ——

# *Living With a Great Man*

*IT IS OFTEN* presumed that a man or woman who has had a long and loving relationship is ideally suited to give the most complete picture of their partner, but this is not necessarily so. If you look at a picture closely you will see all the details, but for the whole effect you must go further away. I intend to give the details of living with John in the hope that the whole picture will come to life, so I will start with some of the broader aspects of our relationship. When our families were told that we intended to marry soon, since John's divorce had been finalised, their reactions varied. John's relatives were delighted; I had got to know them all very well over the years. My own rather more conventional family were slightly doubtful, despite the fact that they all liked John greatly. My father was especially mistrustful: with his Victorian outlook he felt that a man who was a foreigner (although he was born and educated in England), a Roman Catholic, a divorcé and a musician was unlikely to be a suitable husband for his only daughter! Even the more sympathetic members of my family thought that we might find life too complicated, particularly as we came from such different backgrounds.

John and I discussed their doubts and we were convinced that such matters could be resolved. Admittedly we were in love, so we may have been biased, but we were convinced that between two people like ourselves there must be important basic qualities which could override all inconvenient details. Consideration for other people, lack of jealousy, a sense of humour, generosity (not only about money but of speech and thought), and courtesy in the good old-fashioned sense, which encompasses sensitive consideration and deep understanding of the other's point of view: all these qualities John observed throughout his life. He was no saint, but he was a good and greatly caring man. During our life together I understood that music must come first with him; for his part, he always wanted me to play, and was unstinting in his praise and encouragement.

Many people used to ask me if John was difficult to live with because he had such a passionate temperament when conducting. John himself often said, 'I keep my temperament where it belongs, on the platform.' The only difficulty I had was my inability to help him in his fits of depression. He told me that he had inherited this unfortunate tendency from a great-uncle. His sister and one of her sons suffered in the same way. I have often wondered if John's depressions were more prevalent because of his lack of confidence in himself. It seems strange that a man who was so successful and so much loved, could be so doubtful of his own abilities, but it was so. Maybe his work was all the more inspired because of his insecurity and self-criticism. As he got older, the depressions became more frequent and more severe. He tried the medications available at the time, but they were ineffective. His own remedy was never to stop working, and for this reason he refused to take holidays lest depression should come upon him. There seems to be no way in which one can help in these bad times; I believe Winston Churchill suffered in the same way, and used to refer to these periods as his 'black dog'.

One part of our everyday life was eating and drinking. We all eat and drink to live, and some live to eat and drink, while others are just extremely interested in the subject. John certainly belonged to the last category. He had a genuine interest in food and drink which undoubtedly came from his mother's influence. He had inherited her gift for cooking, and loved to make use of this talent.

I was always delighted to see him heading purposefully to the kitchen, because cooking was the only activity which switched him off music. He was completely focused on it, just as he was when working at scores, and he could produce wonderful sauces and imaginative dishes. Our entertaining at home was done on a small scale; dinner for a few close friends, often Michael and Eslyn Kennedy, never a large party. John was a splendid host, and was delighted when his guests were pleased, but he himself seldom ate the tasty fare he prepared with such loving care. He preferred quite plain food; most of all he loved steamed fish with homemade mayonnaise (to me a most boring meal!). I have already mentioned how little he ate, except in his early adult years; no breakfast (just a cup of coffee or tea), and only a small sandwich for lunch (which he often left untouched if he was busy during rehearsal breaks). Even his only real meal at night was not large.

Except for simple Italian trattorias he disliked restaurants, and when we were on tour we picnicked in our hotel room, as I have described in Chapter 18. When cooking he never used a recipe but started with an idea of his own and went on from this, apparently by instinct. He loved pasta and made excellent sauces for it, but he could also cook many other things with equal expertise. He enjoyed Italian food, except gnocchi and polenta, which he disliked. John sometimes asked his mother to show him how she did certain things, but she was far too naturally talented and instinctive a cook to be able to do so. Sometimes John and I

171

cooked together, which was always great fun. I had certain regular tasks, such as cooking the pasta and making the mayonnaise, which I did by hand, as we had no machines or gadgets during the war. John liked pasta 'al dente' and hated it overcooked ('Like paste to apply wallpaper' he used to say) so it had to be taken off the heat at exactly the right moment.

Although he was such a fanatical worker, and thought constantly about music, he had remarkably wide interests. In our early married years we walked a great deal, often for quite long distances. John also liked being driven in my modest little car, sometimes stopping for a picnic, or perhaps visiting a country pub (one of our favourites in Litlington, Sussex, was The Plough and Harrow, which was kept by a fascinating Cockney couple, Fred and Doll), or a beautiful old village church, where we would go in and light a candle and say a short prayer. He appreciated beautiful country, fine buildings in the lovely streets of old towns, and the charm of ancient, sleepy villages. He loved strolling around to get what he called 'the sniff of the place' or to revisit favourite spots. He did not drive at all and was absurdly ignorant about driving rules and road sense. For instance, if he saw a building and wanted to look at it more closely, he could not understand why it might be dangerous to stop and leave the car on a blind bend in the road by the building concerned. 'Surely just a few minutes would be all right,' he would say. He loved anything beautiful: eighteenth-century English furniture, china, and particularly glass. Curiously enough, we had both begun to collect eighteenth-century drinking glasses before we knew each other, so our glass collection grew out of a mutual passion. In our early collecting years it was comparatively easy to find good specimens around the country, but we used also to enjoy visiting a well-known antique glass shop, Churchills, which was manned by a zestful, knowledgeable Cockney called Paddock and a younger man of equal expertise, Howard Phillips, who later became the doyen of antique glass dealers. We learnt a lot from both of them.

John had been a wine drinker since childhood (oddly enough though English I had been brought up in the same way) and we always enjoyed wine with meals. During the rationing years, when wine was almost unobtainable, we drank an excellent type of cider made with pears (called perry) which was sent to us by the case from the West Country, where it was made. During the day, at lunch and later, John would sip Scotch whisky, well diluted with soda water. He suffered, as did Churchill, from being considered a man who drank too much, a reputation neither man deserved. Churchill was reputed to drink all day, but his whisky or brandy and water was quite weak, and for the most part he only sipped it. John too sipped well-diluted whisky. He was never affected by alcohol, nor was it ever an addiction. Someone said of Churchill, 'I never saw him the worse for drink – only the better'. It is unfortunate that certain ill-natured people have exaggerated the modest sipping of both John and Churchill. At least John was in good company. He met Churchill once, though only briefly, when he was about to speak at the annual dinner given by the Royal Academy of Arts, at which John was an honoured guest. He was introduced to the great man, who was sitting outside the banqueting room waiting to go in when John arrived rather late. John shook his hand (surprisingly Churchill had rather a limp handshake – at any rate on that occasion). Churchill was obviously tired and out of humour, and was disinclined to say anything, but it was nevertheless exciting to see him in the flesh.

John was given many honours, including some very beautiful medals from France and Italy, but he valued most highly the English ones: his knighthood, the Royal Philharmonic Gold

Medal and the Companion of Honour. This last very special honour, given only to a limited number of people, is traditionally presented to the recipient privately by the Queen. I drove John to Buckingham Palace and was permitted to sit and wait for him in my parked car. He stayed for a good 30 minutes alone with the Queen in a small sitting room, just chatting. He found her enchanting, very quick-witted and extremely intelligent; she smiled and laughed a lot and seemed to enjoy John's company. Perhaps she is shy with large numbers of people? John regretted that she does not smile or laugh much when 'on show'; maybe she does not realise how much she is admired and respected and how much her public would enjoy seeing her smile more. John was also very proud of being given the Freedom of the City of Manchester, and the Freedom of King's Lynn.

John had a lively sense of humour and was a good raconteur. He was a good writer and public speaker with an easy and wide command of words. He disliked the four-letter words that are so commonly used today and his humour was never smutty, except sometimes in a schoolboy sort of way.

As he slept so little, three or four hours at most, he loved working at night (as I have described in Chapter 21) and he read a great deal in bed. At home we had special bedside lamps, but in hotels elaborate shading with bath towels had to be organised so that his light would not disturb me. (This was typical of his thoughtful consideration.) He enjoyed reading the biographies and letters of people he admired, for example, Nelson, Henry Irving, Ellen Terry, and the great men of medicine such as Pasteur and Lister, and of law such as Birkenhead and Marshall Hall. Occasionally he liked a good detective story, and he was particularly partial to Agatha Christie.

John smoked, though less in later life, and almost always cigarettes. On rare occasions he enjoyed a good cigar, and in his younger adult life he smoked a pipe, but he gave this up when he became such a busy conductor. He said he hadn't got time to fiddle with it, it took too long!

He was endearingly childlike in little ways. For example, on a visit to Russia we bought some enchanting wooden toys, including a bear playing the piano. Its hands could move on and off the keyboard and John insisted that they must always be left on the keys. If he came in and found the bear's hands in the wrong place he would correct it immediately! He loved children and was good with them, but before marrying we made the decision that we would not have a family. John disliked travelling abroad alone and as a conductor's life involves so much of this, either our children would have been left at home without a parent, or John would have had to travel miserably alone while I stayed with the children. We both felt that if we were to have children one of us at least should be with them during their formative years. No doubt our mothers could have looked after them, but the children might have become confused between southern French and middle-class British habits, food and bedtimes. Nevertheless we often regretted our decision, but we still felt it wise not to alter it. Life would have become too complicated and probably unhappy for all concerned.

John seldom looked at television though he liked the news and loved watching cricket. When we were in Manchester we went occasionally to Old Trafford to see live cricket, but sadly, Manchester lived up to its reputation and too often rain stopped play.

In our peripatetic lives we always tried to make a home, even in a hotel room, but we usually had a flat or a house for more permanent occupation. For many years our main home was in Manchester. The first was in 1943, a small flat in a block called Appleby Lodge, opposite Platt Fields Park. Its great advantage (as I mentioned earlier) was central heating, a rare luxury in Manchester during those wartime years, and it was conveniently placed for stations and the centre of the town. After a while we were able to rent a larger flat in the same building and we were happy and comfortable there for some time. In later years we owned a house, Walton Lodge, off Bury New Road, near Prestwich. We had spacious rooms and an attic for storing; our secretary had a large room with plenty of space for her files (and for our old Bechstein concert grand), and there was a pleasant flat on the ground floor which was occupied by the married couple we engaged later on. It was most comfortable.

In London, we stayed at first with Mémé in her Streatham Hill flat. Later, after her death, we bought a very small but pleasant and comfortable house in a mews near Baker Street station, wonderfully central for London recording studios and concert halls. I have already described our beautiful apartment in Hampshire House, New York, and the houses we rented in Vancouver and California. John loved home wherever it was, and was interested in furniture, curtains and carpets, etc.

When we moved into Walton Lodge we had much more space. Tim McOstrich took back the furniture which had been so vital to us in our early days in Manchester, so we enjoyed ourselves arranging everything and living in a more civilised way. We had some fine antique furniture for which before we never had adequate space. Many years earlier, John had given me a lovely early eighteenth-century bureau bookcase. It is made of a handsome hardwood called Padouk, which is impervious to termites, and it was reputedly made for a sea captain. I love it, and so did John – it is a rare piece. A beautiful chair arrived from New York – miraculously it seemed, because it was a wedding present shipped during the war. We bought in Brighton a small, charming commode (which John called his little French Piece with the lovely legs) and for our 25th wedding anniversary we gave each other an elegant little chandelier which we bought in Venice. For John's 25th anniversary with the Hallé he was given a fine antique glass-fronted bookcase from the late eighteenth century. We enjoyed choosing carpets and curtains together: John was interested in such things and had great taste. At last we could display our glass collection which was a great joy.

The actress Yvonne Arnaud was an old friend of John's and when she was in Manchester (where the pre-London productions are often shown) she always came to supper. She loved the glasses in our collection, particularly a large one which we knew as a Toastmaster's glass of the mid-eighteenth-century. After one of our suppers, Yvonne was going on to play in Edinburgh, from where a few days later there arrived a carefully packed parcel. Inside was a tiny eighteenth-century glass, an exact miniature of our large one, with a note from Yvonne saying, 'It must have pupped – with much love'. She had started performing live as a pianist at an early age and she once played a concerto with John and the Hallé at a concert in aid of the orchestra's Benevolent Fund, giving a beautiful performance of the Schumann Piano Concerto – musical and of fine professional standard. It was all the more remarkable as she had not played in public for many years. She was an adorable person on and off the stage. When plans were made after her death to found the Yvonne Arnaud Theatre in Guildford (she had lived nearby with her husband), John played the cello at a fundraising concert in Paul Getty's house, Sutton Place.

I remember that John's cello was locked in a small room which contained also some valuable pictures, and the detectives would not let him in to get his cello. It was kind of Mr Getty to allow his house to be used as a venue, and a lot of money was raised that night. But he did not appear to enjoy himself at all. It is always said that riches do not bring happiness.

Clothes were not of great interest to John, though he was conventional and insisted on wearing the right outfit for any occasion. He had his formal clothes made by an expert tailor. As they were well cut, and made of the finest material available, they would last him for years. At home he would wear casual trousers and shirts, or maybe a dressing gown. He had a number of jackets especially to wear at rehearsals.

My family's pessimistic prognostications about the difficulties of our everyday lives, proved unfounded. True, John ate only once a day, often in the late evening, and I was hungry more frequently and at more normal times, but meals were easily arranged, separately or together, according to my appetite or our mutual convenience. Our schedules also were simple to plan. Conductors arrange their engagements some years in advance; music societies and more modest concerts are booked only a year or so ahead. I used to keep free the times when I would be travelling abroad with John, and when he was working with the Hallé, and well looked after, I would sometimes do some concerts. When he was away conducting the Hallé for the two-week autumn series of concerts in cathedrals in the West Country, I used to take my mother on holiday.

Occasionally, I would play in the city where he was conducting: perhaps a recital on radio or in a small hall, or chamber music with colleagues in the district, and very rarely with John in a more important concert. I could usually practise while he was rehearsing, but if ever I had an urgent need to practise and John was working in our hotel room, this was no problem for him. He had the most remarkable powers of concentration and was able to shut out any sounds he did not want to hear. He put this down to having been brought up in a noisy Italian family, but his ability to focus in this way was remarkable. If he were studying on his bed I might be playing scales in the room at the same time, yet he promised that it did not disturb him, or prevent him from studying his own scores, and I'm sure that this was true. He was always helpful if I was worried about a concert and for example would advise me about the choice of an oboe reed's sound.

John was an excellent traveller. If a plane was delayed and there was obviously nothing he could do about arriving late, he would settle down with his scores and work. He was fatalistic and never worried when flying. If the time came for him to die it would come, he was sure. John was not religious, though his way of living and behaviour was truly Christian. He hardly ever went to church, but though he might justifiably have been called a 'lapsed Catholic', he was relieved and happy when his Church altered its ruling against cremation. John had always wanted to be cremated and to have his ashes buried in his mother's grave, and these wishes were fulfilled.

In money matters, his behaviour was inconsistent. When an old colleague asked him for a large loan (which John was fully aware was most unlikely to be repaid) he would write the cheque immediately and without hesitation, but if he were waiting for a bus in pelting rain he would not dream of taking a taxi for himself. We had a joint bank account and he never even enquired what I spent; in general, he was far too trusting. Although he was careful with money he did not really think about it a great deal. He disliked carrying it, for the sensible reason that he would have nowhere to put it safely when he was conducting – artists' rooms are often vulnerable to casual thieves. He was not a lover of luxury even when he could well afford to be. We did travel first class on planes, but we always stayed in a hotel room rather than taking a suite. His one prerequisite when choosing hotels was not that of price but of position: he loved to stay really near his place of work. In Milan we used to stay in a comfortable hotel (sadly, it no longer exists) opposite the stage door of La Scala; and in Rome there was one hotel that was even more convenient, because there was a pass-door from it into the theatre. We usually stayed at the Embassy when in Rome, but on one occasion the hotel pass-door was irresistible. John always said that he loved the smell of size backstage, and for two weeks of recording Puccini's *Madame Butterfly*, he made full use of that pass-door!

Healthwise, John was strong and resilient until the last two years or so of his life. He suffered from kidney stones at one time and took pills for the pain, but this trouble soon cleared up. Unlike most men (who often complain more about their ailments than women do) he used to put up with trouble uncomplainingly, and usually (too often I fear) worked through it. He had great courage, physically and mentally. Once, when recording in Manchester's Free Trade Hall, he caught his foot in a cable and fell several feet from the platform to the floor of the hall. Miraculously, although he hurt his back quite badly, it was not as serious as it might have been. He picked himself up, went on recording and next morning was back at work on the platform. But during his late sixties his health did begin to deteriorate. This proved to be due to blockages of the main arteries. These caused him small but frequent heart attacks, which he described as his 'blackouts', but courageously he always went back to conduct soon after one. On the advice of our excellent and much loved doctor, Michael Linnett, we went to see an eminent heart specialist, who warned John that he could neither overcome nor afford to ignore this condition, and that one day he would have an extremely serious heart attack, one which might well prove fatal. John's only comment after the specialist's sad prognostication was that he would not die during a concert, and that he would continue working till the end.

Both these things came to pass. John's last heart attack took place during the night when he was in bed in our little mews house. It was very sudden and I do not think he would have felt anything. I dialled 999, and the ambulance came promptly and rushed him to hospital but the experts there failed to resuscitate him. It was better that they did fail because he could only have survived as an invalid, impaired physically and probably mentally. I often wonder if today, with the great advances of open-heart surgery and arterial repairs, something might have been done to help his condition – at the time of his death in 1970 such surgery and treatment was only in its early stages – but looking back is a profitless and sad occupation. His life ended as he wanted, in the midst of work. The day before his death (on 29 July 1970, at the age of 70) he rehearsed hard and happily all day. Janet Baker described this rehearsal as 'the best of her life' and said that John was in great form. He asked for kippers for supper and ate them with relish, while describing the rehearsals, talking about Janet Baker, and saying how fit he felt in readiness for going to Japan in two days' time. The end came as he had wished.

# — 25 —

# *After John*

*WHEN YOUR EXISTENCE* has been disrupted by the loss of someone who filled your whole life for many years, it is sadly difficult to go on living normally, because it really does not seem to matter. At first there will be routine tasks to perform, but after these are finished it helps to try to keep yourself occupied, rather than sit around in grief. I was wonderfully lucky in having work ready and waiting for me but I am aware that for many less fortunate people an occupation has to be found, possibly through voluntary organisations. Family and close friends can be very helpful and understanding, but it is you yourself who must make the effort to continue your life as constructively as possible.

For the first year of my widowhood I sorted out papers that might be useful to Michael Kennedy who, as John had always wanted, was writing John's biography. In addition, I spent time looking for somewhere to live in or near London. I wanted to leave our house in Manchester, which was anyway too large, to be closer to both our families (John's relatives lived in London and mine about 50 miles out of it). I found a most convenient house, 28 Ivor Place, within a stone's throw of our little pied-à-terre where John had his fatal heart attack. It was a typical London house of four floors, plus an accessible attic and what the builder called an 'area' (a small outside space round my basement, a little larger than usual because the house was on a corner). The house was spacious enough to take almost all our furniture and I had the top floor soundproofed in case I decided to teach or practise in the future. I had not yet decided whether to continue playing, but I was persuaded to do so for two reasons. First, I had received invitations for professorships at the Royal Academy of Music and the Royal College of Music, both in London. The Academy was near my house, and my close friend Janet Craxton was head of the oboe department there, so I accepted their offer. The other reason concerned my playing and this came through Ruth Fermoy. A series of midday recitals at the King's Lynn Festival was nearing an anniversary date (I can't recall which!) and Ruth had engaged for one concert a famous artist who was well-known and loved by the regular midday audience. Unfortunately, the artist concerned fell ill and Ruth was searching for a suitable replacement. She implored me to start playing again and offered to accompany me. Ruth was a beautiful accompanist, with whom I'd often played before, so this was in itself an inducement. She persuaded me to do the concert with her, saying that I might as well try once to see if I wanted to go on playing. I practised hard in the short time available and when the concert came I thoroughly enjoyed it. Having found that playing was a relieving solace, I contacted my agents, Ibbs and Tillett, who already had many enquiries from music societies. My partner was Iris Loveridge, a solo pianist of distinction who was also an excellent ensemble player. We got on extremely well together on and off the concert platform and soon became exceedingly busy.

It was through Iris and her dear husband, Harry, that I became interested in gardening. They both came to lunch one day for Iris to rehearse, and when Harry saw my 'area' he decided that I should not continue to live in the house without something growing and flowering. He arrived at the weekend with tubs, sacks of soil, a large bag of daffodil bulbs and all the necessary tools. The bulbs flowered in the spring. Of course I was delighted, and from that moment I became a passionate gardener! Gardening is a wonderfully, healing occupation and I can never be grateful enough to Harry and Iris for setting me on this path. I knew nothing about gardening, but after reading a good deal, joining the Royal Horticultural Society, and talking to Harry and other gardeners, I decided that I must move from my house with its 'area' in order to have a 'proper' garden. After much searching I found the ground floor flat, with garden, where I have lived for nearly twenty years. The previous owner was Mary Stein, the talented gardener of its third-of-an-acre plot, which though rather neglected was well designed and full of potential. I was joined by John Galvin who has been my gardener for some fifteen years. When we began, neither of us knew a great deal, but as the years have gone by I have learnt a little more, and John has become a full-time gardener of considerable skill and knowledge and a good friend. He still comes to me once a week to look after 'our garden'. Some years ago, the then garden editor of *Country Life* magazine, Tony Venison, wrote an article about my garden, which was a great honour. He is truly my garden 'guru', his knowledge is encyclopaedic, his friendship a joy, and his expert help invaluable. After several busy years, Iris and I decided to retire from playing concerts. She and Harry moved into a Cotswold village without a railway station, and as I've sold my car, our communication has been mainly on the telephone. Sadly she died recently.

I have few connections with music these days. I am retiring from my post as Artistic Director of the Isle of Wight International Oboe Festival but I still attend meetings of the

Musician's Benevolent Fund and I do some adjudicating, which I enjoy greatly. In both musical occupations I work with colleagues whom I might not see otherwise, and I keep in touch with the younger generation of oboe players.

For me, the happiest and most exciting occasion of recent years was when celebrations in Manchester marked the centenary of John's birth on 2 December 1999. These events are described in Appendix 2, and were truly worthy of the occasion. I attended them all, of course. They were wonderful, unforgettable. It was heart-warming and most moving to know how warmly and lovingly John is remembered after so many years; he would have been extremely happy and proud.

On 2 December 2000, his next birthday anniversary, a bust of John, larger than life-size, was unveiled by the Duke of Devonshire. He was charming, warm and courteous to everyone, and the proceedings were watched by a large crowd. The bust, sculpted by Byron Howard, is truly wonderful. Byron has truly 'caught' John, in my opinion, and others feel the same. It is in a perfect position, just by the entrance to the Bridgewater Hall, and is designed to exist in all weathers, made of bronze on a stone plinth. It will be a lasting memorial to John. I shall always be deeply grateful to Ivan Saxton, who has worked so hard and so selflessly on this project for the past eight years. Many people came afterwards to the Barbirolli Room in the Bridgewater Hall for tea and buns and the company there included many ex-Hallé members and a number of other old friends, so the whole affair was a warm and wholly delightful occasion.

# Appendix 1

John's article published in 1947 by Penguin Books in their *Music Magazine*, still makes interesting reading and shows his natural gift for expressing himself.

## THE ART OF CONDUCTING
*by John Barbirolli*

The history of conducting can be traced back at least to the fifteenth century, by which time it seems it had become customary to beat time at the performances of the 'Sistine Choir in Rome with a roll of paper called a 'Sol-Fa'. In the next century, about 1516, we find writings describing performances of concerted vocal music at which these writings refer to 'a certain motion made by the hand of the chief singer according to the nature of the marks, which motion directs a song according to measure'. This rather tends to show that by the beginning of the sixteenth century the practice was universal: as does also a passage from Galilei's *Dialogo* (1583), where he mentions that the ancient Greeks did not beat time 'as is customary now'.

However, with the decline of polyphonic music and its

attendant rhythmic subtleties, the time-beater must have become less necessary, and as the idea of the conductor as an interpreter as well as a time-keeper was not yet born, the practice of directing music with the conducting-stick seems to have fallen into disuse.

How and when the change came about I am not certain, but by 1740 or so it was customary to direct opera performances sitting at the harpsichord, at least in Italy and Germany, and we have also, of course, descriptions of Bach to prove that he, in any case, was in the habit of directing the music while he himself played the organ. In France, though, the practice of using the stick seems to have continued, for someone writing in England in 1709 has rather an amusing account of the art as he saw it practised in Paris and apparently copied with assiduous indiscrimination in London. I don't think I can do better than quote the passage as it stands:

'The Master of Musick in the Opera at Paris had an Elboe Chair and Desk placed on the Stage where, with the Score in one hand and a stick in the other, he beat time on a table put there for that purpose, so loud, that he made a greater Noise than the whole Band, on purpose to be heard by the Performer. By degrees they removed this Abuse [not the most polite way of referring to practitioners of my craft] from the Stage to the Musick Room [which must mean what we now term the orchestra pit], where the Composer beats the time in the same manner and as loud as ever, but since the Italian Masters [this must refer to the Italian Opera composers who enjoyed great popularity in the town at that time] have come among us, they have put a stop to that ridiculous custom, because the Eye was too much distracted, being obliged to mind the beating of the measure and the score at the same time: besides, [and this will please some of my friends who sing in opera, if not my colleagues who conduct it] it kept the singer in too much subjection, and Fear of Errors.'

To make some singers fear errors is something of an achievement; unless they happen to be singing the wrong opera, they seem blissfully unaware of them.

By the beginning of the nineteenth century, however, the practice of beating time seems to have become firmly established in Germany, though it was not until 1820 that conducting with a stick at orchestral concerts was tried and became an institution in London, where it was introduced by Spohr at a Royal Philharmonic Society concert. Until then the orchestra was guided by the joint efforts of the principal violin or leader, and a gentleman at the harpsichord who came to the rescue with a few chords if things got a bit shaky. It was received, as I suppose all innovations are fated to be, with the most profound distrust by the directors. But in Spohr's own words: 'The triumph of the baton was complete.'

Spohr's account of this historic occasion is very interesting: 'I took my stand in front of the orchestra, drew my directing baton from my coat pocket, and gave the signal to begin. Quite alarmed at such a novel proceeding, some of the directors protested against it, but the triumph of the baton as a time-giver was decisive, and no one was seen any more seated at the piano during the performance of Symphonies and Overtures.'

The most famous practitioner of the art of conducting at this period was probably Mendelssohn, who presided over the Gewandhaus Concerts in Leipzig from 1835 to 1843. As prime inspirer and founder of the modern school of conducting, I think we can safely point to Wagner, and a survey of his chief disciples, such as Bülow, Richter, Levi, and Mottl, quickly brings us to our own times.

Now I should like to say a little about the practical application of the conductor's art as a means of making orchestral or concerted music more easily intelligible by clarity and eloquence of presentation. This practical application of the art I divide into two sections: (1) the physical, with which I incorporate the psychological, and (2) the purely musical mathematics of the art. The possession of gifts of the former I regard as essential to the fulfilment of the other; for have we not often had the spectacle of a great musician unable to secure even a mediocre interpretation of a work of his own? Wagner laid it down that the two fundamental principles underlying the art were: (1) giving the true tempo to the orchestra; (2) finding the 'melos', which means the unifying thread of line that gives a work its form and shape. Given these two qualities, of course, we have the conductor in excelsis, and most of our lives must be spent in trying to obtain these qualities, more especially the first. It is surprising how few conductors are capable of setting and maintaining a tempo for more than a few bars.

Having stressed the importance of tempo to this extent, I have sometimes advised students as a guiding principle that *no tempo should be so slow as to make it difficult for a melody to be recognisable, and no tempo so fast as to make a melody unrecognisable*, and that composers' metronome marks, though sometimes inaccurate, can be at any rate a guide which it would be dangerous to ignore. This is not to suggest that accuracy of this kind alone can make a perfect performance, for accuracy without imagination is useless, and some small, subtle, barely perceptible modifications of tempo will ever be necessary to a living rendering of any music. From the foregoing it will be realised that the possession and understanding of these fundamental principles laid down by Wagner can only be claimed by very sensitive musical minds endowed with the will, energy, and patience to probe them to the full in the interests of their art.

Now I would say a word on the physical-psychological aspect of conducting, which is so important because, however splendid a conductor's musical ideas may be, they will be nullified if these qualities are not present.

When I speak of the physical aspect I mean a natural gift of gesture which should be at once clear and eloquent, and in the term 'gesture' is included the beat. I do not personally believe in any standardisation in this respect, but I would always ask that every gesture should have a definite meaning, and only be inspired by the most complete sincerity towards the music, oneself, and the public.

By psychological aspect I mean the early divination of the types of players with whom you have to deal and your power of making them do their 100 per cent best for you and the music.

This brings us to a very delicate and important problem - the latitude one can allow to players regarding expression in the rendering of their solos. No hard-and-fast rules can be laid down here, as some players need more guidance than others, and the conductor must be quick to realise these points. It is dangerous to worry a very sensitive player too much; on the contrary, during an important and difficult solo the conductor should provide him with a background of sympathy, trust, and help. I have sometimes been approached to explain various interpretations of the same piece due supposedly to 'moods' of mine. But the explanation is not concerned with moods. This freedom, however, must not extend so as to permit any anachronisms in phrasing, and no 'selfish' player, however good, should ever be tolerated in any first-class orchestra.

I think it could hardly be called a digression from my subject if I said something about the general duties and problems of conducting, which more or less bring us up to the immediate present. Few people seem to realise that conducting at the perfomance is the least important part of the business of conducting. I am not even referring to the continual rehearsals during the season, but to all the work of annotating parts, editing, the one hundred and one points of technical elucidation of scores which has to go on unceasingly.

Of course one of the most formidable tasks that faces the conductor of an organisation such as the Hallé, for instance, is to make programmes – programmes that must have as a basis the great classical masterpieces, what we might call a representative selection of modern classics, and such contemporary music as might interest the public to hear – not forgetting the encouragement, which it is our duty to extend to young and perhaps unknown composers. I myself have sometimes spent weeks reading scores, of which more than 90 per cent must finally be rejected, not because they are all unworthy of performance, but because I do not believe that the Hallé concerts should become merely an experimental forum. When the programme material is all gathered together, I must try to obviate too many repetitions of items played during previous seasons, and, to ensure the retention of some degree of sanity to myself, must not attempt to please everybody. It is easy, by the way, to assemble four great pieces of music and produce a badly balanced programme. Also, in a well-balanced programme the substitution of one piece can completely ruin it. I can say without any exaggeration that it has taken me months to compile programmes for one season, and obviously with the compilation of these programmes there must be constant study. I personally find that after weeks spent in research and study the actual period of conducting comes as a kind of blessed release: musical thoughts that have been singing inside one's mind for months can be expressed at last.

Some questions which I am often asked, and which I might take the opportunity of dealing with here, concern the seating of the orchestra, the most suitable type of baton, accompaniment of soloists, and whether it is best to conduct with or without a score. These things are so personal that I can only state my own methods. First, the question of seating. The main bone of contention is that of the disposition of the strings. It has become usual of late years, both here and abroad, to mass the deeper-toned strings on the outside of the orchestra to the right of the conductor in the traditional place allotted the second violins. Sometimes the violas are placed immediately on the right of the conductor or sometimes even the cellos, and the first and second violins are massed together on the conductor's left. This perhaps creates an extra brilliancy of violin tone, while the proximity of the lower strings to the outside of the orchestra makes for a deep and dark sonority.

This method, however, has its drawbacks. The main one, I think, is that it tends to a preponderance of the bass parts. An even more vital one, especially in the performance of the older classical works where there is so often visual and melodic interplay between the first and second violins — is that when they are massed together it is not so easy to distinguish between the two parts. It is difficult to deny the fact that this 'visual' interplay which takes place aids the 'aural' interplay when each section is placed on either side of the conductor. Obviously, as I have said, there can be no hard-and-fast rule laid down, and the conductor in the end seats his orchestra in the way in which he himself feels most comfortable and will satisfy his musical consciousness, which must always be his guide.

On the subject of batons, here again the choice is a personal one; but perhaps a much more important, sensitive, and delicate choice than is commonly imagined. It is a rather curious fact, which I have noted almost subconsciously, that some conductors change types of batons in different stages of their musical development. In my own case the batons that I find have suited me best have changed during what might be called the brilliant and showy period of my youth and the more sedate and sober period to which I am rapidly approaching. Apart from personal consideration, here as in everything, good taste and good sense should determine. It is as absurd to use a baton which resembles a diminutive lead pencil as it is to wave a weapon of exceeding length and frailty.

I have always taken pleasure in the compliments paid me by artists for my so-called accompaniments. I have used the word 'so-called' advisedly, because with the majority of the great concertos, such as those of Mozart, Beethoven, Brahms, etc., to call the orchestra and conductor the 'accompaniment' is about as accurate as referring to the piano parts of the Mozart, Beethoven, and Brahms Violin Sonatas as 'accompaniments.' Such success as may have attended my labours in this sphere is because I treat a concerto not as a virtuosic display by one individual, but as a collective musical accomplishment, and I spare no pains to that end. It must not be forgotten that the performance of the great concertos provided during a season is not merely a question of presenting soloists, but it is a part of a definite plan to put before the public as many of the symphonic masterpieces as possible. We must not forget that the great concertos should always be a considered part of the orchestral repertoire.

A still more controversial topic is the use or non-use of scores. I would like to say immediately that it is foolish to imagine that a man knows less about a work because he uses a score. On the other hand, it is just as foolish to accuse all those who dispose of them of being bluffers and charlatans. The prime duty of any conductor is to secure the best possible performance of any work with which he is entrusted, and to use such means as he conscientiously believes will ensure the best possible results. To some conductors a score may be an impediment, to others, even though they refer to it very seldom, it is a release from any anxiety which enables them to give a much freer vent to their imagination. At the outset of my career I did a considerable amount of conducting from memory, but I placed on myself the extremely arduous demand that what I conducted from memory I should also be able to write down from memory. As I could not continue to discharge faithfully this onerous conscientiousness, I reverted to scores. On the last occasion when I conducted *Die Meistersinger* some years ago in London, I amused myself by conducting the dress rehearsal without a score, but for the performance I decided it was more sensible and more respectful to the members of the company to have the music before me.

There is one last point I should like to make. I would venture the assumption, without any qualification whatever, that a  conductor is born and not made. By this I am not referring to a musical quality, but rather to a purely technical capacity; and I also do not mean that a born conductor cannot find room for improvement. Some of the most involved technical problems are to be found in the opera house. I would advise any young man with the opportunity for doing so to graduate from the opera house, and it is an indisputable fact that some of the greatest conductors have come from there: 'Richter, Levi, Mottl, Weingartner, Nikisch, Toscanini, and Beecham. For there the conductor is faced with sudden and curious  emergencies of all kinds. He cannot always proceed according to plan, not only because of the performances of singers, but also because of elements of an even more unnerving disposition. The number of little things that can happen for which the conductor is technically responsible are, I am sure, not realised by the audience. For instance, a character has to rush in and sing something and the door sticks – a little delay ensues, and yet all must be made to seem as if everything is proceeding smoothly. With choruses singing off-stage, calculations of distance and sound are necessary that make the conductor's task more complicated, yet all must sound entirely unified in the front of the house.  Experience of these things combines to equip an artist and make him a master of his craft.

Before I conclude, I would like to say to any young musician who contemplates this most arduous and responsible of careers, make your watchwords 'integrity and sincerity to yourself, and loyalty to the man whose music you are seeking to interpret'. Never think, 'What can I make of this piece?' but try to discover what the composer meant to say. We must bear in mind that the conductor has become, for good or ill, one of the most important and responsible personalities in the musical world, and by fine stylistic performances can do much towards a purification of musical perception amongst the general public. On the other hand, performances that are merely the vehicle for indulging the vanity of a personality, however gifted, can only tend to lead us farther from that which should be the goal of all true musicians: service to that great art which it is our privilege to practise.

*Music Magazine*
1947

*Appendix 2*

# Celebrations in Manchester for the Centenary of John's Birth

John was born on 2 December 1899, so 1999 was the centenary year of his birth. The BBC were generous with their time during the period around the date, and in Manchester the Barbirolli Society and, following their example, the Hallé Society, held celebratory events. On 1 December in the Bridgewater Hall, there was an evening given by a Symposium of Talkers, instigated and arranged by the Barbirolli Society. Lyndon Jenkins was the chairman, and eloquent responses to his promptings were given by Daniel Barenboim, Michael Kennedy, Clive Smart, two members of the Hallé Orchestra, Sarah Crouch and Peter Worrall, and myself. I have quoted generously from this event because the participants, in their varying ways built up a vivid general portrait of John. The whole evening was most enjoyable and successful, not least because of the splendid chairmanship of Lyndon Jenkins, who kept us all in order and effortlessly created a good balance of humour and interest. However good the chairman and however eager the responses, there are bound to be a few hesitations, 'ums' and 'ers', so I have done a little judicious editing without, I trust, removing anything of interest.

On 2 December, the day after the symposium, a wonderful concert was given in the Bridgewater Hall by the Hallé Orchestra conducted by Kent Nagano, at which the soloist was Daniel Barenboim, playing Brahms' First Piano Concerto. It was a performance I shall always remember, as I'm sure all the audience will. Daniel played with complete mastery, and such heart and warmth, a truly great performance of a mighty work. Kent Nagano, who at the time of writing is about to leave the Hallé, conducted supportively and well, and the orchestra took part splendidly. I am deeply grateful to all concerned, and most particularly to Daniel Barenboim, who has been so loyal to John's memory over the years and has so unstintingly given of his time and his enormous gifts to honour John's memory.

After these two memorable days, the Barbirolli Society gave an equally unforgettable 'Weekend', arranged perfectly and imaginatively. We watched old films, gazed with admiration and fascination at a marvellous exhibition of photographs etc. arranged by David Jones, listened to some excellent speeches (including an outstanding one from John's niece Cecilie Jaggard) and ate and drank well. It was a heartfelt finale. John would have been proud and very touched by the warm and affectionate remembrances of all present. He counted loyalty high among attributes; surely nobody has been more loyal to him than the Barbirolli Society and Daniel Barenboim. It is thanks to the Barbirolli Society that we now have so many wonderful remastered CDs of John's conducting, so that his memory is evergreen and warmly alive.

Now to the Symposium itself and a key to those who took part:

LJ  – Lyndon Jenkins – chairman
MK – Michael Kennedy
DB  – Daniel Barenboim
EB  – Evelyn Barbirolli
CS  – Clive Smart
SC  – Sarah Crouch
PW  – Peter Worrall

**LJ**  Tonight is a very special occasion, as we gather to honour on what is the eve of what would have been his centenary, one of the greatest names in British music this century, and one who meant so much to this great city of Manchester. Sir John Barbirolli came here in 1943 as conductor of the Hallé Orchestra and he remained faithful to the city and to the orchestra to the end of his life in 1970.

Tomorrow evening, on this platform, the orchestra to which he gave so much will pay him a musical tribute. Tonight our tribute is in words, and a number of people of great distinction have gathered to talk about and to share with us their memories of a great man and a great musician. And what a team it is, led of course by someone who needs no introduction in Manchester, Lady Barbirolli. Then there is the distinguished pianist and conductor, Daniel Barenboim; Michael Kennedy, the author, critic and broadcaster; Clive Smart, who was general manager of the Orchestra for over 30 years from 1960 to 1991, and two members of the Hallé Orchestra who both played for Barbirolli during his last decade – Sarah Crouch and Peter Worrall. A very fine team, I think you will agree, and this marvellous team of contributors are here at the invitation of the Hallé Concert Society and the Barbirolli Society who have jointly put this evening together for our pleasure. My pleasant duty is simply to act as chairman and try and keep them all in order.

It's not only good manners that dictate that I begin with Lady Barbirolli. Can you take us back to 1931 when you first met JB, and tell us what was your first impression of him?

**EB**  He offered me an audition and I was still more or less at college – I was in the profession as well, but I used to go to

College to collect my letters. There was a letter there from what looked like John Barkworth, and it invited me to be in the Covent Garden Crush Bar on a certain date, at a certain time. When I got there it wasn't Mr Barkworth – it was Mr Barbirolli. He gave me an audition – we did the slow movement of a Handel sonata, I remember because I don't think he could play the quick ones [laughter] and he gave me some rather exacting sight-reading, particularly the *Bartered Bride* overture, *very* fast. I couldn't play that, really, and I said I'd practise very hard, and he gave me the job as second oboe in what was then the Covent Garden Touring Opera Company, the successor to the British National Opera Company. That was my first job and my first meeting, when I was nineteen.

LJ    Thank you very much. Daniel Barenboim, let me say first of all that you first met John in 1963 when you came to Manchester to play a concerto with the Hallé Orchestra. You were immediately struck by what you called his 'individual way of conducting.' Can you tell us a bit about that?

DB  I think that his whole way of conducting and his way of preparing for performance was very particular and rather complex. Unfortunately, anybody who comes on the stage for a reasonable amount of time is very often put in some kind of compartment, so and so is an intellectual musician, so and so is emotional, or romantic, etc., and Sir John was considered a very emotional conductor. I might add, without offending anyone, that especially by British standards, it was supposed to be very un-British to be so emotional and feel so deeply about the music which of course is as you would say in Manchester 'total roobish'. I also knew that first hand, because my first wife was accused of very similar crimes. But in fact Barbirolli was a meticulous worker before he was the great artist of the evening. This lady and gentleman at the end will be able to confirm that and elaborate on that. He marked the string parts especially, in such detail that when he wanted something at the point of the bow, God forbid that there was one person in the sixth stand who was in the middle of the bow!

He believed in very conscientious preparation of string parts, but also for the wind, which has to do with balance. I know because through the kindness of Evelyn I now possess his score of the Seventh Mahler which she very kindly gave me, and it is amazing with what care and almost scientific precision he prepared his scores. I had the fortune to play with him very often in the sixties when he was introducing the Mahler symphonies to Manchester and therefore they always needed somebody to play something that was not too complicated. Clive Smart engaged me to play Mozart concertos before the Mahler symphony and this is how I got to know the Mahler symphonies, because I sat at all the split rehearsals. They went on for days, first the strings alone and then the wind alone and then the wind and the brass and then everybody together, and it is this combination of meticulous preparation with great artistic spontaneity which inevitably came out in the evening. When he let loose, since everything had been so meticulously prepared at the rehearsals, the orchestras could really fly away with him. This was true not only of the Hallé, which was after all his orchestra for so many years – and they knew every little gesture – but I also played with him with the Berlin Philharmonic, with the Philharmonia, with many different orchestras, and they all were able to take off in this way. And he had another characteristic which was very difficult, if Michael Kennedy will forgive me, for the gentlemen of the press to accept, in that he was no specialist. There he was, half Italian, half French, and born in London, with a particular affinity of the works of Mahler, for instance, which were really not popular in those days, and for the French impressionists. I remember a performance of *La Mer* with L'Orchèstre de Paris which was quite unique. Some of the most wonderful Haydn symphonies I have heard were conducted by Sir John, especially, I must say, with the Berlin Philharmonic, not to speak of Elgar, or of so many other things. In fact he was in many ways ahead of his time because you could not put him in any kind of compartment. He may have been relatively small, but he was larger than life.

LJ  Michael Kennedy, you were still serving in the Forces when you came under what we might call 'the Barbirolli spell', were you not?

MK  Just about to go. I wasn't already serving, but I first saw Sir John when, after he'd come to Manchester in June 1943, I went to the last concert of what we call the old Hallé a memorial concert for Leslie Heward, given in the Longford Cinema, Stretford. Malcolm Sargent was conducting and there was a little man there with a brown overcoat on, I think, in June. It wasn't hot – well, it was an English summer day! We all said 'This is the new man', because we wondered where he'd come from, as if it was from another planet. I was seventeen or something at the time, he'd been in New York, out of our range as it were. But as soon as he started with the Hallé we heard very good concerts. It was a good orchestra under Malcolm Sargent and Leslie Heward and Basil

Cameron and all these people, but when I went to this concert – and I'm not at all sure that it wasn't a performance of *La Mer* – it was like a blinding revelation because of the wonderful sense of colour, the excitement of the music-making and the feeling (and I got from him from that day until the last concert I ever heard him conduct), that the concert he was conducting at that moment was the most important thing that was going on in the world and certainly in his life. He once described it as a mission, there was a kind of evangelistic, crusading element to his coming to the Hallé. He made a wonderful statement that he had a vision of a great orchestra and a conductor adventuring together on a journey through the great works of music. This is what one felt when he did all the Sibelius symphonies. We had all the Beethoven symphonies, all the Brahms symphonies and Vaughan Williams. It was an exploration, even though some of my colleagues – I've always been cross with them – used to say he was just a specialist in romantic music. He had the most extraordinary range of repertoire. He was very good in a great deal of music, and I'm sure Clive, in planning the programmes, must have realised that he wasn't a conductor of whom you say, 'This is the only possible work there.' He could have done the lot if it had been necessary. That's what I felt about him.

LJ  Thank you. Clive Smart, you joined in 1960. What was your impression of JB on a day-to-day basis?

CS  Totally dedicated. He created the Hallé. It was his family, his baby. He lived for the orchestra and he was such a hard-working man, he was very hard to keep up with. Working in the orchestral world is a very, you know, time-consuming business, but John would rehearse from ten till one, two till five, six till nine; strings in the morning, wind in the afternoon, the full orchestra at night. The next day at 9 a.m. I'd be at his bedside planning next season's programmes. In the afternoon he'd go off and rehearse and then he'd do the Thursday night concert, and the next morning I'd be there again at the bedside planning what we were going to do, we'd sit there discussing programmes for the next season until half past one and after. Life was very hard for orchestras in the sixties. Money was short. The Hallé had major financial problems but John would always recognise these and the important thing was that from his point of view the orchestra always came first. He made tremendous financial sacrifices in the interests of the orchestra. He never sought any increased fees for himself. If there was any money available, it was to go to the orchestra. He would sacrifice an increase in fee for one year on the understanding that the next year we would go on a tour of Germany or an overseas tour. Any resources that the Hallé had were for the orchestra and not for him, and this is something that, clearly, has gone out of the window these days. People are not prepared to make those sacrifices.

LJ   Now our two players. I must bring you in, Sarah Crouch and Peter Worrell.

PW   At rehearsals I mean there was always a search for the colouring, the fingerings, the slides, how you bowed. As Dr Daniel Barenboim said, woe betide me when I was on the wrong part of the bow, because he had an eagle eye and he'd shout at you – he'd shout at you at the rehearsal, but if you did it right at the concert you'd get a grin. He never forgot to acknowledge it at the concert. Can I just add a story now – it's a very personal thing and I find it quite moving – but I have a certain inbuilt non-conformist reserve which didn't go well with Sir John; his only contact with Methodism would be the methodism of the warmed heart. I sensed that something was not right, and I had a word with Martin Milner who said, 'Well, it's funny that you should say that, because he is a bit concerned that you're not very demonstrative in your playing – he feels you could put more effort into it.' So I tried to do that. The next time he came back he noticed the difference. I had to go to his room and he said to me, 'Oh, that's better. There's a bit of life there now, my boy.' Then he said something that still cuts me to the quick: 'You see, you won't have me with you much longer.' And we didn't.

SC   He would take particular notice for example, of impressive playing. If we were playing things like Elgar or Mahler he would be very angry with somebody if he saw them crossing over the strings on a fifth or sixth instead of going up the string, creating the sound that the single string would make with a little *portamento* perhaps. He was very keen, watching us, and would give people a hard time if they were slacking and not doing what he wanted them to do.

DB   People forget, maybe, that he was a very fine cellist himself.

LJ   In 1925, he himself gave one of the early performances of Elgar's Cello Concerto, in Bournemouth with Dan Godfrey. JB's incessant cry, which I heard when I went to his rehearsals was 'Play it at the point, dammit.' So much so that in Berlin, where the point is called the *spitze*, he became known as 'Herr Spitze'.

SC He used to want us to use full bows when a piece required full bows, but if it was just an accompanying passage he wanted the whole string section to play in the same part of the bow – often at the point, sometimes in the middle, sometimes at the heel, but he wanted us all to be there, together. Not only for the visual aspect but for the *sound*, which was very important to him.

PW There was always a search for colour. He could change the mood of the music so quickly: one minute would be tremendously dynamic and rhythmic and the next minute he'd have a lovely vibrato, *flautando* sound, absolute magic, and I think a lot of it was he created these tremendous contrasts. He had so much imagination, so much sensitivity, so much commitment, in the end so much love, both for the music and the players. And the effect was quite over-whelming.

PW If you didn't use enough bow, he'd say: 'Do you practise in a telephone kiosk?'

DB I remember passages like the scherzo of the Elgar First Symphony or the beginning of the allegro of the 'Prometheus' Overture of Beethoven, where very often it's played in the middle of the bow as *spiccato*, he insisted you should get that at the point and really get the articulation. It was said, sometimes unkindly, 'he wants it like this because it's safer to play together,' but it's really not true, because it is a different sound. He was looking for that kind of sound first and for the comfort of the player second. He made it absolutely clear why he wanted a certain passage at a certain part of the bow, with a little bow or with a lot of bow. He was always able to explain that, which is unfortunately not very often the case.

MK As an example, if anybody has got that splendid video *The Art of Conducting,* there's a long extract of John rehearsing the Hallé. It's a scherzo of one of the Bruchner symphonies, and there's something not right in it. He keeps on stopping them until he gets that, and he must have had an absolutely incredible ear, because he says 'It's over there, it's in the basses, in the basses...' He found it in the end, but it takes him about four or five minutes. It must have driven you mad, sometimes.

CS The other thing about John was that he really understood what motivated orchestral musicians and made them tick. He'd been one himself under very difficult circumstances in the twenties and he knew exactly how to get the best out of orchestral players. He knew what their problems were; he sympathised, he understood how difficult it was playing in an orchestra and he was one of the very few conductors at that time who could get the best out of the players that were working for him.

LJ Lady Barbirolli, you went often with him abroad and you say that you would go to his first rehearsal with a foreign orchestra and that by the time the first break occurred in the rehearsal he would be getting what we call 'the Barbirolli sound' from that orchestra.

EB Yes, that's true. I don't know, it was a kind of magic. I used to joke and call him *Il Mago* (the magician) because this always happened, even if the orchestra was not that marvellous. If it was a good orchestra, obviously it was easier. Sometimes on tour, especially going round America where there were so many orchestras, there were some that weren't first class but even they sounded like him. I can't tell you how or why. It was a kind of magic.

LJ It was something to do with the bowing, I know, which we'll come to in a moment or two.

EB Yes, it's not only that. Stresemann, who was the Intendant of the Berlin Philharmonic for many years and a great friend and admirer of John's (he himself was a very fine musician), told me that when John was conducting the rehearsal for the recording of Mahler Nine, which was the first time he'd ever conducted the Berlin Philharmonic, Stresemann went to listen to find out how it was going. He said at the first interval, after perhaps an hour or an hour and a half, a deputation came from the orchestra committee saying 'Sign up this man. Don't wait, don't let's lose him.' And this always touched John very much.

LJ When he conducted orchestras in Europe where they can't always speak English, how did he manage the language? He used to say 'I only speak two languages – Venetian and Cockney.' So how did he get on in Germany and France?

EB He spoke fluent French of course and fluent Italian, but his German wasn't at all good. He spoke his own sort of pidgin German, and he made them understand. He even used to make little jokes in his pidgin German. He had a pair of glasses, the kind of sunglasses in which the dark parts are on a hinge. They were used in a James Bond film at the time, and the players used to point to them and say 'James Bond, James

Bond'. When I go to Berlin now there isn't anyone left who was in the orchestra in John's day, but I met someone at a concert backstage. He had been one of the cellists, and he said 'James Bond' as he greeted me.

LJ   Daniel Barenboim, you saw him at work in Berlin. He was very much admired there, wasn't he?

DB   He was, first of all he was greatly loved by the orchestra, because he appreciated the warmth of the sound of the orchestra in those days very much and he knew how to get out of them what he wanted. For string players there was not only something very knowledgeable about him, there was a real physical pleasure; he would take somebody's cello and show how he wanted a certain *portamento*, and therefore they identified not only with his music making but with a sense of physical pleasure in playing. And I remember, funnily enough, the same piece that we are playing tomorrow, here. I played the Brahms D Minor with him for the Berlin Philharmonic sometime in the mid-sixties – it must have been '65 or '66 – and the Berlin Philharmonic in those days had a very easily recognisable sound, always very sustained, very rich, every sound held until the very end without any diminishing of intensity. It was very much the way of playing of the orchestra then for Karajan (who was then permanent conductor of the Berlin Philharmonic until his death). Everything had a quite incredible sustaining power.

    John started the Brahms D Minor Concerto in the rehearsal and gave his upbeat. A few seconds later [makes *vroom* noise] the orchestra started and then, although he used to ask the strings to play with two down bows, at the beginning [sings] in that orchestra there was simply no air between the notes, it was *vroom, vroom, vroom*...He went on with a few bars of that, and then he agitated his stick on the stand and stopped them and – in English, obviously – he said 'No, no, no, no.' 'This passage is like one long *wurst*'. He looked at them and he said, 'You understand, *wurst*. Sausage'. They all giggled and then he said: 'Well, this long *wurst* you understand to eat the long *wurst*, you have to cut it [laughter] in little pieces.' He said 'No, you must articulate properly' [sings]. And that's how he got it [laughter]. I've always remembered the *wurst* of the Brahms D Minor.

LJ  You mentioned the word *portamento* which is the business, in the old days and in the twenties when JB was starting, of sliding up and down on the violins. He would sometimes try and get you to do that to get a particular effect even in many later years, wouldn't he? I wanted to ask Sarah Crouch and Peter Worrell what he used to say about that. He said jokingly, 'I will pay for any damage it does to your instruments.' But how did he get you to do it?

SC  He wanted us to make a very sympathetic sound and to use the same string and to slide up to third, fourth, fifth position, wherever we had to, with a nice tasteful little *portamento*. Nothing too heavy or 1920ish.

LJ  In which composers, Peter Worrell?

PW  Obviously in Mahler, we would do the *glissandi* in Mahler again and again. He had a tremendous affinity with Mahler because it seemed to me that he could take all the diverse elements in a Mahler symphony – the dark elements, the majesty, the neurotic bits – and they would all come together as absolutely fantastic music. In the end it became a music of joy, but I think deep joy can actually contain deep insecurity and deep suffering. I think this is why his Mahler was so tremendous – it seems to me he took all the diverse elements, in a way exaggerated them and put them all together, and the music was truly marvellous. That's why he would get the absolutely glorious passages, but the next minute he'd be telling the orchestra to play like a café band because the music needed it. And the *spiccato* was something else again; it got the effect – the nervous neuroses of the music as a whole.

LJ   Michael Kennedy: he would use these same effects sometimes in Elgar, wouldn't he? Because when he started, Elgar was still alive and *portamento* was very strong in those days.

MK  Yes. He didn't do the old-fashioned *portamento*, but it needs it. I can remember hearing him rehearse once and he said about these *glissandi* in Mahler, 'You know, outside they'll think it's indecent, but don't worry – it's me that could go to prison.'

PW  Of course there's the absolutely overwhelming instance in the slow movement of Elgar Two, the climax at the end with the *glissandi* was absolutely fantastic. Many of the audience will know the recording . . .

MK  I don't think that passage has ever been done by anybody like that. In that recording, that great moment creases you every time you hear it. You hear many other recordings, go to other performances, but nobody gets near that climax. It was marvellous. That is great string playing as well as having the emotion behind it but it is wonderful.

211

DB At the risk of being a little bit too specific, I don't know whether one should in two or three words, explain *portamento* for the audience; I don't know that everybody is necessarily aware of it. I think what guided John's whole idea of the string sound was the fact that string players have no idea of the geographical distance between the notes because their instruments are tuned in fifths. A pianist who plays a sixth has an idea of the distance, but for a string player, since the strings are tuned in fifths, it's enough for him to put the same finger over two strings and get a fifth, and this is of course the most *in*expressive way of playing for the string instrument. This is what he fought against. And it was not just for the effect, or not necessarily even for the colour, it was really for the expressivity which you cannot get in certain cases if you simply use the most comfortable fingerings as is very often taught and played today. I think the whole element of colour, and of sonorous fantasy, disappears when you don't use that. Of course the danger with the *portamento* which is going up or coming down on one string, is that if there is too much pressure of the finger or of the bow or bows it creates the impression of bad taste which is of course not what he wanted. I think he would have a more difficult time today with many orchestras because young people who learn to play stringed instruments today are taught not to do that, as if it was something which was not an inherent and coherent part of the expression of the music, which of course it is.

LJ Lady Barbirolli, could I return to you, because clearly you spent more time with him than anybody else. He was a tremendously hard worker, we've heard that expression before. He spent hours bowing his parts and writing in the bowings. This was how the Barbirolli sound was obtained, wasn't it?

EB I'm a wind player, as you know, not a string player, but I know that was not the whole story. He was a very fine cellist and I think that the bowings did help; certainly to save rehearsal time, because he didn't have to explain it all, and the players had to do it if the string was designated or the bow or whatever was there. So that in that case it did help. But I think that it was his own conviction of the *sound* he wanted which came out to the players, if I can put it that way. I don't think it was only the purely mechanical help of the bowings, although of course that was a great time saver.

SC Just occasionally the bowing that a cellist will use didn't suit a fiddle player, in which case Martin Milner would say 'Sir John, that's not really working. Can we try this?' He'd answer, 'Yes, of course,' and that would be a good collaboration between the two of them.

LJ He relied on Martin, didn't he?

PW Yes, he did, especially.

SC Certainly.

DB One has to say that Martin Milner was not just a normal leader of the sections. He was one of the most consummate leaders of the string section that I have come across anywhere and his knowledge and his help in the music-making went far beyond his playing the violin.

PW I think the fact that he'd been through it part by part and marked in all the bowings gave him a tremendous insight. He was immersed in the parts, he had a feel with all the parts.

DB  And you go on feeling that he was playing everybody's parts as he was conducting.

PW  The bowings brought a tremendous cohesion. And of course he did a tremendous amount of work with the orchestra so we got used to his bowings. He was meticulous, and had a tremendous eye for detail. If he said 'Play at the point' it was no good being a quarter of an inch away. It had to be at the point. The bowings were always geared to the *sound*.

PW  So it was a full sound, a spiky, *ponticello* sound; you really had to play *ponticello*, and in Debussy's *La Mer* you had to slap the bow on, almost as if it was waves. You could feel the splash! [Laughter]. I did an audition once and played some of Debussy's *La Mer* and JB said it was all right, we could feel the splash. He was very practical. He'd say 'Play semiquavers' and I think Martin or somebody said to him, 'But Sir John, it's marked tremolo'. And he said, 'Yes, but if I ask for semiquavers I shall get more notes'.

I don't want to be too lighthearted, but there's a very difficult passage in Nielsen Four ('The Inextinguishable'), in the last movement, which he used to take so fast. Again, I think Martin said to him: 'Sir John, couldn't we take that passage a bit slower?' And he said, 'No, my boy, if we take it any slower people'll hear what you're playing.'

LJ  I'd like to round off this first half by asking Michael Kennedy to speak for a moment about JB's simple dedication to the Hallé.

MK  Well, the dedication we all know about – he gave 27 years of his life to this orchestra and there must have been many times when he was very tempted to leave the Hallé. He told me once, and I think Evelyn will corroborate what I am saying, 'You know I had no intention of staying much more than about a year.'

EB   Yes, that's right.

MK   At the time he was in the USA and he explained that he had wanted to get back to his family and his mother in London; it was in the middle of the war and he hated being an Englishman out of England. He wanted to come back.. Here was a lifeline. He came. And I don't think he realised what was going to happen. We all know how he arrived and found that half the players had thrown in their lot with the BBC so he had a month to find an orchestra in the middle of the war. So that was the first example of his dedication. He did it. He took them to the Western Front and played not far from the enemy lines. Whether he knew it or not, a whole lot of emotional experiences were binding him to this orchestra. When the London Symphony Orchestra, within a year, asked him to go with them (he'd been a member of the London Symphony Orchestra and had conducted it many times), I think he was considering it, round about the time when there was a performance, I think, of an Elgar symphony at Belle Vue, he said to you [Evelyn] 'How can I leave this?'

EB   Yes, I remember it well.

MK   But there must have been times after that when he did think of leaving it, I mean for the BBC. I don't think for a minute that he ever seriously considered becoming conductor of the BBC Symphony Orchestra as successor to Adrian Boult –

imagine John playing works selected for him by a committee which is what the BBC conductor did in those days. But of course as was being said earlier by Clive, it was a way in which he could hold his own fame, which by then was tremendous, and what he'd done with the audience over the Hallé committee and the city and say, 'If you don't let me enlarge the orchestra, if you don't pay them more so that all the players that I train don't go immediately off to London and get more money there, if we don't have more foreign tours because tours are good for an orchestra and they're good for the reputation of this city, then I shall go.' He used this – blackmail, it was – several times to very good effect, when he really had no intention of going at all. People forget now that there was no Arts Council grant in those days. When he came, Manchester Council didn't give anything to the orchestra at all, no city council gave anything to any orchestra in this country in those days – there weren't government grants, they had to earn the money at the box office. He conducted, in the first eighteen months, something like 230 Hallé concerts. It is absolutely stupid and ridiculous, but he did it. And in the end – after these experiences, like going over the Pennines on a winter's night in the war, while it was snowing, where they used to sell pork pies so that he could buy one for Gladys Yates, the cellist, this kind of thing, quite apart from the satisfaction that he had – he used to say to me quite often, 'You know, capital cities aren't the places where the greatest music is made. If you look it's often made in the non-capitals.' That is what he felt about Manchester. He could make these adventures and take the audience with him, week by week, and when he talked about the Hallé family, he meant not only the orchestra, he meant his audience. There was a kind of rapport, people romanticised about him, and it was a tremendous community feeling. And certainly, those of us who grew up under him were educated by him; even when I became a critic I could still learn a lot. It was something that you were marked for life.

LJ  Thank you very much. That's a great moment at which to pause.

## Second Half

LJ  We've had a few lighter things already, but this might be the time now, in our second half, for some more. Martin Milner's here.

EB  Oh, is he here? How marvellous. Isn't that lovely, I'm so glad.

LJ  Not many orchestral leaders get a standing ovation. It's so nice, I had no idea that Martin was there. How lovely, we must talk afterwards.

  We'll try and make this second half lighter because all these people are full of the most wonderful JB stories, but, Lady Barbirolli, can I start with you? Tell us about John's superstitions, would you, because as an Italian and a Catholic he had many superstitions, didn't he?

EB  Oh, yes, all Italians do, I think. But he did rather particularly. He had normal, little ones, about the house – you've got to put the left sock on first and you mustn't put the hat on the bed. You can't wear anything new for a concert. I have a memory of his sitting in a new dress suit in our modest kitchen eating a modest meal, with a great big towel around him. Also he would not use a new baton for a concert. I used to mark them with a cross when they had been used, for instance at a rehearsal.

There's one very important superstition, though; this really shows how strong it was. When he first started to conduct he had his own little orchestra of fifteen or so good players and he gave a series of concerts in London, which were a great success. Frederic Austin, the head of the British National Opera Company, came to one of these concerts and offered John a job at tuppence ha'penny a week with almost no rehearsal and five operas in the first eight days! He hadn't conducted anything except a fifteen-part chamber orchestra and so it was naturally very exciting. He went home and told the family about it. They were thrilled – but there was a snag ... The family pointed out that the first six of his nine hours of rehearsals were on a Friday, and Italians will not start any new enterprise on a Friday – it's disaster. So there was a great family conference and all the family said he couldn't possibly start on a Friday. He went back to Mr Austin, the head of the opera company, and said he'd forgotten a quartet concert or something and he couldn't do the rehearsals on a Friday – could they be changed? Austin said he was very sorry that the rehearsal schedule couldn't possibly be changed that late and the only thing he could offer him was three hours' rehearsal on a Saturday. So he took the three hours' rehearsal and gave up the six hours on a Friday. That shows you, that's a fairly strong superstition, isn't it?

LJ   Five operas on three hours' rehearsal!

EB   Ever after he used to say, 'You see, I was quite right.' And of course he was!

MK   I'd like to talk about John as a cook. He was a very good cook.

EB  Yes, he was.

MK  If you were going to dinner he would tell you that he'd been at the market at about six o'clock in the morning to make sure he got the right piece of halibut or pheasant or something, and he used to make the most wonderful sauce with it. He never seemed to eat anything himself, but he used to prepare wonderful meals. My first wife and I would sometimes go there for dinner, he would put the food in front of you and then stand over you and say, 'Go on, what do you think? Taste it. What's it like?' It was just the main course that interested him. He knew I had a sweet tooth and afterwards he used to say, 'And as for that sort of strawberry muck you like, Evelyn'll see to that.'

But the other thing that I found so inspiring about him was not only his musicianship, he had a tremendous knowledge not only about the notes of music, but (and this isn't true of all conductors) he actually knew a lot about the composers. He loved reading composers' letters and he loved reading their biographies. He really thought about them as people. I can remember his sending me a postcard from Vienna or somewhere he'd been conducting Schubert's Great C Major Symphony and all he put on it was 'Just imagine – he never heard this work.' It bothered him that Schubert hadn't ever heard his masterpiece. I can remember going up to see him after an Elgar First Symphony in the Free Trade Hall. He was just sitting there and then, five minutes later he suddenly gripped my hand and with tears in his eyes said, 'God, I love that piece.' This was what made him so wonderful, you know, you can't imagine... I loved Adrian Boult but you can't imagine Adrian saying that to you after a concert.

He had a terrifically wide interest in politicians, and he

knew everything about Admiral Nelson, he was passionately interested in the actor Henry Irving. He was a very well read, broadly interesting man as well as a great musician, and this is partly what made him a great musician, I think.

EB   Could I add just one thing. This is rather light, but it's going back to your cooking, Michael. John used to cook a lot, because for one thing it really switched him off music. Sometimes he would start on his own, sometimes we'd do it together. But if he started on his own, most of the pasta sauces and others begin with onion and garlic in olive oil, cooking slowly. I used to adore the smell of this, and if I was doing something else, perhaps practising or writing letters, he would come in and call me, he'd say 'Come on, there's Rothwell No. 5 waiting for you.' (In passing, John didn't greatly like normal perfumes, except Chanel No. 5, which I use!)

MK  I can remember one occasion when, I think, it may have been Clifford Curzon playing a Brahms Piano Concerto with him (not Danny on that occasion) and between the first and second movements, when there's a gap, and they're retuning, he got off the rostrum went and had a word with Clifford, and he got back on the rostrum again. I said to Sir Clifford afterwards, 'Was JB worried about something?' 'No,' he said 'he just came down, to tell me the supper's in the oven. It's all been prepared.'

LJ   There you are, ladies and gentlemen, culinary lessons from Lady Barbirolli and Michael Kennedy. Clive Smart. Once, when he was being interviewed, talking about contemporary music, Barbirolli said, 'If you look back over my Hallé programmes you will find that I have played the largest possible number of modern works consistent with the orchestra not going bankrupt.' Now you would know about that, wouldn't you?

CS  It's probably true. I don't think that criticism concerned him greatly, but he could get very annoyed about the way some of his critics would write off the fact that he did not, in his later years, do a lot of contemporary music. He suggested that it would not do them any harm to look back and see how much contemporary music he'd done in the early days of the Cheltenham Festival, for example, how expensive the cost of rehearsing a lot of these contemporary works is, and how little all too often, they were appreciated by the audiences. He also felt that it consumed a great deal of his personal time, possibly there would be just one performance which he could not then take to any of the orchestras throughout the world that he was going to conduct as a guest conductor. So, in his later years, he felt that it wasn't the best use of his time, and in that in any event he had been an outstanding pathfinder in the earlier years that he'd spent with the Hallé. I think he was quite often very annoyed that some of his critics didn't recognise that fact.

MK  It was only a certain part of contemporary music – he wasn't particularly interested in the serialists. If I may be rude with this audience (we're all used to Channel 4 and things these days), he said, 'You know, these works that are like three farts and a raspberry.'

CS  He was devoting a great deal of time, during that period to introducing the Mahler symphonies to Manchester and many parts of the world. These took a great deal of his personal preparation time. They were new works to a lot of audiences at that time. I remember on tour we'd very often be travelling in the coach to wherever we were going in Germany; he'd have conducted a concert the night before in Munich and we'd be on our way to Hamburg. He'd be sat there in the coach with his Mahler score on his knee, doing the bowings and preparing a Mahler symphony that he wasn't going to do tomorrow but in two years' time. But he was working on that score then.

LJ He thought touring was very important for the orchestra's health, didn't he?

CS He thought touring was very important for a lot of reasons. One thing that John was very strong about was teamwork. He was a part of the team. Unlike a lot of conductors that I've worked with since John, he believed that if we were staying in Hotel Grot in Vienna he was going to stay in Hotel Grot. There was no way he was going to go to the five-star hotel. Anything the orchestra had to do, he would do. He led by example all the time. He worked hard, he drove himself harder than anybody else, and he was a great example to all the players who worked for him. I think he got a lot of respect from the players because they recognised that they were not being asked to do anything that he wasn't going to do himself.

MK Lyndon, can I just comment about the contemporary works. Critics' and audiences' views on what is adventurous can differ considerably. And you must remember, thinking back to the early years of the Hallé – '43, '44, '45, when he would do something like *La Mer* – that there were no LPs in those days. People didn't have great record collections, and there wasn't a Radio 3. You went to a concert to hear music and that was probably the only time you heard it. But a work like *La Mer* was being played in Preston and Blackburn and Accrington and all these other places in those days. Not many people knew it, but this was the considerable thing to do. All right, we all know *La Mer* backwards, we sing it in our baths now, but it was a brave thing to do in those years and he carried on doing it. We all know Mahler now but we didn't all know Mahler in 1940-something.

LJ Daniel Barenboim, you wrote once: 'As far as orchestral playing is concerned, I learned most of what I know from Barbirolli.' That's an astonishing tribute to a man.

DB It's the truth. I mean that I learned how to learn. I learned how to study a score, I learned how to prepare, in those days when I used to come and conduct in the sixties. I had, through his generosity and Clive's help, access to all the music. I saw all the parts. A lot of things that are marked in my parts now stem from that, so it is, it is absolutely clear to me, it's not paying tribute in any empty way – it is very clear what it was and what it was that I learned. You know, I conducted many of the great works of the repertoire for the first time in Manchester. The first time I conducted the Ninth Beethoven was here. The first time I conducted the Ninth Bruckner was here, in the same week.

And I would have not been able to do all that if I had not had access to so much information. In other words, it wasn't only that his parts for the orchestra were put at my disposal, it was that I was able to get all the information of how he arrived at certain decisions. He was always available for me to ask him, and I remember asking about the scherzo of the

Ninth Bruckner with all those upbows [sings] and orchestra musicians still complain to this day when I conduct this. I know that comes from here but I don't tell them!

LJ Of course not. Well, we must wrap this evening up. But I'd like to ask you all for a final comment, if you would care to. I don't know whether I should start with you, Sarah, throwing you in rather at the deep end.

SC I joined in 1960. I was trained in London and lived in London but I was very keen on Barbirolli and the Hallé and I thought well I'll stay for five years. Thirty-eight years later I'm still here! I'll always be grateful for the ten years I spent with JB.

CS I came to the Hallé in 1958 as an administrator, knowing very little about orchestral life and everything I know about orchestral music and about how to treat orchestral musicians and get the best out of them I learned from John. I will forever be grateful for that.

DB I think that not enough mention was made, maybe, about John's great talent as a raconteur and as a mimic. He was very aware of the theatrical aspect of concert giving and concert going and he knew quite well how to get what he wanted from the public as well as from the orchestral players.

CS Could I interject a small story about JB's 21st anniversary at the Hallé? In those days all the national press was published here in Manchester, and the music critics and the journalists of this city were so grateful for the way John treated them. Whenever they wanted an interview he would always grant them one, would always talk to them, so on his 21st anniversary with the Hallé they gave him a party. We did a concert in the Free Trade Hall on the Thursday night, and after the concert we adjourned to the Grand Hotel, which sadly I think isn't here any more. (John would be distraught, because he thought it was the only decent hotel in Manchester.) We went there for the party that these hard-bitten journalists were throwing for John. The party progressed, and we were having a great time. The northern editor of *The Times*, or the *Sunday Times*, did a headstand in the middle of the party and at about half past one in the morning, it was John's turn to say something to the journalists. About three o'clock he was still on his feet, recounting various tales that had happened to him during his early career.

Anyway this went on until three o'clock and then there was more talk, and at five o'clock we thought it was probably time that we went, because John had to go home, collect his suitcase, and be on the nine o'clock plane to London en route for Houston where he had a rehearsal that day. That was a day in the life of JB.

DB  I don't know what programme it was, but I think it was on the television where he tells the story of the double bass player. 'Oop theer?, never bin oop theer before.' I love that.

EB  And then there's the other one. Another double bass player was given the scherzo of the Beethoven Five. He played it with enormous energy and verve, but he never moved his left hand, so it was all on one note!

LJ  Now, a serious note for a second. Lady Barbirolli, I think we're all delighted now that it's finally been put to rest that the New York years – which you knew, which preceded the

Hallé years – are supposed not to have been a success at all. They were a tremendous success.

EB   Yes, they were actually. And that was a sort of political cabal which I can't go into now – it's not the time or place. We didn't quite realise it at the time, but now the results from the audience attendances have been published. They were 85 per cent for all concerts, which was more than Toscanini ever got.

And the orchestra adored him, always, of that there was no question. Some of the recordings which have been remastered show that he really loved conducting them and they loved playing for him.

LJ   Michael Kennedy – a last thought?

MK   When I was a young man, John had been very kind to me, and then I started writing about concerts and I thought, this will be the end of that. But friendship remained, and if I'd said something that wasn't quite right, it was a no-go area between us and we forgot about it. But Danny mentioned about him being a raconteur. Can I tell you the story that he told me that I love probably the most?

Just before coming to Manchester in March 1943, John happened to be in Los Angeles when Rachmaninov died. He'd conducted for Rachmaninov many times. John had greatly admired and liked him, so we thought that we ought to go the funeral, which was a proper Russian Orthodox one. Rachmaninov was known for never smiling (Stravinsky is supposed to have called him a six-foot scowl) and John said to me: 'You know, Mike, I'd forgotten, that they have an open coffin. I was standing there, and there's the old boy laid out  looking a bloody sight more cheerful than he ever looked in life!'

LJ   Peter to round off, are you going to cap that story of Michael Kennedy's?

PW  I wasn't going to tell this, but maybe... We were rehearsing a piece by John McCabe. I've forgotten the title, but in the last movement there were some rhythms – they would be nothing these days, but they were 123, 123, 12345, 123, 123, 12345, and I remember that at the afternoon rehearsal JB had some difficulty getting to terms with all the 3s and the 5s. The next day we came back and he said, 'I've discovered, I've discovered how to beat all that business in the last movement. I've added all those beats together and I find I can beat 4/4 though the lot.'

Ladies and gentlemen, I'm sure you would agree and you will be quite happy if we went on all night, but unfortunately we can't. May I thank on your behalf these wonderful people who've come together to give us such a marvellous evening.

# Discography of Recordings currently available on Compact Disc

The discography is arranged by date of original recording session, followed by recording venue, artist(s), composer, work and current CD number. It should be pointed out that the availability of some discs may be erratic.

I am adding this note to the foregoing excellent discography because I have only just heard that the Bax work discussed herein is to be recorded soon on CD by BBC LEGENDS.

The compiler wishes to express his thanks to John Bryant of Haymarket Publishing for help and assistance with this compilation.

## 1911
October Edition Bell Studios, Elephant and Castle, London
*John Barbirolli* (cello); *Rosa Barbirolli* (piano)
*Van Biene* The Broken Melody
    Dutton CDSJB 1999

## 1925
June Vocalion Studios
*Kutcher Quartet* (with John Barbirolli, cello)
Mozart String Quartet in E flat major, K 428 – Menuetto
    Dutton CDSJB 1999

**1927**

December London

**Lilian Stiles-Allen** (soprano); Orchestra

*Mascagni* Cavalleria Rusticana – Voi lo sapete

Dutton CDSJB 1999

**1928**

1 March & 17 July Queen's Hall, London

**John Barbirolli Chamber Orchestra**

*Haydn* Symphony No. 104 in D major "London"

Barbirolli Society SJB 1899

May 8 Kingsway Hall, London

**Frida Leider** (soprano); orchestra

*Beethoven* Fidelio – Abscheulicher, wo eilst du hin?... Komm

Hoffnung Preiser 89004; 89301

11 May Kingsway Hall, London

**Frida Leider** (soprano); orchestra

*Gluck* Armide – Ah! Si la liberté

Preiser 89004; Pearl GEMMCDS 9926

*Mozart* Don Giovanni – Don Ottavio, son morta... Or sai chi

l'onore

EMI CMS 763750 2; Preiser 89004; 89301;

Memoir Classics CDMOIR 406

*Wagner* Wesendonk-Lieder – Träume

Preiser 89004

18 June Queen's Hall, London

**Renato Zanelli** (tenor); Orchestra

*Verdi* Otello – Dio! mio potevi scagliar

Dutton CDSJB 1999; Testament SBT 0132; Pearl

GEMMCDS 9926

*Verdi* Otello – Niun mi tema

GEMMCD 9028; Pearl GEMMCDS 9926

19 June Queen's Hall, London
  ***Feodor Chaliapin*** (bass); Orchestra
  *Mozart* Don Giovanni – Madamina!
    Pearl GEMMCD 9314

13 July Queen's Hall, London
  ***John Barbirolli Chamber Orchestra***
  *Purcell* The Married Beau – Hornpipe
    Barbirolli Society SJB 1899; Koch 3-7077-2

13 July & 28 January 28 **1929** Queen's Hall, London
  ***John Barbirolli Chamber Orchestra***
  Mozart Serenade in G major, K 525 "Eine kleine
    Nachtmusik"
  Koch 3-7077-2; Barbirolli Society SJB 1899

27 August Royal Opera House, Covent Garden
  *Florence Austral* (soprano); ***Royal Opera Chorus and
  Orchestra, Covent Garden***
  *Sullivan* The Golden Legend – The Night is Calm
    Dutton CDLX 7025

28 August Royal Opera House, Covent Garden
  ***Florence Austral*** (soprano); ***Chorus and Orchestra of the
  Royal Opera House, Covent Garden***
  *Rossini* Stabat Mater – Inflammatus
    Memoir Classics CDMOIR 411; Testament SBT 1008;
    SBT 0132; Dutton CDLX 7025

24 September Queen's Hall, London
**Peter Dawson** (bass-baritone); Orchestra
*Mussorgsky* The Song of the Flea
   Pearl GEMM 040
*Elgar* Caractacus, Op. 35 – O my warriors
   Dutton CDAX 8019; Pearl GEMM 040
*Elgar* Caractacus, Op. 35 – Leap, leap to light
   Dutton CDAX 8019

28 November Queen's Hall, London
**Dusolina Giannini** (soprano); Orchestra
*Verdi* La forza del destino – Son giunta!... Madre pietosa
   Preiser 89044; Malibran CDRG 152; EMI CZS 574217 2;
   Dante Lys LYS 388

6 December Queen's Hall, London
**Joseph Hislop** (tenor); Orchestra
*Puccini* La Bohème – Che gelida manina
Pearl GEMMCD 9956
*Mascagni* Cavalleria Rusticana – Mamma, quel vino è
   generoso Pearl GEMMCD 9956

17 December Queen's Hall, London
**Dusolina Giannini** (soprano); Orchestra
*Verdi* La forza del destino – Pace, pace, mio Dio
Dante Lys LYS 388; Testament SBT 0132

19 January 1929 Queen's Hall, London
 **Walter Widdop** (tenor); Orchestra
 *Handel* Messiah – Comfort ye, my people; Ev'ry valley
  Pearl GEMMCD 9112
 *Handel* Messiah – He that dwelleth in Heaven... Thou shalt
  break them
  Pearl GEMMCD 9112; Symposium 1209
 *Handel* Judas Maccabaeus – Sound an alarm
  Pearl GEMMCD 9112

28 January Queen's Hall, London
 **John Barbirolli Chamber Orchestra**
 *Elgar* Introduction and Allegro for Strings, Op. 47
  Barbirolli Society SJB 1899

7 June Queen's Hall, London
 **New Symphony Orchestra**
 *Delius* A Song before Sunrise
  Dutton CDSJB 1005

13 June Queen's Hall, London
 **Elsie Suddaby** (soprano); Orchestra
 *Handel* Messiah – Rejoice greatly, O Daughter of Zion
  Dutton CDLX 7029; Amphion PHI CD 134
 *Coleridge-Taylor* Scenes from the Song of Hiawatha: Part 3,
  Hiawatha'a Departure – No. 1, Spring had come with all
  its splendour
  Amphion PHI CD 140
 *Bach* Cantata No. 70 – No. 5, Though the reviling tongues
  assail us
 Amphion PHI CD 140

19 June Queen's Hall, London
*Giovanni Inghilleri* (baritone); Orchestra
*Verdi* Un ballo in maschera – Eri tu che macchiavi
  Bongiovanni GB 1151-2
*Puccini* Tosca – La povera mia cena fu interotta
  Preiser 89187; Testament SBT 0132
*Puccini* Tosca – Tre sbirri... una caroza
  Dutton CDSJB 1999; Preiser 89187

19 June Queen's Hall, London
*Giovanni Inghilleri* (baritone); *Octave Dua, Luigi Cilla*
(tenors); Chorus and Orchestra
*Verdi* Otello – Inaffia l'ingola
  Preiser 89187

2 June Queen's Hall, London
*Giovanni Inghilleri* (baritone); Orchestra
*Rossini* Il barbiere di Siviglia – Largo al factotum
  Preiser 89187

21–22 June Queen's Hall, London
*Irene Minghini-Cattaneo* (mezzo-soprano); Orchestra
*Bizet* Carmen – Près des remparts de Seville
  Preiser 89008
*Bizet* Carmen – L'amour est un oiseau rebelle
  Preiser 89008

26 June Queen's Hall, London
*John Barbirolli Chamber Orchestra*
*Rosse* The Merchant of Venice – Suite
  Barbirolli Society SJB 1899

12 July Queen's Hall, London
  *Joseph Hislop* (tenor); Orchestra
  *Wagner* Lohengrin distant lands (Grail Song)
    Pearl GEMMCD 9956
  *Wagner* The Mastersingers of Nuremberg – Morning was
    gleaming (Prize Song)
    Pearl GEMMCD 9956

19–20 December Queen's Hall, London
  *Mischa Elman* (violin); London Symphony Orchestra
  *Tchaikovsky* Concerto for Violin and Orchestra in D, Op. 35
    Pearl GEMMCD 9388; Naxos 8.110912
**1930**
17 May Queen's Hall, London
  *Launtz Melchior* (tenor); New Symphony Orchestra
  *Verdi* Otello – Gott! Warum has du gehauft (Dio! mio potevi
    scagliar)
    Pearl GEMMCD 9500; Danachord DACOCD 315/6;
    Nimbus Nl 7816; Preiser 89006; EMI CZS 574217 2
  *Verdi* Otello – Jeder Knabe kann mein Schwert (Niun mi
    tema)
    Pearl GEMMCD 9500; Danachord DACOCD 315/6;
    Nimbus Nl 7816; Preiser 89006

29 May Queen's Hall, London
  *Lauritz Melchior* (tenor); *New Symphony Orchestra*
  *Wagner* Rienzi – Allmächt'ger Vater
    Danachord DACOCD 315/6; EMI 769789 2; Nimbus NI
    7812; Preiser 89086
  *Meyerbeer* L'Africaine – Mi battre il cor... O Paradiso (Sung
    in German)
    Danachord DACOD 228/9; Nimbus Nl 7816; Preiser 89086

*Leoncavallo* Der Bajazzo – Hüll dich im Tand . . . Lache Bajazzo
  Electrola EJ 582/ Danachord DACOD 228/9; Nimbus NI
  7816; Preiser 89086; Pearl GEMMCD 9500
*Wagner* Tannhäuser – Dir töne Lob
  Danachord DACOCD 315/6; Nimbus NI 7812; Preiser
  89086; Testament SBT 0132

18 December Queen's Hall, London
**Covent Garden Opera Company; London Symphony
Orchestra**
*Johann Strauss II* Die Feldermaus – Brother dear and sister dear
  Dutton CDSJB 1999

**1931**
8 January Queen's Hall, London
**Arthur Rubinstein** (piano); **London Symphony Orchestra**
*Chopin* Concerto for Piano and Orchestra No. 2 in F minor,
  Op. 21
  EMI CHS 7644912; CHS 764933 2; RCA/BMG 09026
  63005-2; HMV Legends 74045 2; Magic Talent CD 48012

9 January Queen's Hall, London
**Arthur Rubinstein** (piano); **London Symphony Orchestra**
*Mozart* Concerto for Piano and Orchestra No. 23 in A major,
  K 488
  RCA/BMG 09026 63009-2

11 May Queen's Hall, London
  *Friedrich Schorr* (bass-baritone); *London Symphony Orchestra*
  *Mendelssohn* Elias – Herr Gott Abrahams
    Pearl GEMMCD 9398; Memoir Classics CDMOIR 411; Preiser 89127
  *Haydn* Die Jahreszeiten – Schon eilet from der Ackersmann
    HMV DB 1564/ Pearl GEMMCD 9398; Preiser 89127

16 May Kingsway Hall, London
  *Elisabeth Schumann* (soprano); *Gladys Parr* (contralto); *Lauritz Melchior, Ben Williams* (tenors); *Freidrich Schorr* (baritone); *London Symphony Orchestra*
  *Wagner* Die Meistersinger von Nürnberg – Selig wie die Sonne (Quintet)
    Danachord DACOCD 315/6; EMI CMS 764008 2; Pearl GEMMCD 9944; Preiser 89214; Music Memoria MM 30283

16 May Kingsway Hall, London
  *Lauritz Melchior* (tenor); *London Symphony Orchestra*
  *Wagner* DieWalküre-Act 1, Winterstürme Wichen dem Wonnemond
    Symposium 1209
  *Wagner* Die Meistersinger von Nürnberg – Morgenlich leuchtend
    Danachord DACOCD 315/6; Beulah 2PD 4; Pearl GEMMCD 9040

18 May Queen's Hall, London
  *Frida Leider* (soprano); *London Symphony Orchestra*
  *Wagner* Tristan und Isolde – Mild und leise
    Preiser 89004; Pearl GEMMCD 9331; Nimbus NI 7818; Legato Classics LGD 146

*Wagner* Parsifal – Ich sah das Kind
    Preiser 89004; EMI CDS 764008 2, Pearl GEMMCD 9331
    Memoir Classics CDMOIR 408; Music Memoria MM 30285
*Wagner* Wesendonk-Lieder – Schmerzen
    Preiser 89004

26 June Queen's Hall, London
  **Beniamino Gigli** (tenor); Orchestra
  *Massenet* Manon – O dolce incanto . . . Chiudo gli occhi
    EMI CDH 761051 2; Nimbus 7817; Opera CD 54505;
    Romophone 88011-2; Romophone 88020-2;
  *Sullivan* The Lost Chord
    Pearl GEMMCD 9033
  *Tosti* Addio
    Pearl GEMMCD 9033; Romophone 82011-2

## 1932

1 April No. 1 Studio, Abbey Road, London
  **Emmi Leisner** (mezzo-soprano); **Friedrich Schorr**
  (baritone); **London Symphony Orchestra**
  *Wagner* Die Walküre – Der alte Sturm, die alte Müh'!
    Pearl GEMMCD 9357; Pearl GEMMCDS 9137

9–10 June No. 1 Studio, Abbey Road, London
  **Arthur Rubinstein** (piano); **London Symphony Orchestra**
  *Tchaikovsky* Concerto for Piano and Orchestra No. 1 in B flat
    minor, Op. 23
    Memoir Classics CDMOIR 450: RCA/BMG 09026 63001-2

2 September No. 1 Studio, Abbey Road, London
  *Yvonne Arnaud* (piano); string orchestra
  *Saint-Saëns* Valse-caprice, Op. 76
    Dutton CDSJB 1999

29 September Kingsway Hall, London
  *Richard Crooks* (tenor); orchestra
  *Stephen Adams* The Holy City
    ASV CDAJA 5240; Memoir Classics CDMOIR 431
  *Nevin* The Rosary
    Pearl GEMMCD 9093

3 October Kingsway Hall, London
  *Richard Crooks* (tenor); orchestra
  *Gounod* Jésus de Nazareth (sung in English)
    Memoir Classics CDMOIR 431

**1933**
20 March No. 1 Studio, Abbey Road, London
  *Beniamino Gigli* (tenor); Orchestra
  *Handel* Serse – Frondi tenere e belle ... Ombra mai fù
    Romophone 82020-2; Opera CD 54505
  *Cottrau* Santa Lucia
    Romophone 82020-2; ASV CDAJA 5122; Opera CD 54516;
    Memoir Classics CDMOIR 425; Pearl GEMMCDS 9176
  *Donizetti* L'Elisir d'amore – Una furtiva lagrima
    Romophone 82020-2; Nimbus NI 7817; EMI CDM 566809
    2; Memoir Classics CDMOIR 417; Pearl GEMMCDS 9176
  *Leonvacallo* Pagliacci – No! Pagliaccio non son!
    Romophone 82020-2; Opera CD 54505; Pearl GEMMCDS
    9176

20 July Kingsway Hall, London
**London Philharmonic Orchestra**
*Tchaikovsky* Swan Lake, Op. 20 – Suite
Koch Legacy Series 3-7077-2

18 October No. 1 Studio, Abbey Road, London
**London Symphony Orchestra**
*Balfe* The Bohemian Girl – Overture
Dutton CDSJB 1999

**1934**
23 February No. 1 Studio, Abbey Road, London
**Jascha Heifetz** (violin); **London Philharmonic Orchestra**
*Mozart* Concerto for Violin and Orchestra No. 5 in A major,
K219
EMI CDH 565191 2; RCA 09026 61733 2; Biddulph LAB
012; Pearl GEMMCDS 9157; Naxos 8.110941; 8.107001

28 March No. 1 Studio, Abbey Road, London
**Jascha Heifetz** (violin); **London Philharmonic Orchestra**
*Glazunov* Concerto for Violin and Orchestra in A minor, Op. 82
Biddulph LAB 026; EMI CDH 764030 2; RCA 09026
61778 2; Pearl GEMMCDS 9157
2 May No. 1 Studio, Abbey Road, London
**Arthur Schnabel** (piano); **London Symphony Orchestra**
*Mozart* Concerto for Piano and Orchestra No. 27 in B flat
major, K 595 Arabesque Z 6592; Grammofono AB 78531;
Pearl GEMS 0006

18 May No. 1 Studio, Abbey Road, London
**Gregor Piatigorsky** (cello); **London Philharmonic Orchestra**
*Schumann* Concerto for Cello and Orchestra in A minor,
Op. 129
Pearl GEMMCD 9447; Music and Arts CD 674

**1935**

14 March No. 1 Studio, Abbey Road, London
*Jascha Heifetz* (violin); *London Philharrnonic Orchestra*
*Vieuxtemps* Concerto for Violin and Orchestra No. 4 in D
  minor, Op. 31
  Biddulph LAB 025; EMI CDH 7642512; Pearl
  GEMMCDS 9167

18 March No. 1 Studio, Abbey Road, London
*Jascha Heifetz* (violin); *London Philharmonic Orchestra*
*Saint-Saëns* Introduction and Rondo Capriccioso in A minor,
  Op. 83
  Biddulph LAB 025; EMI CDH 764 2512; RCAIBMG 09026
  61778 2; 09026 617735 2; Pearl GEMMCDS 9167;
  Gammofono AB 78511; Naxos 8.110943; Naxos 8.107001
*Wieniawski* Concerto for Violin and Orchestra No. 2 in D
  minor, Op. 22
  Biddulph LAB 026; EMI CDH 764 251 2; RCA/BMG
  09026 61778-2; 09026 61734-2; Gammofono AB 78511;
  Naxos 8.110938; Naxos 8.107001; Pearl GEMMCDS 9167

25 May No. 1 Studio, Abbey Road, London
*Lily Pons* (soprano); Orchestra
*Mozart* La Flûte enchantée – Ah, je le sais
  Pearl GEMMCD 9415
*Rossini* Il barbiere di Siviglia – Una voce poco fà
  Pearl GEMMCD 9415; RCA/BMG 09026 61411 2;
  Mastersound DFCDI-111

6 June No. 1 Studio, Abbey Road, London
*Edwin Fischer* (piano); Orchestra
*Mozart* Concerto for Piano and Orchestra No. 22 in E flat
  major, K 482
  APR APR 5523; Pearl GEMS 0042

8 July No. 1 Studio, Abbey Road, London
  *Alfred Cortot* (piano); Orchestra
  *Chopin* (ed. Cortot) Concerto for Piano and Orchestra No. 2 in
    F minor, Op. 21
    Pearl GEMMCD 9491; EMI CZS 767359 2;
    Grammophono AB 78501; Naxos 8.110612

**1936**

16–17 & 22 June No. 1 Studio, Abbey Road, London
  *Fritz Kreisler* (violin); *London Philharmonic Orchestra*
  *Beethoven* Concerto for Violin and Orchestra in D major, Op. 61
    Biddulph LAB 001/3; LAB 100; Pearl GEMMCDS 9362;
    Iron Needle IN1328

18 & 22 June No. 1 Studio, Abbey Road, London
  *Fritz Kreisler* (violin); *London Philharmonic Orchestra*
  (solo oboe: Léon Goossens)
  *Brahms* Concerto for Violin and Orchestra in D major, Op. 77
    Biddulph LAB 001/3; Pearl GEMMCDS 9362; Naxos
    8.110925

29 November Carnegie Hall, New York City (public concert)
  *Philharmonic-Symphony Orchestra of New York*
  *Mozart* Symphony No. 33 in B flat major, K 319
    Dutton CDSJB 1011

29 November Carnegie Hall, New York City *Robert Casadesus*
  (piano); *Philharmonic-Symphony Orchestra of New York*
  *Weber* Konzertstück for Piano and Orchestra, J 262
    APR APR 5601
  *Franck* Variations symphoniques
    APR APR 5601

6 December Carnegie Hall, New York City (public concert)
**Philharmonic-Symphony Orchestra of New York**
*Loeffler* Memories of my Childhod "Life in a Russian village"
New York Philharmonic NYP 9904

13 December Carnegie Hall, New York City (public concert)
**Philharmonic-Symphony Orchestra of New York**
*Beethoven* Symphony No. 4 in B flat major, Op. 60
Dutton CDSJB 1011
*Mendelssohn* Octet in E flat major, Op. 20 – Scherzo
Dutton CDSJB 1011

27 December Carnegie Hall, New York City (public concert)
**Josef Hoffmann** (piano); **Philharmonic-Symphony Orchestra of New York**
*Chopin* Concerto for Piano and Orchestra No. 2 in F minor, Op. 21
Dante HPC 002; Video Artists International VAIA 1002

**1937**
25 March No. 1 Studio, Abbey Road, London
**Jascha Heifetz** (violin); **London Philharmonic Orchestra**
*Tchaikovsky* Concerto for Violin and Orchestra in D, Op. 35
EMI CDH 764030 2; Biddulph LAB 026; RCA/BMG 09026 61778-2; 09026 61749-2; Pearl GEMMCDS 9157; Naxos 8.110938; Naxos 8.107001

5 April No. 1 Studio, Abbey Road, London
**Arthur Rubinstein** (piano); **London Symphony Orchestra**
*Chopin* Concerto for Piano and Orchestra No. 1 in E minor, Op. 11
Memoir Classics CDMOIR 450; EMI CHS 764491 2; CHS 74933 2; RCA/BMG 09026 63005-2; Magic Talent CD 48012

9 April No. 1 Studio, Abbey Road, London
*Jascha Heifetz* (violin); *London Symphony Orchestra*
*Sarasate* Zigeunerweisen, Op. 20 No. 1
    Biddulph LAB 026; EMI CDH 764 2512; Pearl
    GEMMCDS 9167; RCA/BMG 09026 61778 2; 09026
    617735 2
*Saint-Saëns* Havanaise in E major, Op.83
    Biddulph LAB 025; EMI CDH 764 2512; Pearl GEMMCD
    9023; GEMMCDS 9167; RCA/BMG 09026 61778 2;
    09026 617735 2; Gammofono AB 78511; Naxos 8.110943;
    Naxos 8.107001

5 May Royal Opera House, Covent Garden (public performance)
*Dame Eva Turner* (soprano) *Turandot*; *Mafalda Favero*
(soprano) Liù; *Giovanni Martinelli* (tenor) *Calaf*, *Octave Dua*
(tenor) Emperor; *Chorus of the Royal Opera, Covent
Garden; London Philharmonic Orchestra*
*Puccini* Turandot – In questa reggia and Riddle Scene
    Pearl GEMS 0094

10 May Royal Opera House, Covent Garden (public performance)
*Dame Eva Turner* (soprano) *Turandot*; *Licia Albanese*
(soprano) *Liù*; *Giovanni Martinelli* (tenor) *Calaf*, *Octave Dua*
(tenor) Emperor; *Chorus of the Royal Opera, Covent
Garden; London Philharmonic Orchestra*
*Puccini* Turandot – In questa reggia and Riddle Scene
    Pearl GEMS 0094

7 November Carnegie Hall, New York City (public concert)
*Philharmonic-Symphony Orchestra of New York*
*Schumann* Symphony No. 4 in D minor, Op. 120
    Dutton CDSJB 1007

19 December Carnegie Hall, New York City (public concert)
**Philharmonic-Symphony Orchestra of New York**
*Beethoven* Coriolan Overture, Op. 62 Dutton CDSJB 1011

**1938**
7 February Carnegie Hall, New York City
**Philharmonic Symphony Orchestra of New York**
*Purcell* (arr. Barbirolli) Suite for Strings with horns, flutes and
cor anglais
Dutton CDEA 5019; Pearl GEMMCDS 9922
*Respighi* Antiche danze ed arie – Suite No. 3: Arie di corte
Dutton CDEA 5019
*Debussy* Images – No. 2, Iberia
Dutton CDEA 5000; Pearl GEMMCDS 9922

9 February Carnegie Hall, New York City
**Philharmonic-Symphony Orchestra of New York**
*Tchaikovsky* Francesca da Rimini, Op. 52
Dutton CDEA 5000

9 February Carnegie Hall, New York City
**Yehudi Menuhin** (violin); **Philharmonic-Symphony
Orchestra of New York**
*Schumann* Concerto for Violin and Orchestra in D minor,
Op. posth
Biddulph LAB 047

13 March Carnegie Hall, New York City (public concert)
**Josef Hoffman** (piano); **Philharmonic-Symphony Orchestra
of New York**
*Chopin* Concerto for Piano and Orchestra No. 1 in E minor,
Op. 11
Video Artists International VAIA 1002

20 March Carnegie Hall, New York City (public concert)
**Robert Casadesus** (piano); **Philharmonic-Symphony Orchestra of New York**
*Mozart* Concerto for Piano and Orchestra No. 23 in A major, K 488
APR APR 5601

20 November Carnegie Hall, New York City (public concert)
**Philharmonic-Symphony Orchestra of New York**
*Wagner* Rienzi – Overture
Dutton CDSJB 1001
*Wagner* Tristan und Isolde – Act 1, Prelude and Liebestod
Dutton CDSJB 1001
*Wagner* Tannhäuser – Venusberg Music
Dutton CDSJB 1001
*Wagner* Die Meistersinger von Nürnberg – Suite from Act 3
Dutton CDSJB 1001
*Wagner* Siegfried Idyll
Dutton CDSJB 1001

**1939**
21January Carnegie Hall, New York City
**Philharmonic Symphony Orchestra of New York**
*Schubert* Symphony No. 4 in C minor, D 417 "Tragic"
Dutton CDEA 5000

21 February Carnegie Hall, New York City
**Philharmonic Symphony Orchestra of New York**
*Schubert* Five German Dances and Seven Trios, D 90
Dutton CDEA 5019
*Respighi* Fontane di Roma
Dutton CDEA 5019; Pearl GEMMCDS 9922

29 October Carnegie Hall, New York City (public concert)
*Josef Lhévinne*, *Rosina Lhevinne* (pianos); *Philharmonic-Symphony Orchestra of New York*
*Mozart* Concerto for Two Pianos and Orchestra in F major, K 242
New York Philharmonic NYP 9701

November (exact date not known). Utica, New York State (public concert)
*Philharmonic-Symphony Orchestra of New York*
*Tchaikovsky* Symphony No. 5 in E minor, Op. 64
Dutton CDSJB 1007

24 December Carnegie Hall, New York City (public concert)
*Philharmonic-Symphony Orchestra of New York*
*Weinberger* Christmas
Dutton CDSJB 1999

**1940**
31 March Carnegie Hall, New York City (public concert)
*Vladimir Horowitz* (piano); *Philharmonic-Symphony Orchestra of New York*
*Tchaikovsky* Concerto for Piano and Orchestra No. 1 in B flat minor, Op. 23
APR APR 5519; Urania 22.160

24 June Carnegie Hall, New York City
*Philharmonic-Symphony Orchestra of New York*
*Sibelius* Symphony No. 2 in D major, Op. 42
Dutton CDEA 5016

16 December Carnegie Hall, New York City
**Benny Goodman** (clarinet); **Philharmonic-Symphony Orchestra of New York**
*Debussy* Première Rapsodie pour clarinette et orchestre
   Clarinet Classics CC 0010; Pearl GEM 0057

16 December Carnegie Hall, New York City
**Philharmonic-Symphony Orchestra of New York**
*Bach* (arr. Barbirolli) Cantata No. 208 – Sheep may safely graze
   Biddulph 83069/70

**1941**
30 March Carnegie Hall, New York City (public concert)
**Philharmonic-Symphony Orchestra of New York**
*Britten* Sinfonia da Requiem, Op. 20
NMC Archive Series D030

4 May Carnegie Hall, New York City (public concert)
**Vladimir Horowitz** (piano); **Philharmonic-Symphony Orchestra of New York**
*Rachmaninov* Concerto for Piano and Orchestra No. 3 in D
   minor, Op. 30
APR 5519; Urania URN 22.160

29 October Carnegie Hall, New York City
**Josef Hoffman** (piano); **Philharmonic-Symphony Orchestra of New York**
*Beethoven* Concerto for Piano and Orchestra No. 4 in G
   major, Op. 58
Intaglio INCD 7651 (unauthorised release)

3 November Carnegie Hall, New York City
  *Robert Casadeus* (piano); *Philharmonic-Symphony*
  *Orchestra of New York*
  *Mozart* Concerto for Piano and Orchestra No. 27 in B flat
    major, K 595
    Dante HPC 100

**1942**
Exact date not known. Carnegie Hall, New York City (public
  concert) *Philharmonic Symphony Orchestra of New York*
  *Menotti* The Old Maid and the Thief – Overture
  CDEA 501 9

Exact date not known. Carnegie Hall, New York City (public
  concert) *Philharmonic Symphony Orchestra of New York*
  *Creston* Threnody
    Dutton CDEA 5019

22 March Carnegie Hall, New York City (public concert)
  *Philharmonic-Symphony Orchestra of New York*
  *Anthony Collins* Sir Toby and Sir Andrew – Overture
    Dutton CDSJB 1999

12 Apri Carnegie Hall, New York City
  *Nathan Milstein* (violin); *Philharmonic-Symphony*
  *Orchestra of New York*
  *Bruch* Concerto for Violin and Orchestra No. 1 in G minor,
    Op. 26
    Biddulph LAB 096; Pearl GEMMCD 9259

31 December 1943 & 12 January 1944 Houldsworth Hall,
Manchester
*Hallé Orchestra*
*Bax* Symphony No. 3 in C major
    Dutton CDLX 7111

**1944**

17 February Houldsworth Hall, Manchester
*Hallé Orchestra*
*Vaughan Williams* Symphony No. 5 in D major
    Avid Classics AMSC 599; Pearl GEMS 0062

18 September Houldsworth Hall, Manchester
*Hallé Orchestra*
*Wagner* (arr. Barbirolli) Die Meistersinger von Nürnberg –
    Suite from Act 3
    Dutton CDEA 5504

**1945**

16 February Houldsworth Hall, Manchester
*Hallé Orchestra*
*Mendelssohn* A Midsummer Night's Dream, Op. 61 – Scherzo
    Memoir Classics CDMOIR 446

20 March Houldsworth Hall, Manchester
*Hallé Orchestra*
*Michael Heming* (arr. Anthony Collins) Threnody for a
    Soldier killed in Action
    EMI CDM 566053 2

**1946**
6 June Houldsworth Hall, Manchester
*Hallé Orchestr*a
*Vaughan Williams* Fantasia on a Theme by Thomas Tallis
Dutton CDSJB 1022

6–7 June Houldsworth Hall, Manchester
*Hallé Orchestra*
*Richard Strauss* (arr. Rodzinski) Der Rosenkavalier – Suite
Dutton CDSJB 1004

7 June Houldsworth Hall, Manchester
*Hallé Orchestra*
*Wagner* Lohengrin – Act 1, Prelude
Dutton CDSJB 1004
*Wagner* Lohengrin – Act 3, Prelude
Dutton CDSJB 1004
*Weber* Euryanthe – Overure
Dutton CDSJB 1004

**1947**
24 January Houldsworth Hall, Manchester
*Hallé Orchestra*
*Berlioz* Symphonie fantastique, Op. 14
Dutton CDEA 5504

4 January Houldsworth Hall, Manchester
*Hallé Orchestra*
*Elgar* Elegy for Strings, Op. 58
Dutton CDSJB 1017
*Fauré* Shylock, Op. 37 – Nocturne
Dutton CDEA 5504

12 May Kingsway Hall, London
**Hallé Orchestra**
*Elgar* Variations on an Original Theme, Op. 36 "Enigma"
   (previously unpublished takes)
   Dutton CDSJB 1020

19 May No. 1 Studio, Abbey Road, London
**Hallé Orchestra**
*Beethoven* Symphony No. 5 in C minor, Op. 67
   Dutton CDSJB 1014

29 May Kingsway Hall, London
**Hallé Orchestra**
*Elgar* Introduction and Allegro for Strings, Op. 47 Dutton
   CDSJB 1017

30 May Kingsway Hall, London
**Hallé Orchestra**
*Elgar* Bavarian Dances, Op. 29 – No. 2, Lullaby
   Dutton CDSJB 1017
*Elgar* Bavarian Dances, Op. 29 – No. 2, Lullaby (previously
   unpublished take)
   Dutton CDSJB 1020

27 August Festspielhaus, Salzburg (public concert)
**Wiener Philharmoniker**
*Delius* (arr. Beecham) A Village Romeo and Juliet – Walk to
   the Paradise Garden
   Dutton CDSJB 1999
*Weber* Euryanthe – Overture
   Dutton CDSJB 1999

23 October Kingsway Hall, London
**Hallé Orchestra**
*Elgar* Variations on an Original Theme, Op. 36 "Enigma"
Dutton CDSJB 1017

**1948**
25–26 February Houldsworth Hall, Manchester
**Hallé Orchestra**
*Mendelssohn* Symphony No. 4 in A major, Op. 90 "Italian"
Memoir Classics CDMOIR 446

26 February, 1 May Houldsworth Hall, Manchester
**Hallé Orchestra**
*Delibes* Sylvia – Suite from the Ballet
Memoir Classics CDMOIR 446

26 February Houldsworth Hall, Manchester
**Hallé Orchestra**
*Grainger* Irish Tune from County Derry "Londonderry Air'
Memoir Classics CDMOIR 446

10 March Houldsworth Hall, Manchester
**Hallé Orchestra**
*Stravinsky* Concerto in D for string orchestra
Dutton CDSJB 1999

28 April & 31 1949 May Free Trade Hall, Manchester & No. 1
Studio, Abbey Road, London
**Hallé Orchestra**
*Schubert* Die Zauberharfe – Overture, D 644
Dutton CDSJB 1020

29 April–1 May Houldsworth Hall, Manchester
 **Theo Olof** (violin); **Hallé Orchestra**
 *Britten* Concerto for Violin and Orchestra, Op. 15 (original
  version)
 EMI CDM 566053 2

30 April Houldsworth Hall, Manchester
 **Hallé Orchestra**
 *Mendelssohn* The Hebrides Overture, Op. 26 "Fingals' Cave"
 Memoir Classics CDMOIR 446

1 May Houldsworth Hall, Manchester
 **Parry Jones** (tenor); **Hallé Choir and Orchestra**
 *Ireland* These Things shall be
  Dutton CDSJB 1022

1 May Houldsworth Hall, Manchester
 **Hallé Orchestra**
 *Delius* (arr. Fenby) Two Aquarelles
  Dutton CDSJB 1005

4 December Houldsworth Hall, Manchester
 **Hallé Orchestra**
 *Grieg* Peer Gynt – Suite No. 1, Op. 46
  Memoir Classics CDMOIR 446

**1949**
3 and 5 March No. 1 Studio, Abbey Road, London
 **Hallé Orchestra**
 *Sibelius* Symphony No. 7 in C major, Op. 107
  Dutton CDSJB 1018

5 March No. 1 Studio, Abbey Road, London
**Hallé Orchestra**
*Mozart* Le nozze di Figaro, K 492 – Overture
Dutton CDSJB 1004

28 April No. 1 Studio, Abbey Road, London
**Hallé Orchestra**
*Beethoven* Egmont, Op. 84 – Overture
Dutton CDSJB 1014

30 April No. 1 Studio, Abbey Road, London
**Hallé Orchestra**
*Elgar* Serenade in E minor, Op. 20
EMI CMS 566543 2

31 May No. 1 Studio, Abbey Road, London
**Hallé Orchestra**
*Ireland* Mai-Dun – symphonic rhapsody
Dutton CDSJB 1022
*Ireland* The Forgotten Rite – Prelude for Orchestra
Dutton CDSJB 1020
*Mendelssohn* Octet in E flat major, Op. 20 – Scherzo
Dutton CDSJB 1020

15 and 17 December Kingsway Hall, London
**Hallé Orchestra**
*Haydn* Symphony No. 83 in G minor "La Poule"
Dutton CDSJB 1003

15 December & 1950 2 February Kingsway Hall & No. 1
Studio Abbey Road, London
**Hallé Orchestra**
*Elgar* Cockaigne Overture, Op. 40 "In London Town"
EMI CMS 566543 2

**1950**

1 January No. 1 Studio, Abbey Road, London
*Hallé Orchestra*
*Elgar* Dream Children No. 1, Op. 43 No. 1
    EMI CDM 566399 2

2 February No. 1 Studio, Abbey Road, London
*Hallé Orchestra*
*Delius* A Song of Summer
    Dutton CDSJB 1005
*Mozart* Cassation in G major, K 63
    Dutton CDSJB 1999

19 October Kingsway Hall, London
*Hallé Orchestra*
*Bizet* L'Arlésienne – Suite No. 1
    Dutton CDSJB 1002

14–15 December No. 1 Studio, Abbey Road, London
*Hallé Orchestra*
*Rubbra* Symphony No. 5 in B flat major, Op. 63
    EMI CDM 566053 2

18 December No. 1 Studio, Abbey Road, London
*Hallé Orchestra*
*Rubbra* Improvisations on Virginal Pieces by Giles Farnaby,
    Op. 50 – No. 4, Loth to depart
    EMI CDM 566053 2

**1951**
9 March Free Trade Hall, Manchester (public concert) *Kathleen Ferrier* (contralto); *Hallé Orchestra*
*Chausson* Poéme de l'amour et de la mer, Op. 19
Decca 433 472-2DM

19 December Free Trade Hall, Manchester
*Hallé Orchestra*
*Turina* Danzas Fantásticas
     Dutton CDSJB 1013

20 December Free Trade Hall, Manchester
*Hallé Orchestra*
*Weber* Der Freischütz – Overture
     Dutton CDSJB 1004

**1952**
5 April Free Trade Hall, Manchester
*Hallé Orchestra*
*Haydn* Symphony No. 96 in D major "The Miracle"
     Dutton CDSJB 1003
*Lehár* Gold und Silber, Op. 75 – Walzer
     Dutton CDSJB 1013
*Mozart* Divertimento No. 11 in D major, K 251 – Minuet
     Dutton CDSJB 1999

21–22 May Free Trade Hall, Manchester
*Hallé Orchestra*
*Brahms* Symphony No. 3 in F major, Op. 90
     Dutton CDSJB 1020

18–19 December Free Trade Hall, Manchester
*Hallé Orchestra*
*Sibelius* Symphony No. 2 in D major, Op. 42
    Dutton CDSJB 1018

19 December Free Trade Hall, Manchester
*Hallé Orchestra*
*Grieg* (orch. Barbirolli) Lyric Pieces – Book 6, Op. 57–No. 4,
Secret
    Dutton CDSJB 1999

## 1953

4 June Royal Opera House, Covent Garden, London (public
performance)
*Maria Callas* (soprano) Aida; *Giulietta Simionato* (mezzo-
soprano) Amneris; *Kurt Baum* (tenor) Radames; *Jess
Walters* (baritone) Amonasro; *Guilio Neri* (bass) Ramfis;
*Michael Langdon* (bass) The King; *Dame Joan
Sutherland* (soprano) Priestess; *Chorus and Orchestra of
the Royal Opera House, Covent Garden*
*Verdi* Aida
    Golden Melodram GM 20035; Eklipse EKRCD 14
    (unauthorised version)

15–16 June Free Trade Hall, Manchester
*Margaret Ritchie* (soprano); *Hallé Choir and Orchestra*
*Vaughan Williams* Sinfonia Antartica
    EMI CMS 566543 2
*Nb*: the organ part, played by Lawrance Collingwood, was
recorded at No. 1 Studio, Abbey Road on September 29
1953

16 June Free Trade Hall, Manchester
*Hallé Orchestra*
*Vaughan Williams* The Wasps – Overture
EMI CMS 566543 2

31 August Free Trade Hall, Manchester
*Hallé Orchestra*
*Haydn* Symphony No. 88 in G major "Letter V"
Dutton CDSJB 1003

1 September Free Trade Hall, Manchester
*Hallé Orchestra*
*Elgar* Introduction and Allegro for Strings, Op. 47
EMI CMS 566543 2

21 & 23 December Free Trade Hall, Manchester
*Hallé Orchestra*
*Schubert* Symphony No.9 in C major, D 944 "Great"
Dutton CDSJB 1020

23 December Free Trade Hall, Manchester
*Hallé Orchestra*
*Debussy* Prélude à l'après-midi d'un faune
Dutton CDSJB 1002

31 December Free Trade Hall, Manchester
*Jean Bell* (harp); *Hallé Orchestra*
*Vaughan Williams* Five Variants on "Dives and Lazarus"
EMI CMS 5CC543 2

**1954**

1 January Free Trade Hall, Manchester
*Hallé Orchestra*
*Ibert* Divertissement
   Dutton CDSJB 1002

2 January FreeTradeHall, Manchester
*Hallé Orchestra*
*Verdi* La traviata – Act 1, Prelude
   Dutton CDSJB 1004
*Verdi* La traviata – Act 3, Prelude
   Dutton CDSJB 1004
*Chabrier* España – rapsodie
   Dutton CDSJB 1013

4 January Free Trade Hall, Manchester
*Hallé Orchestra*
*Faure* Pelléas et Mélisande – Suite, Op. 80
   Dutton CDSJB 1002
*Elgar* Cockaigne – Concerto Overture, Op. 40 "In London
   Town"
   EMI CDM 566399

5 January Free Trade Hall, Manchester
*Hallé Orchestra*
*Barbirolli* (arr.) An Elizabethan Suite
   Dutton CDSJB 1020

10–11 February Free Trade Hall, Manchester
*Marion Rawicz & Walter Landauder* (piano duet); *Hallé
Orchestra*
*Saint-Saëns* Le Carnaval des animaux – fantaisie zoologique
   Dutton CDSJB 1002

11 February Free Trade Hall, Manchester
   ***Marion Rawicz & Walter Landauder*** (piano duet); ***Hallé Orchestra***
   *Strauss Family* (arr. Landauer) A Strauss Fantasy
      Dutton CDSJB 1010

11 February Free Trade Hall, Manchester
   ***Hallé Orchestra***
   *Suppe* Der schöne Galathée – Overture
      Dutton CDSJB 1013

8–9 June Free Trade Hall, Manchester
   ***Hallé Orchestra***
   *Elgar* Symphony No. 2 in E flat major, Op. 63
      EMI CDM 56639/2

9 June Free Trade Hall, Manchester
   ***Hallé Orchestra***
   *Vaughan Williams* (arr. Greaves) Fantasia on "Greensleeves"
      EMI CMS 566543 2

14 June No. 1 Studio, Abbey Road, London
   ***Philip Catelinet*** (tuba); ***London Symphony Orchestra***
   *Vaughan Williams* Concerto for Bass Tuba and Orchestra
      EMI CMS 566543 2

**1955**

12 January Free Trade Hall, Manchester
*Hallé Orchestra*
*Sibelius* Lemminkainen Suite, Op. 22 – No. 2, Swan of
Tuonela
Dutton CDSJB 1018
*Richard Strauss* (arr. Clemens Krauss) Die Liebe der Danae –
Symphonic Fragments
Dutton CDSJB 1004

12–13 January Free Trade Hall, Manchester
*Hallé Orchestra*
*Villa-Lobos* Bachianas Brasileiras No. 4
Dutton CDSJB 1004

13 January FreeTrade Hall, Manchester.
*Hallé Orchestra*
*Johann Strauss II* Kaiser-Walzer, Op. 437
Dutton CDSJB 1010

4–5 July No. 1 Studio, Abbey Road, London
*Evelyn Rothwell* (oboe); *London Symphony Orchestra*
*Vaughan Williams* Concerto for Oboe and String Orchestra in
A minor
EMI CMS 566543 2

**1956**

19 June Free Trade Hall, Manchester
*Hallé Orchestra*
*Vaughan Williams* Symphony No. 8 in D minor
Dutton CDSJB 1021
*Johann Strauss* II Di Zigeunerbaron – Overture
Dutton CDS JB 1010

20 June Free Trade Hall, Manchester
*Hallé Orchestra*
*Butterworth* A Shropshire Lad – Rhapsody
   Dutton CDSJB 1022
*Johann Strauss II* G'schichten aus dem Wienerwald, Op. 325
   Dutton CDSJB 1010
*Johann Strauss I* (arr. Gordon Jacob) Radetzky Marsch, Op.
   228 Dutton CDSJB 1010
*Johann Strauss II* Die Fledermaus- Overture
   Dutton CDSJB 1010
*Johann Strauss II & Josef Strauss* Pizicato Polka
   Dutton CDSJB 1010

21 June Free Trade Hall, Manchester
*Hallé Orchestra*
*Bax* The Garden of Fand
   Dutton CDSJB 1020
*Johann Strauss II* An die schön, blauen Donau, Op. 314 –
   Walzer
   CDSJB 1010

22 June Free Trade Hall, Manchester
*Hallé Orchestra*
*Delius* (arr. Beecham) A Village Romeo and Juliet – The Walk
   to the Paradise Garden
   Dutton CDSJB 1005
*Delius* (arr. Fenby) Fennimore and Gerda Intermezo
   Dutton CDSJB 1005; EMI CMS 565119 2; HMV Classics
   574054 2
*Delius* Irmelin Prelude
   Dutton CDSJB 1005
*Delius* On hearing the First Cuckoo in Spring
   Dutton CDSJB 1005

23 June Free Trade Hall, Manchester
*Hallé Orchestra*
*Johann Strauss II* Perpetuum mobile, Op. 257 – Polka schnell
Dutton CDSJB 1010
*Johann Strauss II* Annen Polka, Op. 117
Dutton CDSJB 1010

11 December Free Trade Hall, Manchester
*Sylvia Fisher* (soprano); Jess Walters (baritone); *Hallé Orchestra*
*Delius* Idyll: "Once I passed through a populous city"
Dutton CDSJB 1005

11–12 December Free Trade Hall, Manchester
*Hallé Orchestra*
*Elgar* Symphony No. 1 in A flat major, Op. 55
Dutton CDSJB 1017

12 December Free Trade Hall, Manchester
*Hallé Orchestra*
*Elgar* Introduction and Allegro for Strings, Op. 47
Dutton CDSJB 1017
*Elgar* Elegy for Strings, Op. 58
Dutton CDSJB 1017

**1957**
3 May Free Trade Hall, Manchester
*Hallé Orchestra*
*Lehár* Gold und Silber, Op. 75 – Walzer
Dutton CDSJB 1010
*Waldteufel* Les Patineurs – Valse [Op. 183]
Dutton CDSJB 1013
*German* Nell Gywn – Dances: Pastoral Dance; Country
Dance; Torch Dance
Dutton CDSJB 1006

4 May Free Trade Hall, Manchester
*Marina da Gabarain* (mezzo-soprano); *Hallé Orchestra*
*Falla* (orch. Ernesto Haffter) Siete canciones populares
españolas – Seduilla murciana
Dutton CDSJB 1004

21–22 May Free Trade Hall, Manchester
*André Navarra* (cello); *Hallé Orchestra*
*Elgar* Concerto for Cello and Orchestra in E minor, Op. 85
Testament SBT 1204

21–22 May Free Trade Hall, Manchester
*Hallé Orchestra*
*Berlioz* La Damnation de Faust, Op. 24 – Marche hongrois –
Danse des sylphes – Menuet des follets
Royal Classics ROY 6467
– Menuet des follets (rehearsal sequence)
Dutton CDSJB 1004

24 May Free Trade Hall, Manchester
*Evelyn Rothwell* (oboe); *Hallé Orchestra*
*Corelli* (arr. Barbirolli) Concerto for Oboe and Orchestra
Dutton CDSJB 1009

24–25 May Free Trade Hall, Manchester
*Evelyn Rothwell* (oboe); *Hallé Orchestra*
*Pergolesi* (arr. Barbirolli) Concerto for Oboe and Strings
Dutton CDSJB 1009

27 May Free Trade Hall, Manchester
*Hallé Orchestra*
*Tchaikovsky* Symphony No. 4 in F minor, Op. 36
HMVD 573077 2; Royal Classics HR 704032

28 May Free Trade Hall, Manchester *Hallé Orchestra*
   *Sibelius* Symphony No. 5 in E flat major, Op. 62
      Dutton CDSJB 1018

29 May Free Trade Hall, Manchester *Hallé Orchestra*
   *Grainger* Irish Tune from County Derry "Londonderry Air"
      Dutton CDSJB 1006
   *Grainger* Mock Morris
      Dutton CDSJB 1006
   *Grainger* Molly on the Shore
      Dutton CDSJB 1006
   *Grainger* Shepherd's Hey
      Dutton CDSJB 1006
   *Grainger* Shepherd's Hey (Rehearsal excerpt leads into a
   previously unpublished stereo 'test' recording)
      Dutton CDSJB 1006

11–12 June Free Trade Hall, Manchester
*Hallé Orchestra*
   *Mahler* Symphony No. 1 in D
      Dutton CDSJB 1015

12 June Free Trade Hall, Manchester
*Hallé Orchestra*
   *Verdi* La forza del destino – Overture
      Dutton CDSJB 1006

13 June Free Trade Hall, Manchester
*Hallé Orchestra*
   *Tchaikovsky* Romeo and Juliet – Fantasy Overture
      Disky DCL 705902; Royal Classics HR 704032

28 June Free Trade Hall, Manchester
***Hallé Orchestra***
*Dvořák* Scherzo capriccioso, Op. 66
Royal Classics HR 703992
29 June Free Trade Hall, Manchester
***Hallé Orchestra***
*Dvořák* Symphony No. 8 in G major, Op. 88
Royal Classics HR 703992

8 August Free Trade Hall, Manchester
***Hallé Orchestra***
*Ponchielli* La Gioconda – Dance of the Hours
Dutton CDSJB 1006
*Dvořák* Symphony No. 7 in D minor, Op. 70
Royal Classics HR 703992

9–10 August Free Trade Hall, Manchester
***Hallé Orchestra***
*Grieg* Peer Gynt – Suite No. 1, Op. 46
Dutton CDSJB 1013
*Tchaikovsky* Andante cantabile, Op. 11
Royal Classics HR 704032

10 August Free Trade Hall, Manchester
***Hallé Orchestra***
*Grieg* Two Elegiac Melodies, Op. 34
Dutton CDSJB 1013

10 and 13 August Free Trade Hail, Manchester
***Members of the Hallé Orchestra***
*Dvořák* Serenade in D minor, Op. 44
Royal Classics HR 703992; Disky DCL 705902

11 August Free Trade Hall, Manchester
*Hallé Orchestra*
*Grieg* Symphonic Dances, Op. 64
   Dutton CDSJB 1012
*Massenet* Scènes alsaciennes – Sous les tilleuls
   Dutton CDSJB 1006
*Chabrier* Marche joyeuse
   Dutton CDSJB 1006

13 August Free Trade Hall, Manchester
*Evelyn Rothwell* (oboe); *Hallé Orchestra*
*Haydn* (attributed) Concerto for Oboe and Orchestra in C
major
   Dutton CDSJB 1016

15 November Turin, Italy
*Orchestra Sinfonica di Torino della RAI*
*Elgar* Variations on an Original Theme, Op. 36 "Enigma"
   Hunt 2CDHP 584 (unauthorised release)

20 November Rome, Italy
*Constance Shacklock* (mezzo-soprano); *Jon Vickers* (tenor);
*Marian Nowakowski* (bass); *Orchestra Sinfonica e coro di
Roma della RAI*
*Elgar* The Dream of Gerontius, Op. 38
   Hunt 2CDHP 584 (unauthorised release)

28–29 December Free Trade Hall, Manchester
*Hallé Orchestra*
*Vaughan Wlliams* A London Symphony (No. 2)
   Dutton CDSJB 1021

30–31 December Free Trade Hall, Manchester
  *Hallé Orchestra*
  *Sibelius* Symphony No. 1 in E minor, Op. 39
    Dutton CDSJB 1018

**1958**
1 January Free Trade Hall, Manchester
  *Hallé Orchestra*
  *Beethoven* Symphony No. 1 in C major, Op. 21
    Dutton CDSJB 1014

2 January Free Trade Hall, Manchester
  *Hallé Orchestra*
  *Beethoven* Symphony No. 8 in F major, Op. 93
    Dutton CDSJB 1014

20 August Free Trade Hall, Manchester
  *Hallé Orchestra*
  *Tchaikovsky* Symphony No. 6 in B minor, Op. 74 "Pathetique"
    HMVD 573077 2; Royal Classics HR 704032

2 September Free Trade Hall, Manchester
  *Evelyn Rothwell* (oboe); *Hallé Orchestra*
  *Handel* (ed. Mackerras & Rothwell) Concerto for Oboe and
    Strings No. 1 in B flat major
    Dutton CDSJB 1009

3 September Free Trade Hall, Manchester
  *Hallé Orchestra*
  *Dvořák* Legends, Op. 59 – No. 4 in C major; No. 6 in C sharp
    minor, No. 7 in A major
    Royal Classics HR 703992

4 September Free Trade Hall, Manchester
**Hallé Orchestra**
*Mascagni* Cavalleria Rusticana – Intermezzo
    Dutton CDSJB 1006
*Rossini* (arr. Charles Godfrey Jnr) Guillaume Tell – Ballet
    Music
    Dutton CDSJB 1006

**1959**
10 January Carnegie Hall, New York City (public concert)
**New York Philharmonic Orchestra**
*Mahler* Symphony No. 1 in D
    New York Philharmonic NYP 9801

April. Free Trade Hall, Manchester
**Mindru Katz** (piano); **Hallé Orchestra**
*Beethoven* Concerto for Piano and Orchestra No. 5 in E flat
    major, Op. 73 "Emperor"
    Dutton CDSJB 1014

April (exact dates not known). Free Trade Hall, Manchester
**Hallé Orchestra**
*Beethoven* Leonore Overture No. 3, Op.04, 72
    Dutton CDSJB 1014
*Tchaikovsky* Marche slave, Op. 31
    Royal Classics HR 704032
*Dvořák* Symphony No. 9 in E minor, Op. 95 "From the New
    World"
    Royal Classics HR 703992
*Tchaikovsky* Symphony No. 5 in E minor, Op. 64
    HMVD 573077 2; Royal Classics HR 704032; Disky DCL
    705702

5–6 June St Gabriel's Church, Cricklewood, London
**Evelyn Rothwell** (oboe) **Pro Arte Orchestra**
*Albinoni* Concerto for Oboe and Strings in B flat major, Op. 7
No. 3
Dutton CDSJB 1009
*Albinoni* Concerto for Oboe and Strings in D major, Op. 7 No. 6
Dutton CDSJB 1009
*Cimarosa* (arr. Arthur Benjamin) Concerto for Oboe and Strings
Dutton CDSJB 1009

2–3 September Free Trade Hall, Manchester
**Hallé Orchestra**
*Berlioz* Symphonie fantastique, Op. 14
Disky DCL 705902
*Berlioz* Symphonie fantastique, Op. 14 – No. 3, Scene aux
champs
Disky DCL 705902

17–18 September Free Trade Hall, Manchester
**Alfredo Campoli** (vn); **André Navrra** (cello); **Hallé
Orchestra**
*Brahms* Concerto for Violin, Cello and Orchestra in A minor,
Op. 102
Dutton CDSJB 1020; Disky DCL 705902;
Royal Classics HR 703992

**1960**
20 October Free Trade Hall, Manchester (public concert)
**Hallé Orchestra and BBC Northern Symphony Orchestra**
*Mahler* Symphony No. 7 in E minor
BBC Legends BBCL 4034–2

25 November Turin, Italy (public concert)
***Orchestra Sinfonica di Torino della RAI***
*Mozart* Symphony No. 34 in C major, K 338
 Hunt CDHP 584
*Mahler* Symphony No. 9 in D
 Hunt CDLSMH 34003

**1961**

11 April Teatro Kursaal, Lugano, Switzerland (public concert)
***Hallé Orchestra***
*Rimsky-Korsakov* Capriccio espagnole, Op. 34
 Ermitage ERM 181–2
*Chabrier* España – rapsodie
 Ermitage ERM 181-2
*Barbirolli* (arr.) An Elizabethan Suite
 Ermitage ERM 181–2
*Vaughan Williams* Symphony No. 8 in D minor
 Ermitage ERM 181–2 1962

23–25 March House of Artists, Prague, Czechoslovakia
***Czech Philharmonic Orchestra***
*Franck* Symphony in D minor
 Supraphon 11 06132

**1962**

8–9 May Kingsway Hall, London
***Philharmonia Orchestra***
*Vaughan Williams* Symphony No. 5 in D major
EMI CDM 5651 12

9 May & 27 August Kingsway Hall, London
***Philharmonia Orchestra***
*Elgar* Variations on an Original Theme, Op. 36 "Enigma"
 EMI CDM 566332 2

10 May Kingsway Hall, London
*Sinfonia of London*
*Elgar* Serenade in E minor, Op. 20
EMI CDM 567240 2

*Sinfonia of London*
*Vaughan Williams* Fantasia on "Greensleeves"
EMI CDM 567240 2

11 May Kingsway Hall, London
*Allegri Quartet; Sinfonia of London*
*Elgar* Introduction and Allegro for Strings, Op. 47
EMI CDM 567240 2

17 May Temple Church, London
*Sinfonia of London*
*Vaughan Williams* Fantasia on a Theme by Thomas Tallis
EMI CDM 567240 2

27 August Kingsway Hall, London
*Philharmonia Orchestra*
*Elgar* Cockaigne – Concerto Overture, Op. 40 "In London
Town"
EMI CDM 566323 2

28–29 August Kingsway Hall, London
*Philharmonia Orchestra*
*Elgar* Symphony No. 1 in A flat major, Op. 55
EMI CDM 764511 2

29 August Kingsway Hall, London
*Philharmonia Orchestra*
*Elgar* Pomp and Circumstance March No. 1 in D major, Op. 39
EMI CDM 566323 2
*Elgar* Pomp and Circumstance March No. 4 in G major, Op. 39
EMI CDM 566323 2

1 and 9 October Walthamstow Assembly Hall, London
**Royal Philharmonic Orchestra**
*Sibelius* Symphony No. 2 in D major, Op. 42
   Chesky CD 3

8 December Philharmonic Hall, Lincoln Center, New York City
(public concert)
**New York Philharmonic Orchestra**
*Mahler* Symphony No. 9 in D New York Philharmonic
   NYP 9801

17–18 December No. 1 Studio, Abbey Road, London
**John Ogdon** (piano); **Philharmonia Orchestra**
*Tchaikovsky* Concerto for Piano and Orchestra No. 1 in B flat
   minor, Op. 23
   Dutton CDSJB 1019

**1964**
10–11,14 and 16 January Jesus Christuskirche, Berlin-Dahlem
**Berliner Philharmoniker**
*Mahler* Symphony No. 9 in D
   EMI CDM 763115 2; HMV Classics 574364 2

20–21 April Kingsway Hall, London
**Hallé Orchestra**
*Elgar* Symphony No. 2 in E flat major, Op. 63
   EMI CDM 764724 2

21 April Kingsway Hall, London
**Sir John Barbirolli** in an impromptu conversation with EMI
recording producer Ronald Kinloch Anderson talking
primarily about Elgar and Mahler
Dutton CDSJB 1004

1 June Kingsway Hall, London
**Hallé Orchestra**
*Elgar* Falstaff – Symphony Study in C minor, Op. 68
    EMI CDM 566322 2

1–2 September Kingsway Hall, London
**London Symphony Orchestra**
*Tchaikovsky* Serenade in C major, Op. 48
    EMI CMS 764843 2; Royal Classics HR 704032; Disky
    DCL 705702
*Arensky* Variations on a Theme of Tchaikovsky, Op. 35
    EMI CZS 5693612

14 October Symphony Hall, Boston (public concert)
**Boston Symphony Orchestra**
*Elgar* Symphony No. 2 in E flat major, Op. 63
    Music and Arts CD 251 (unauthorised release)

30 October Symphony Hall, Boston (public concert)
**Boston Symphony Orchestra**
*Purcell* (arr. Barbirolli),"Suite for Strings with horns, flutes
    and cor anglais",
    Music and Arts CD 251 (unauthorised release)
*Delius* (arr. Beecham) A Village Romeo and Juliet – The Walk
    to the Paradise Garden
    Music and Arts CD 251 (unauthorised release)
*Vaughan Williams* Symphony No. 6 in E minor
    Music and Arts CD 251 (unauthorised release)

27–30 December Free Trade Hall, Manchester
  **Dame Janet Baker** (mezo-soprano); **Richard Lewis** (tenor);
  **Kim Borg** (bass); **Ambrosian Singers**; **Sheffield
  Philharmonic Chorus**; **Halle Choir & Orchestra**
  *Elgar* The Dream of Gerontius, Op. 38
    EMI CZS 573579 2

## 1965
(exact date unknown). Manchester (film recording of rehearsal
  sequence for BBC TV "Monitor" programme)
  **Hallé Orchestra**
  *Bruckner* Symphony No. 7 in E major – No. 3, Scherzo
    (opening)
    Teldec (video) 4509-95038-3; 4509-95038

19 August Kingsway Hall, London
  **Jacqueline Du Pré** (cello); **London Symphony Orchestra**
  *Elgar* Concerto for Cello and Orchestra in E minor, Op. 85
    EMI CDC 556219 2; CDC 556806 2; CDC 55527 2; CMS
    769707 2; CMS 567341 2; CZS 568132 2

24 August Kingsway Hall, London
  **London Symphony Orchestra**
  *Delius* (arr. Beecham) A Village Romeo and Juliet – The Walk
    to the Paradise Garden
    EMI CMS 565119 2; HMV Classics 574054 2

25–27 August No. 1 Studio, Abbey Road, London
   *Victoria de los Angeles* (soprano) Dido; *Peter Glossop*
   (baritone) Aeneas; *Heather Harper* (soprano) Belinda;
   *Patricia Johnson* (contralto) Sorceress; *Elisabeth Robson*
   (soprano) Second Woman; *Clare Walmesley* (soprano) First
   Witch; *Sybl Michelow* (contralto) Second Witch, Spirit;
   *Robert Tear* (tenor) Sailor; *Raymond Leppard* (harpsichord
   continuo); *Ambrosian Singers; English Chamber Orchestra*
   *Purcell* (ed. Boyling) Dido and Aeneas
      EMI CDM 565664 2

30 August No. 1 Studio, Abbey Road, London
   *Dame Janet Baker* (mezzo-soprano); *London Symphony*
   *Orchestra*
   *Elgar* Sea Pictures, Op. 38
      EMI CDC 556806 2
   *Elgar* Sea Pictures, Op. 38 – No. 4, Where corals lie only
      Philips 465 253-2PH

28 December Kingsway Hall, London
   *London Symphony Orchestra*
   *Ireland* A London Overture
      EMI CDM 565109 2
   *Bax* Tintagel
      EMI CDM 565110 2; Reader's Digest RDCD 1941/5

**1966**
13 January Philharmonie, Berlin (public concert)
   *Berliner Philharmoniker*
   *Mahler* Symphony No. 6 in A minor "Tragic"
      Hunt CD 702 (unauthorised release)

23 January No. 1 Studio, Abbey Road, London
**Hallé Orchestra**
*Sibeilus* Karelia Suite, Op. 11
   EMI CMS 567299 2
*Sibelius* Kuolema – incidental music, Op. 44: Valse triste
   EMI CMS 567299 2
*Sibelius* Finlandia – symphonic poem, Op. 26
   EMI CMS 567299 2
*Sibelius* Lemminkaïnen Suite, Op. 22 – No. 2, Swan of
   Tuonela
   EMI CMS 567299 2

23–24 January No. 1 Studio, Abbey Road, London
**Hallé Orchestra**
*Sibelius* Lemminkaïnen Suite, Op. 22 – No. 4,
   Lemminkaïnen's Return
   EMI CMS 567299 2

24 January No. 1 Studio, Abbey.Road, London
**Hallé Orchestra**
*Sibelius* Pohjola's Daughter – symphonic fantasia, Op. 49
   EMI CMS 567299 2

14 July Kingsway Hall, London
**New Philharmonia Orchestra**
*Elgar* Pomp and Circumstance March No.2 in A minor, Op. 39
   EMI CDM 566323 2
*Elgar* Pomp and Circumstance March No.3 in C minor, Op. 39
   EMI CDM 566323 2
*Elgar* Pomp and Circumstance March No.5 in C major, Op. 39
   EMI CDM 566323 2

14 July Kingsway Hall, London
**London Symphony Orchestra**
*Delius* Irmelin Prelude
   EMI CMS 565119 2; HMV Classics 574054 2
*Delius* A Song of Summer
   EMI CMS 565119 2; HMV Classics 574054 2

15 July Kingsway Hall, London
**New Philhannonia Orchestra**
*Elgar* Froissart – Concert Overture, Op. 17
   EMI CDM 566323 2

16 July Kingsway Hall, London
**New Philharmonia Orchestra**
*Elgar* Elegy for Strings, Op. 58
   EMI CDM 567240 2
*Elgar* Sospiri, Op. 70
   EMI CDM 567240 2

25–26 July Kingsway Hall, London
**Hallé Orchestra**
*Sibelius* Symphony No. 2 in D major, Op. 42
   HMV ASD 2302, EMI CMS 567299 2

26–27 July Kingsway Hall, London
**Hallé Orchestra**
*Sibelius* Symphony No. 5 in E flat major, Op. 62
   EMI CMS 567299 2

27–28 July Kingsway Hall, London
**Hallé Orchestra**
*Sibelius* Symphony No. 7 in C major, Op. 107
   EMI CMS 567299 2

16–18 and 20–27 August Teatro dell'Opera, Rome, Italy
  ***Renata Scotto*** (soprano) Cio-Cio-San; (tenor); ***Anna di
  Stasio*** (mezzo-soprano) Suzuki; ***Silvna Padoan*** (mezzo-
  soprano) Kate Pinkerton; ***Carlo Bergonzi*** (tenor) B. F.
  Pinkerton; ***Rolando Panerai*** (baritone) Sharpless; ***Piero de
  Palma*** (tenor) Goro; ***Giuseppe Morresi*** (tenor) Prince
  Yamadori; ***Paolo Montarsolo*** (bass) ll Bonzo; ***Mario
  Rinaudo*** (bass) Il Commissario; ***Orchestra e Coro del Teatro
  dell'Opera di Roma***
  *Puccini* Madama Butterfly
     EMI CMS 769654 2; HMVD 572886 2

6–8 December Grosser Saal, Musikverein, Vienna
  ***Wiener Philharmoniker***
  *Brahms* Symphony No. 2 in D major, Op. 73
     Royal Classics HR 703992; Disky DCL 707132

28–30 December Kingsway Hall, London
  ***Hallé Orchestra***
  *Sibelius* Symphony No. 1 in E minor, Op. 39
     EMI CMS 567299 2

30–31 December Kingsway Hall, London
  ***Hallé Orchestra***
  *Lehár* Gold und Silber – Walzer, Op. 75
     Dutton CDSJB 1004

31 December Kingsway Hall, London
  ***Hallé Orchestra***
  *Berlioz* Le Carnaval romain – Overture, Op. 9
     Royal Classics ROY 6467

**1967**

3 January Smetana Hall, Prague, Czechoslovakia (public concert)
**BBC Symphony Orchestra**
*Berlioz* Le Corsaire, Op. 21
  Dutton CDSJB 1014

3 January Smetana Hall, Prague, Czechoslovakia (public concert)
**Heather Harper** (soprano); **BBC Symphony Orchestra**
*Mahler* Symphony No. 4 in G
  BBC Legends BBCL 4014-2

22 January Royal Festival Hall, London (public concert)
**New Philharmonia Orchestra**
*Mahler* Symphony No. 6 in A minor "Tragic"
  Hunt CDGI 726 (unauthorised release)

3 May BBC Studios, Maida Vale, London
**Hallé Orchestra**
*Britten* Variations and Fugue on a Theme by Purcell, Op. 34
  BBC Legends BBCL 4013 2

4 May No. 1 Studio, Abbey Road, London
**Dame Janet Baker** (mezzo-soprano); **Hallé Orchestra**
*Mahler* Ruckert Lieder – No. 4, Ich bin der Welt abhanden
  EMI CDM 5669812
*Mahler* Lieder eines fahrenden Gesellen
  EMI CDM 5669812; CZS 569665 2; Disky DCL 705902

18–19 May No. 1 Studio, Abbey Road, London
**BBC Symphony Orchestra**
*Beethoven* Symphony No. 3 in E flat major, Op. 55 "Eroica"
  Dutton CDSJB 1008

19 May No. 1 Studio, Abbey Road, London
**BBC Symphony Orchestra**
*Barbirolli* (arr.) An Elizabethan Suite
Dutton CDSJB 1008

11–14 July No. 1 Studio, Abbey Road, London
**Hallé Orchestra**
*Vaughan Williams* A London Symphony (No. 2)
EMI CDM 565109 2

12–13 July No. 1 Studio, Abbey Road, London
**Dame Janet Baker** (mezzo-soprano); **Hallé Orchestra**
*Mahler* Kindertotenlieder
EMI CDM 566981 2; CZS 569665 2

13 July No. 1 Studio, Abbey Road, London
**Hallé Orchestra**
*Sibelius* Pelléas et Mélisande – Suite from the incidental
music, Op. 46: No. 1 At the Castle Gate
EMI CMS 567299 2

14 July No. 1 Studio, Abbey Road, London
**Hallé Orchestra**
*Sibelius* Pelléas et Mélisande – Suite from the incidental
music, Op. 46: No. 2, Melisande",
EMI CMS 567299 2
*Sibelius* Pelléas et Mélisande – Suite from the incidental
music, Op. 46: No. 7, Melisande at the Spinning Wheel",
EMI CMS 567299 2
*Sibelius* Pelléas et Mélisande – Suite from the incidental
music, Op. 46: No. 9, The Death of Melisande",
EMI CMS 567299 2

8 August Royal Albert Hall, London (public concert)
**BBC Symphony Orchestra**
*Britten* Sinfonia da Requiem, Op. 20
    BBC Legends BBCL 4013 2

17–19 August Kingsway Hall, London
**New Philharmonia Orchestra**
*Mahler* Symphony No. 6 in A minor "Tragic"
    EMI CZS 569252 2; CZS569349 2

19 August Kingsway Hall, London
**New Philharmonia Orchestra**
*Richard Strauss* Metamorphosen
    EMI CZS 569252 2

20–21 August No. 1 Studio, Abbey Road, London
**Daniel Barenboim** (piano); **New Philharmonia Orchestra**
*Brahms* Concerto for Piano and Orchestra No. 1 in D minor,
    Op. 16
    EMI CZS 572649 2; Philips 456 721-2PM2

21, 27–28 August No. 1 Studio, Abbey Road, London
**Daniel Barenboim** (piano); **New Philharmonia Orchestra**
*Brahms* Concerto for Piano and Orchestra No. 2 in B flat
    major, Op. 83
    EMI CZS 572649 2

23 August No. 1 Studio, Abbey Road, London
**Dame Janet Baker** (mezzo-soprano); **New Philharmonia
Orchestra**
*Berlioz* Les Nuits d'été
    EMI CZS 572640 2; HMV Classics 573446 2

4–6 December Grosser Saal, Musikverein, Vienna
*Wiener Philhannoniker*
*Brahms* Symphony No. 1 in C minor, Op. 68
  Royal Classics HR 703992

6–8 December Grosser Saal, Musikverein, Vienna
*Wiener Philharmoniker*
*Brahms* Symphony No. 4in E minor, Op. 98
  Royal Classics HR 703992

8 and 15 December Grosser Saal, Musikverein, Vienna
*Wiener Philharmoniker*
*Brahms* Symphony No. 3 in F major, Op. 90
  Royal Classics HR 703992

13 December No. 1 Studio, Abbey Road, London
*Jacqueline Du Pre* (cello); *London Symphony Orchestra*
*Haydn* Concerto for Cello and Orchestra in D major,
  Hob.Vllb/2
  EMI CDM 566896 2; CMS 769707 2; CMS 5673412; CZS
  568132 2

17 December Grosser Saal, Musikverein, Vienna (public concert)
*Wiener Philharmoniker*
*Debussy* La Mer
  Hunt CD 731 (unauthorised release)

18 December Grosser Saal, Musikverein, Vienna
*Wiener Philhannoniker*
*Brahms* Tragic Overture, Op. 81
  EMI CZS 572649 2; Royal Classics HR 703992
*Brahms* Academic Festival Overture, Op. 80
  EMI CZS 572649 2; Royal Classic HR 703992

19 December Grosser Saal, Musikverein, Vienna
*Wiener Philhannoniker*
*Brahms* Variations on a Theme by Brahams, Op. 56a "St.
   Antoni"
   Disky DCL 705902; EMI CZS 572649 2; Royal Classics
   HR 703992

27–28 December Kingsway Hall, London
*Dame Janet Baker* (mezzo-soprano); *New Philharmonia
Orchestra*
*Ravel* Shéhérazade
   EMI CZS 568667 2; HMV Classics 573446 2

**1968**
5 January Naples
*Dino Ciani* (piano); *Sinfonia Orchestra di Napoli*
*Mozart* Concerto for Piano and Orchestra No. 25 in C major,
   K 503
   Stradivarius STR 10005; Curcio-Hunt CON 7
   (unauthorised releases)

28–29 January and 6 August No. 1 Studio, Abbey Road, London
*Sheila Armstrong, Patricia Clarke* (sopranos); *Ambrosian
Singers, Hallé Orchestra*
*Grieg* Peer Gynt – incidental music
   Disky DCL 706482

6 August No. 1 Studio, Abbey Road, London
*Hallé Orchestra*
*Delius* (arr. Fenby) La Calinda
   EMI CMS 565119 2
*Delius* On hearing the First Cuckoo in Spring
   EMI CMS 565119 2

7 August No. 1 Studio, Abbey Road, London
*Hallé Orchestra*
*Delius* A Song before Sunrise
  EMI CMS 565119 2
*Delius* (arr. Beecham) Hassan – Intermezzo; Serenade with
  *Robert Tear* (tenor)
  EMI CMS 565119 2
*Delius* In a Summer Garden
  EMI CMS 565119 2; HMV Classics 574054 2

7–8 August No. 1 Studio, Abbey Road, London
*Hallé Orchestra*
*Delius* (arr. Fenby) Sonata for Strings – Movement 3, Late
  Swallows
  EMI CMS 565119 2; HMV Classics 574054 2

8 August No. 1 Studio, Abbey Road, London
*Hallé Orchestra*
*Delius* Summer Night on the River
  EMI CMS 5651192

12–21 August and 8, 10 and 30 October Walthamstow
  Assembly Hall, London
  *James McCracken* (tenor) Otello; *Dietrich Fischer-Dieskau*
  (baritone) Iago; *Piero de Palma* (tenor) Cassio; *Florindo*
  *Andreolli* (tenor) Roderigo; *Alfredo Giacomotti* (bass)
  Lodovico; *Leonardo Monreale* (bass) Montano; *Glynne*
  *Thomas* (tenor) A Herald; *Dame Gwynneth Jones* (soprano)
  Desdemona; *Anna de Stasio* (mezo-soprano) Emilia;
  *Ambrosian Chorus; Children's Chorus of Boys from Upton*
  *House School and Girls from Hammersmith County*
  *School; New Philharmonia Orchestra*
  *Verdi* Otello
  EMI CMS 565296 2

13 September Royal Festival Hall, London (public concert)
*Henryk Szeryng* (violin); *Helsinki Philharmonic Orchestra*
*Sibelius* Concerto for Violin and Orchestra in d, Op. 47
   Intaglio INCD 7171(unauthorised release)

13 September Royal Festival Hall, London (public concert)
*Helsinki Philharmonic Orchestra*
*Sibelius* Symphony No. 7 in C major, Op. 107
   Intaglio INCD 7171(unauthorised release)

20 September No. 1 Studio, Abbey Road, London
*Jacqueline Du Pre* (cello); *Valda Aveling* (harpsichord
continuo); *London Symphony Orchestra*
*Monn* Concerto for Cello and Orchestra in G minor
   EMI CMS 5673412; CZS 568132 2

2 November No.1 Studio, Abbey Road, London
*Evelyn Rothwell* (oboe); *New Philharrnonia Orchestra*
*Corelli* (arr. Barbirolli) Concerto for Oboe and Orchestra
   Dutton CDSJB 1016

12–13 December Salle Wagram, Paris
*Orchestre de Paris*
*Debussy* La Mer
   EMI CZS 762669 2; Disky DCL 705902; DCL 707142;
   Royal Classics ROY 701172

18 & 20 December Salle Wagram, Paris
*Maîtrise de l'O.R.T.F.; Orchestre de Paris*
*Debussy* Trois Nocturnes
   EMI CZS 762669 2; Royal Classics ROY 701172

**1969**

Exact date not known
*Sir John Barbirolli* talking about Jacqueline Du Pré
  EMI Video 724349 218813

8 March Philharmonie, Berlin (public concert)
  *Lucretia West* (contralto); *Frauen und Knabenchor der St*
  *Hedwigs Kathedral, Berlin; Berliner Philharmoniker*
  *Mahler* Symphony No. 3 in D minor
    Hunt CD 719 (unauthorised release)

30 April Royal Festival Hall (public concert)
  *Hallé Orchestra*
  *Berlioz* Symphonie fantastique, Op. 14
    Hunt CD 731 (unauthorised release)

23 May Free Trade Hall, Manchester
  *Kirsten Meyer* (mezzo-soprano); *Ladies of the Hallé Choir;*
  *Boys of Manchester Grammar School; Hallé Orchestra*
  *Mahler* Symphony No. 3 in D minor
    BBC Legends BBCL 4007-7

27 May Kingsway Hall, London
  *Hallé Orchestra*
  *Purcell* (arr. Barbirolli) Suite for Strings with horns, flutes and
    cor anglais
    Dutton CDSJB 1015
  *Bach* (arr. Barbirolli) Cantata No. 208 – Sheep may safely graze
    Dutton CDSJB 1004

27–28 May Kingsway Hall, London
  *Hallé Orchestra*
  *Sibelius* Symphony No. 3 in C major, Op. 52
    EMI CMS 567299 2

29–30 May Kingsway Hall, London
*Hallé Orchestra*
*Sibelius* Symphony No. 4 in A minor, Op. 63",
  EMI CMS 567299 2

16–18 July Town Hall, Watford
*New Philharmonia Orchestra*
*Mahler* Symphony No. 5 in C sharp minor
  EMI CDM 566910 2

17–18 July Town Hall, Watford
*Dame Janet Baker* (mezzo-soprano); *New Philharmonia*
*Orchstra*
*Mahler* Rückert-Lieder
  EMI CDM 5669812; CZS 569665 2

19 July Town Hall, Watford
*New Philharmonia Orchestra*
*Tchaikovsky* Romeo and Juliet (omits coda – never recorded)
  Dutton CDSJB 1019

29 July Royal Albert Hall, London (public concert)
*Hallé Orchestra*
*Bruckner* Symphony No. 9 in D minor
  BBC Legends BBCL 4034–2

4 August Kingsway Hall, London
*Hallé Orchestra*
*Sibelius* Scènes historiques, Op. 25 – Suite No. 1: No. 1, All'
  overtura
  EMI CMS 567299 2
*Sibelius* Scènes historiques, Op. 25 – Suite No. 1: No. 2, Scena
  EMI CMS 567299 2
*Sibelius* Scènes historiques, Op. 25 – Suite No. 1: The Hunt
  EMI CMS 567299 2

5 August Kingsway Hall, London
*Hallé Orchestra*
*Sibelius* Romance in C major for strings, Op. 42
   EMI CMS 567299 2
*Sibelius* Rakastava for strings and percussion, Op. 14
   EMI CMS 567299 2


5 August No. 1 Studio, Abbey Road, London
*Evelyn Rothwell* (oboe); *Hallé Orchestra*
*Marcello* (arr. Barbirolli) Concerto for Oboe and Strings
   Dutton CDSJB 1016

6 August No. 1 Studio, Abbey Road, London
*Hallé Orchestra*
*Grieg* Lyric Suite, Op. 54
   Dutton CDSJB 1012; Disky DCL 706482
*Grieg* Sigurd Jorsalfar, Op. 56 – No. 3, Homage March
   Dutton CDSJB 1012

8 August Royal Albert Hall, London (public concert)
*Hallé Orchestra*
*Walton* Partita for Orchestra
   BBC Legends BBCL 4013 2

9 August Royal Albert Hall, London (public concert)
*Hallé Orchestra*
*Haydn* Symphony No. 83 in G minor"La Poule"
   BBC Legends BBCL 4038–2
*Lehár* Gold und Silber, Op. 75 – Walzer
   BBC Legends BBCL 4038-2
*Johann Strauss II* Perpetuum mobile, Op. 257 – Polka schnell
   BBC Legends BBCL 4038-2
*Johann Strauss II* Kaiser-Walzer, Op. 437
   BBC Legends BBCL 4038-2

*Johann Strauss II* Tritsch-Tratsch Polka, Op. 214
　BBC Legends BBCL 4038-2
*Johann Strauss II* Die Fledermaus – Overture
　BBC Legends BBCL 4038-2
*Richard Strauss* (arr. Artur Rodzinski) Der Rosenkavalier –
　Suite
　BBC Legends BBCL 4038-2
Impromptu speech by Sir John Barbirolli
　BBC Legends BBCL 4038-2

18–19, 21–22, 25–27 and 30 August Town Hall, Watford
*Montserrat Caballé* (soprano); *Fiorenza Cossotto* (mezzo-
soprano); *Jon Vickers* (tenor); *Ruggero Raimondi* (bass);
*New Philharmonia Chorus and Orchestra*
*Verdi* Messa da Requiem
　EMI CZS 568412 2

26–27 September No. 1 Studio, Abbey Road, London
*London Symphony Orchestra*
*Richard Strauss* Ein Heldenleben, Op. 40
　EMI CZS 569349 2

28 September Royal Festival Hall, London (public concert)
*London Symphony Orchestra*
*Mozart* Symphony No. 36 in C major, K 425 "Linz"
　BBC Legends BBCL 4055-2
*Richard Strauss* Ein Heldenleben, Op. 40
　BBC Legends BBCL 4055–2

1 October No. 1 Studio, Abbey Road, London
*New Philharmonia Orchestra*
*Tchaikovsky* Francesca da Rimini, Op. 32
　Dutton CDSJB 1019

## 1970

10 April Herkulessaal der Münchner Residenz, Bavaria, Germany
**Symphonieorchester des Bayenschen Rundfunks**
*Brahms* Symphony No. 2 in D major, Op. 73
    Orfeo C 265 921B
*Vaughan Williams* Symphony No. 6 in E minor
    Orfeo C 265921 B

20–21 May Kingsway Hall, London
**Hallé Orchestra**
*Sibelius* Symphony No. 6 in D minor, Op. 104
    EMI CMS 567299 2

20 May Royal Festival Hall, London (public concert)
**Hallé Orchestra**
*Elgar* In the South – Concert Overture, Op. 50 "Alassio"
    BBC Legends BBCL 4013 2
*Bruckner* Symphony No. 8 in C minor (Haas edition)
    BBC Legends BBCL 4067-2

22 May No. 1 Studio, Abbey Road, London
**Hallé Orchestra**
*Grieg* Norwegian Dances, Op. 35
    Dutton CDSJB 1012

19 June Stuttgart (public concert)
**Helen Donath** (soprano); **Birgit Finnilä** (contralto);
**Südfunkchor; Chor der Staall Hochschule fur musik und**
**Darstallende Kunst Stuttgart; Radiosinfonieorchester,**
**Stuttgart**
*Mahler* Symphony No. 2 in C minor "Resurrection"
    EMI CZS 75100 2

15–16 July Kingsway Hall, London
   *Alun Jenkins* (baritone); *Ambrosian Singers*; *Hallé Orchestra*

   *Delius* Appalachia
     EMI CMS 565119 2
   *Delius* Appalachia (rehearsal sequence)
     EMI CMS 565119 2

17 July Kingsway Hall, London
   *Hallé Orchestra*
   *Delius* Brigg Fair – An English Rhapsody
     EMI CMS 565119 2; HMV Classics 574054 2

Malcolm Walker
August 2001

# *Index*

293